P9-EDZ-445

PRAISE FOR *One More Step*

"Bonner Paddock is an amazing person with an unconquerable spirit. His story is beyond inspiring, and he personifies what true toughness and heart are all about. Through it all, Bonner Paddock keeps going, and takes all of us along with him."

—Jay Bilas, ESPN basketball analyst and author of the *New York Times* bestseller *Toughness: Developing True Strength On and Off the Court*

"Bonner Paddock's *One More Step* is the triumphant story of a man who accomplishes the impossible. On a deeper level, however, it's about the human bonds that can push us to become heroes. An instantly engaging and wonderful book."

—A. J. Baime, *New York Times* bestselling author of *The Arsenal of Democracy and Go Like Hell*

"*One More Step* is a courageous and heartwarming story of one man's trials and triumphs over cerebral palsy. Packed with adventure, this gripping narrative of summiting Mount Kilimanjaro and becoming a Kona Ironman both exhausts and uplifts the human spirit. An inspiring and irresistible book."

—Lars Anderson, author of *The Storm and the Tide*

"*One More Step* is a riveting story of overcoming the challenge of living with cerebral palsy and conquering the impossible. Bonner Paddock is an inspiration to everyone."

—Nolan Ryan, MLB Hall of Fame pitcher

"[Bonner Paddock's] story of training for these events and the mind-boggling pain he endured to achieve his goals will have readers crying and cheering all the way to the finish line. An emotion- and action-packed story of the author's tenacious, dogged pursuit of his goals."

—*Kirkus Reviews*

"Each step of Paddock's journey is described in vivid and compelling detail. Readers will cheer for this extraordinary man, whose story is solid evidence that limits fall away when confronted with resolve, service, and courage."

—*Publisher's Weekly*

ONE MORE STEP

ONE MORE STEP

My Story of Living with Cerebral Palsy,
Climbing Kilimanjaro, and Surviving
the Hardest Race on Earth

BONNER PADDOCK

WITH NEAL BASCOMB

HarperOne
An Imprint of HarperCollinsPublishers

HarperOne

ONE MORE STEP. Copyright © 2015 by Bonner Paddock. All rights reserved. Printed in the United States of America. No part of this book may be used or reproduced in any manner whatsoever without written permission except in the case of brief quotations embodied in critical articles and reviews. For information address HarperCollins Publishers, 195 Broadway, New York, NY 10007.

HarperCollins books may be purchased for educational, business, or sales promotional use. For information please e-mail the Special Markets Department at SPsales@harpercollins.com.

FIRST HARPERCOLLINS PAPERBACK EDITION PUBLISHED IN 2016

Designed by Ralph Fowler

ISBN 978–0–06–229560–6

Library of Congress Cataloging-in-Publication Data

Paddock, Bonner.
  One more step : my story of living with cerebral palsy, climbing Kilimanjaro, and surviving the hardest race on earth / Bonner Paddock.
pages cm
ISBN 978–0–06–229558–3 (hardcover)
1. Paddock, Bonner. 2. Cerebral palsied—United States—Biography.
3. Mountaineering—Tanzania—Kilimanjaro, Mount. 4. Triathlon—Training.
I. Bascomb, Neal. II. Title.
RC388.P33   2015
616.8'360092—dc23
2014035608

16 17 18 19 20   RRD(H)   10 9 8 7 6 5 4 3 2 1

To Jake,
for igniting this journey and for being there
every step of the way . . . my inspiration.

*You gain strength, and courage, and confidence by
every experience in which you really stop to look
fear in the face . . . you must do the thing
you think you cannot do.*

—Eleanor Roosevelt

*Not everything that is face can be changed, but
nothing can be changed until it is faced.*

—James Baldwin

Contents

ONE MORE STEP

PROLOGUE

Fight Your Fight

Force away the pain. Fight your fight. One more step. You are an Iron-man, Bonner Paddock. You are an Ironman.

    I silently repeat it, over and over. *You are an Ironman.* The words are a promise. They are an aspiration. If I finish—no, *when* I finish—before the midnight cutoff, the announcer will shout them out to the world, and they will become fact. But right now I am running alone in the inky blackness of a Hawaiian island night, my headlamp is casting a small wobbling circle of light on the broken pavement ahead, and I am struggling.

    Passing into my 17th mile, I know I am in trouble. Every inch of my body screams in pain. I want nothing more than to stop, collapse into a heap, and end this torture. With each troubled stride, my knees bend in, and my ankles flail out: my legs are breaking down. At some point, fast approaching, determination will no longer be enough to keep me moving.

    One second I want to quit. The next, I force away the thought. I have battled these doubts throughout the 2.4-mile swim in swelling seas, on the 112-mile bike ride in devil-searing heat, and now during the final miles of the marathon run of the 2012 Ironman World Championship.

You are an Ironman. Force away the pain. Fight your fight. One more step. You are an Ironman. My mantra keeps me moving for another hundred yards, but then I slow down, almost to a walk.

I'm running through the Natural Energy Laboratory property, just off the Queen Ka'ahumanu Highway. The government installation is the farthest point away from Kailua-Kona, home base. The Energy Lab is dark, can't-see-your-hand-in-front-of-your-face dark. Day or night, it is creepy too, with windowless sheet-metal buildings and huge black pipelines that snake through the grounds before plunging into the ocean. Worst of all, the lab boasts the reputation, confirmed many times by my coach, Ironman legend Greg Welch, for being the place that makes or breaks competitors. Top pros have entered this stretch, roughly Miles 16–19 of the marathon, in the lead only to fall far behind by the time they emerge. Many other racers have left on stretchers. The heat, the absence of a breeze, the sheer haunting barrenness—they are often too much to bear.

Time is running out for me. Since 7 A.M., when the sun rose over the summit of Mount Hualalai, one of the Big Island's five active volcanoes, I've been pushing my body. More than fourteen hours with no rest and no reprieve. My legs feel mashed to a pulp. My feet burn with every step, each foot a wet, bloody, swelling mess laced into its shoe. At any moment the race officials—Grim Reapers on scooters—are going to sweep me up.

"Too slow, Bonner. You won't make the cutoff," they will say.

"No can do," they'll continue. "We're sorry. You had a good race. At least you gave it your best."

No.

My best I have yet to give. I dig inside of myself, deeper than before. I quicken my pace slightly, but enough to bring the pain roaring back. So be it. *Use the pain. Ignore the rest. Step after step.* I head down toward the ocean, then bank right, going north now.

I worry that I am sweating too much. I worry that I am moving too fast. Then I worry that I am moving too slowly. I want to know the time, but I worry that if I look at my watch I will lose my balance and fall. I need to use my sight to keep my balance. I worry about the rising twinge in my ankles. I worry that my body is not keeping in any of the liquid I am drinking. I worry that I am hitting the wall, that I'll faint. I worry that I will stumble off the road into the lava fields and that nobody will know where I've gone. There I will lie until they find me, and all that will remain will be the desiccated skeleton of Bonner Paddock. I am not thinking straight, haven't for hours. I feel so isolated and so alone.

"Keep the strides long, mate. Keep your pace even," Welchy says. "Move your arms." I turn to find my coach jogging along beside me. He's wearing flip-flops. How I would love to be wearing flip-flops. His wife, Sian, also an Ironman champion, is chugging down the road on a scooter. Why are they here? I left them back on the Queen K Highway before I turned into the Energy Lab. They said they would meet me at the finish.

"I'll never quit, Welchy," I say.

"I know," he says. "Just remember to drink chicken broth at the next aid station and keep running your own race."

"Okay, okay."

"There's a ton of big blue cowboy hats waiting at the finish for you."

My body trembles. My toes explode with each step. I stare down at the road. When I look back to my coach, he is gone, as is Sian. *Poof.* As if they were never there.

I am not alone, I remind myself. I never have been. My coach is with me. All my friends and family down at the finish line in big blue foam cowboy hats are with me. My brother Mike, who saw me through every bump and roadblock of this journey, is with me. Juliana is with me. Steve Robert and his family are with me. And Jake, dear Jakey, is with me, as he was at the very beginning when I knew absolutely nothing of myself—and accepted even less.

Ahead I see a bright white light. It's not heaven, but close enough. It's the Energy Lab turnaround. Once I reach it, I will be heading back toward the finish, toward home.

Force away the pain. Fight your fight. One more step. You are an Ironman, Bonner Paddock. You are an Ironman.

1

Normal. Happy.

The alarm buzzed. I hit the snooze button. The alarm buzzed again. I hit snooze again and turned over. On the third buzz, I sat up in bed. Time to get the day on. It was March 2005. Life was good. Life was normal. At twenty-nine, I finally had some money in my pocket and a dream sales job on a professional sports team. Yes, I had racked up some serious credit-card and student-loan debt, but who hadn't at my age, I figured.

I lived in Newport Coast, California, a mile from the ocean, in a one-bedroom, 850-square-foot bachelor pad. I had the big-screen TV, racks of CDs, a closet full of suits, an oversized couch, and a refrigerator with all the essentials: beer, mustard, ketchup, Tabasco sauce, and flour tortillas for bean and cheese burritos. The beige walls, which matched the beige carpet, were bare but for a black-and-white photograph of some hanging garlic taken by my grandfather. The apartment complex boasted a pool and a small gym. The silver Lexus parked in the garage was perfect for rolling to work and for getting to parties on the weekends (or even during the week—hey, I was young). Normal. Happy.

The fact of my having cerebral palsy? Only my family and close friends knew about that—and then not all of them did. Because the nature of my cerebral palsy allowed me to keep it a secret, that was exactly what I did. Sitting across from me at a meeting or over dinner, people saw a big guy, six foot four, with the wingspan of a basketball player and hair that was maybe thinning a little too early. I smiled a lot and talked fast and furiously. Nothing wrong with me. All was well.

That morning when I finally rolled out of bed and put my feet on the floor was like every morning. There was no avoiding the stiffness and pain. Try holding your hand tight in a fist for as long as possible. Really concentrate and push yourself. Feel that burn start in your fingers and then move down your wrist into your forearm. That is how my feet, calves, hamstrings, quads, glutes, and lower back feel—all the time. There is no loosening, no release. Every morning it feels as though I hit the gym the night before for the first time ever, really pushing it to the limit, and now my body is mad at me, really mad.

When I finally stood up from the bed, it was snap, crackle, and pop time, from my toes to my ankles to my knees. As I moved about, getting ready for work, my leg muscles were loosening up, but I still made an awful racket, my feet pounding the wooden floor like a troll let loose. I didn't trip on the stairs that morning, and I didn't fall over in my closet putting my shoes on, but neither was unusual.

A half hour later, I parked at the Anaheim Ducks arena, where I was into my second week as the Director of Corporate Sponsorships. Given the NHL lockout over player salaries and the recent cancellation of the season, there was not much to sell. Out in front of the arena, the billionaire founder of Broadcom, Henry Samueli, and his wife, Susan, soon-to-be new owners of the Ducks, were holding a breakfast pep rally for the troops.

Crossing to the buffet, I focused on my walk, trying to minimize my knees' natural inward bend and trying to stop my feet swinging out in a half-moon with each step. Even so, some people noticed my awkward gait, and a nice young woman asked me if I had hurt my leg. "Weekend warrior," I said, smiling but feeling uncomfortable. Nobody but my boss at the Ducks knew I had cerebral palsy. I grabbed some pancakes and bacon, sat down at a table, and introduced myself to a few people.

Samueli stepped up to the podium at the front. He was tall and lanky and wore a very nice suit. We had yet to meet, and I didn't know what to expect. Would he offer words about keeping the faith maybe, about the next season definitely being "on," or about staying the course because we have work to do, and so on? There was some of that, sure.

But then he said, "We have to focus on what we *can* control. This time we have on our hands, it's a great opportunity to help people who need a lot more than we ever will. Go volunteer at your favorite charity, give back to your community."

Give back, huh?

A dutiful new employee, I returned to my desk and googled "cerebral palsy" and "Orange County" and up came the United Cerebral Palsy Foundation of Orange County (UCP-OC). I rang them and said that I wanted to volunteer, and the executive director, Paul Pulver, asked me to lunch. My boss had given me a task, it sounded worthwhile and well-meaning, and given my disability, UCP-OC seemed like the right place to give back. I really didn't think about it any more than that. By no stretch of my imagination did I think my whole life was about to change. After all, I was happy. Good. Normal.

Paul Pulver and I met at a fish restaurant by Angels Stadium. His own son had CP. I gave the broad strokes on my life and my new job and told him that I used to play goalie on my college soccer team. Paul was surprised at how independent and physically able I was. When he asked what specific kind of CP I had, I didn't answer. I didn't know. At the end of our lunch, he invited me to speak to the UCP-OC board, with a mind to joining.

So a few weeks later, early in the morning, there I was. At the time, the UCP-OC was headquartered in a ground-floor office in a business park off I-5. I went through the door. In a room adjacent to the reception area, behind a wall of glass, sat the board members around a big table. A dozen pair of eyes looked at me, and suddenly I felt my heart sink into my wingtip shoes. It's one thing to put in a few hours of volunteering; it's another thing entirely to stand in front of a room to speak about my CP. I had never done it and had never wanted to—ever. Yet there I was.

Paul Pulver came out from the boardroom.

"Hang tight," he said. "We'll be right with you."

Decades passed in those short moments. I sweated. My hand trembled. If someone had opened a window, I might have crawled out of it. Then I was led inside. I shook some hands and introduced myself, but I wasn't seeing or hearing anything. Finally, everybody returned to their seats except me. I stood in front of the table, feeling the way I imagined an alcoholic would at his first AA meeting, admitting my CP as if it were something to be ashamed of. Nervous, staring at a spot on the table in front of me, I told my story—part of it anyway.

On May 22, 1975, during my first seconds out in this world, I gasped for breath. The umbilical cord was wrapped twice around my neck. My mother, Andrea, on her third natural childbirth, wondered why the hospital room was so quiet. I should have been crying, making a big fuss.

"Shouldn't we be hearing from that baby down there?" she asked, worried.

"You will," the doctor answered.

Only after he loosened the accidental noose did my pale, almost lifeless body get some air at last. But the damage to my brain as a result of being starved of precious blood flow was done. Numerous areas suffered from the cerebral anoxia (lack of oxygen) at this precious moment of life—white matter, neural connections, and a bunch of things that go by Latin terms, half of which I don't understand to this day—and maybe for good reason, because the anoxia played havoc inside my head, destroying at random some serious brain matter.

Once I had some air, though, and the doctor gave me a firm slap on my buns, I wailed and flailed like any other newborn. The doctor told my mother and my father, Tom, that there might be some impact from the wrapped cord, but then again there might not. Any tests at that point would be inconclusive. They were to have faith.

Eight hours later, my mother was eager to get home, and I left the hospital, all chubby eight pounds and two ounces of me, swaddled in a blanket and out to make my way in life. To any and all who looked on, I was just another standard-issue baby.

I had two older brothers, Mike and Matt—my mother called me "Me Three"—and I sat up, crawled, stood, and walked earlier than they did, but everything was just that little bit different. When I was sitting on the floor, my legs were angled awkwardly behind me. Crawling, I'd haul my body forward by my arms, dragging my legs behind me like a commando advancing under low barbed wire. Standing, I wobbled in at the knees and curled my toes underneath my feet. Walking, I swung my legs around and rolled inward on my big toes. I lost my balance easily and fell all the time. Truth was, anything that required the use of my body from the waist down was hard to watch—and even harder to do.

In those early years, I looked like a straw with two knots tied at either end, one for my knees, the other for my head. Otherwise, I was straight and skinny, with a sunken chest and no muscles, particularly in my legs. When I was three years old, my mother told the pediatrician that I was tripping a lot. He said I was walking a little pigeon-toed and that some corrective shoes with metal toes would do the trick. These succeeded only in crushing my mother's toes (this being southern California, everyone else was in sandals), but I continued to fall—a lot. Climbing steps, crossing the yard, walking on the beach—you name it, I fell doing it. Running and learning to ride a bike were more exercises in catastrophe than new skills to be learned.

Broken bones came by the score. Toes, fingers, arms, ankles. I spent more time in splints, braces, and plaster casts than Wile E. Coyote. At four, I fell off a jungle gym at preschool and snapped my left arm. According to family legend, I didn't cry, not once. Two days after the cast came off, I crashed my skateboard in the church court-yard and broke the same arm, in the same place.

While I was at the hospital, I walked toward the doctor who had set my arm the first time, and he said to my mother, "Your child doesn't walk right."

"Thank you for noticing," my mother said. "You have no idea what it means for you to notice that it's not an average walk."

The doctor offered to assess me. After stripping down to my underwear, I was asked to walk down the hallway and back (once). His assessment?

"Bonner doesn't have a normal walk."

"What should we do?" my mother asked.

"No further tests required," the doctor said. "He just walks strange."

It was around this time I started to hate doctors.

Over the next five years, as I struggled to keep up with my brothers, at soccer, basketball, swimming, and everything else kids do, my parents assembled a team of orthopedic doctors to see what it was about my walk, the way I moved, that was not normal. One guy—and they were always guys—said I needed occupational therapy. Once a week, he had a therapist push me back and forth in a hammock, so I could learn the position of my body in space. When I was eight, another orthopedic surgeon said I was all out of alignment: the muscles in my legs were too short for my bony frame; my calves were knotted up. The solution? Both legs in plaster casts up to my knees.

I still played baseball. I mean, I could still play defense and swing the bat. The coach got me a designated runner and switched me to catcher. A real pistol I was. Afterward, my mother would have to use a brush to clean the gravel and dirt out of my plastered feet. When the doctors found that their plaster casts hadn't worked, they put me in fiberglass ones, all the way up to my hip flexors. Nothing changed except I missed a season of soccer and swimming in the ocean.

When I was nine years old, my mother took me to see yet another doctor, this time a neurologist. He was not covered by my family's insurance, but he was apparently the smartest guy in the room (the room being Arcadia, California), so they paid cash. My brother Mike, who was sixteen at the time, came with me. The neurologist watched me walk, clipped something to the bottom of my foot, and had me track his finger with my eyes. No MRI, no scans, no nothing. While I was sitting on my brother's lap beside our mother, he gave the diagnosis: syringomyelia, a spinal-cord disorder. The prognosis, which he delivered right then and there, was that I would be in a wheelchair by the age of fourteen and most likely dead by twenty.

Now, none of this fazed me. I simply blocked it out, put it away in a dark corner of my mind. The neurologist recommended a physical therapist and prescribed some pills. The pills made me loopy, so I stopped taking them, and the therapy was so dull and tiresome that I loathed every session. My parents, my brothers, my grandparents, and I never spoke about the doctors, the prognosis, or the therapy. None of it.

Two years later, my brother's near-death experience overturned my own death sentence. Mike was working out at the University of California–Irvine (UCI) gym. Always a big-shot athlete in high school, co-captain of the water polo and swim teams, Mike was involved in both again during his freshman year in college, and he added another sport as well: crew. He was cranking away at the indoor rowing machine, trying to "pull a better erg" (number of strokes and power over time), so that he would be selected to compete that weekend. Suddenly, he got dizzy and lost consciousness. His coach and teammates rushed him to the UCI hospital ER, where he remained over the weekend, with a skull that felt split into a hundred pieces.

By Monday morning, tests had revealed that Mike had suffered a brain hemorrhage from his overzealous workout. By chance, the blood vessel that popped was basically a loop going nowhere; otherwise, he would have died. It was nothing that some bed rest wouldn't heal, but the hospital recommended that Mike also see a neurologist. This doctor asked Mike if there was anything out of the ordinary with his family medical history. Mike, who, like the rest of us, had pushed my syringomyelia diagnosis out of his mind, simply told the doctor that one of his brothers walked kind of weird. The neurologist asked to see me.

My mother was all for it, but I, now eleven years old, wanted nothing more to do with doctors. Mike offered a deal: if I went, I could spend the night with him at college and go to his classes. Bribes worked wonders on me.

It turned out that Mike's neurologist was not just any neurologist. His name was Dr. Arnold Starr, the department head at UCI and a cutting-edge researcher. He was in his late fifties, with a goatee and a "mad professor" shock of hair. He peered around the mountain of patients' files on his desk and took my medical history. My mother mentioned the syringomyelia. Dr. Starr asked if I had ever had an MRI. The answer was no.

Then he leaned over his desk, elbows firmly placed on a low stack of manila folders, and said to my mother, "You *can't* diagnose syringomyelia without an MRI. There is no other diagnostic for the condition. If Bonner didn't have that test, then the diagnosis can't hold."

Dr. Starr then gave me a thorough physical exam and sent me for a battery of tests: MRI, CT, EEG, blood tests, the works. I didn't much want to be rolled into the MRI machine, which looked like a tomb, but Mom dangled the bribe in front of me. Still as a stone, I let the machine make its rat-a-tat-tat ruckus as it peered inside my brain. Then came even more tests, poking, prodding, stabbing, and examining my every movement, hour after hour.

While we were waiting for the test results, my big night on the UCI campus came. Mike lived in an apartment a half block from the beach in an area named, for its wild parties, the "War Zone." I stayed up late, ate pizza, listened to loud music, and fed roaches to

Mike's oscar fish. Gobble. Gobble. All the girls pinched my cheeks, and I felt like a big shot. The next day, I went to his classes with him. Economics was a drag, but next came Humanities. I was sitting in the back row, eyes wide open, when the professor started talking about human sexuality. With details, lots of wondrous details. Mike clamped his hands over my ears and ushered me out the door.

We went back to see Dr. Starr a month later. As he spoke to my mother, his words rolled over me. I was thinking mostly about his black convertible Porsche with the red leather interior that he had promised to take me driving in, once all the tests were done.

"Well, I'll tell you the good news," Dr. Starr said. "There's no way Bonner has syringomyelia."

"No wheelchair at fourteen?" My mother replied. "No—"

"Absolutely not. No demise at twenty years of age either."

"So, what is it?"

"Bonner has cerebral palsy."

"Is that like MS?" my mother asked.

"No, muscular sclerosis is progressive and degenerative. Cerebral palsy is chronic, but nonprogressive." This was doctor speak for, "You got it, and it ain't going away, but it doesn't get better or worse over time."

My cerebral palsy, Dr. Starr went on to say, was the result of the damage inflicted during those precious first seconds of life when I was starved of oxygen. It was a disorder of the brain, causing garbled messages to be sent out to the body, primarily impacting motor function.

No two manifestations of CP were alike. Some of the most severe cases left people unable to control their movements, their arms and their legs often crooked and locked. I fell into the broad CP category of spastic diplegia, in which the lower body is primarily affected. Because Mission Control in my brain was out of whack, the muscles in my legs didn't function as they should. To walk or run normally, some muscles must contract while others elongate; it's a delicate balance. My spastic diplegia threw off that balance, leaving me with poor motor-function control, debilitating tightness in my hips and legs, weak muscle tone, a tendency toward joint breakdown, rapid exhaustion, slow recovery, tendinitis, plantar fasciitis, and plenty of other "-itis" fun. To add to the mix, I had trouble maintaining my balance and equilibrium. Dr. Starr prescribed continuing with my physical therapy and keeping on with the sports. Whatever I was doing was working marvels.

Given my previous diagnosis, all of this came as fantastic news to my mother. Her eyes welled up with tears of relief. For my part, I wanted to go home, kick the ball around, ride my bike, maybe head out for a swim with my grandfather. None of these words, spastic this, palsy that, applied to *me*. They might as well have been referring to some other kid.

At dinner that night, not one word was mentioned about the doctor visit. Later that year, when I won a soccer all-stars award for "overcoming adversity," I didn't know what people were talking about. I was normal, just like everybody else. That's what I told myself.

At the end of my talk to the board at UCP-OC, I offered to do anything I could to help their work, shook hands with everyone, passed out my business cards (a salesman always), and left. As I walked to my car, my hands settling from the shakes, I felt a tremendous weight fall from my shoulders. This was the first time I had been honest about my disability to strangers, to a group of them no less, and they had accepted me—they were even considering me as a candidate for the board.

The next day, at my desk at work, I received an e-mail from one of the board members, Steve Robert. He had been sitting directly to my left, but I had been so nervous throughout that meeting that I couldn't even put a face to the name. His e-mail read:

> *Hi, Bonner.*
>
> *Nice to meet you yesterday. I have a four-year-old son named Jake, who has severe cerebral palsy. I went home last night and shared your story with my wife, Alison, and I wanted to let you know how much hope it gives to us and our little Jakey, seeing what you do, having accomplished what you have with college and your career. You give us hope that if we keep working hard and pushing to help our Jakey, he can get to a better place than he is at.*

Sitting in my office, reading, then rereading the note, I cried, and yet I had absolutely no idea why.

2

A Boy Named Jake

On a crisp Sunday morning, January 8, 2006, I stood at the starting line of the Orange County Marathon in my white microfiber shirt and brand-new Asics running shoes. The sun had just risen over the hills of Newport Beach, and the Pacific Ocean stretched out to the west into the endless distance. Thousands of runners of every stripe—young, old, fit, unfit, eager, and scared senseless (I was in the last category)—milled about, waiting for the race to begin. Even though I was set to only run the half marathon, 13.1 miles still seemed like an immense distance.

Ever since my speech to the UCP-OC board six months before, my idea of normal (and happy) was quickly changing. The same day I received the note from Steve Robert, I was invited to become a member of the UCP-OC board. Spurred on by the feeling of acceptance they gave me for something I had long kept hidden, I dove into the foundation's activities, raising awareness in the community about cerebral palsy and helping families get early-intervention care for their children.

It definitely required more time than I had first thought when I rose to Henry Samueli's challenge. And, with the end of the NHL lockout in July 2005, work was intense. Putting in ten to twelve hours a day, six, often seven, days a week, helping develop the sponsorship division from the ground up, entertaining clients at the games and concerts at the arena, I was burning it at both ends.

At the time, adding a half marathon to the mix had seemed like a great idea. The foundation was one of the charities involved at the event, and every other board member had committed to run at least a 5K. Gung-ho, I went for the half marathon. More miles, more money, no big deal. I trained exactly twice: one run of 3 miles and another of 5. What other training could I possibly need? With e-mails to friends and family, I raised a little over $3,000 on the promise that I would finish.

So there I was at the Orange County Marathon, slathered in Body-Glide to prevent chafing and believing that chafing would be my biggest problem. To my left was Steve Robert, wearing a visor with "Jake" written across the bill. At six foot three, a former jock whose banner days were long past, he was all nervous jokes. To my right was Grant Dunning, another board member and the fittest of our bunch. His young daughter, Paige, who had CP, was strapped into a jogging stroller ahead of him. Steve and Grant were in for the full marathon.

At the gun, Grant pressed ahead, and we lost him pretty quickly. I was thankful for the crush of runners, as it kept the pace slow. Soon, though—too soon for my taste—the pack loosened, and we headed away from the coast along San Miguel Drive.

"How fast are you?" Steve asked about a mile and a half into the race, both of us going at a jog.

"I'm really slow," I said.

"I'll go at your speed then," Steve said with a grin.

We took the next couple of miles at a good pace. The day was gorgeous, the fans along the course were cheering, and the adrenaline was working its magic. Steve asked how I liked being on the board, and we spoke about the foundation's work. Even after his email, the two of us had never really spoken at length, and I had not met his family prior to that morning. But as the miles added up and our pace slowed, Steve opened up about his life and his son Jake, and I started asking a lot of questions.

Born in southern California, Steve married his junior-high sweetheart, Alison. Steve was the general manager at Targus, the laptop-case manufacturer, and Alison was the stay-at-home mother of their two sons, Tyler and Zach, both athletic kids. In the thirty-seventh week of her third pregnancy, Alison and the boys were spending the night at her mother's while Steve was on a business trip. After everybody went to bed, she began experiencing intense abdominal pain. She crawled to her mother's room, and the paramedics arrived soon after. In the hospital, the pain subsided, and everything seemed okay. But when Alison started labor a few hours later, the pain returned, and it was beyond measure. Thirty minutes later, Jake was born. From the expression on the doctor's face, Alison knew that everything was definitely not okay. Jake wasn't breathing, and she was bleeding heavily. While one doctor tended to Alison, another worked to resuscitate Jake. Finally they were both stabilized, and an ambulance whisked Jake to a hospital with better critical infant care.

Meanwhile, in Virginia, Steve was frantically trying to find out what was going on. He called the hospital only to be told that they were very busy down there. In the morning, he was on the first flight to Los Angeles. When he arrived, there was a message from his father on his cell phone. It said, "I'll be at the airport to pick you up." In his heart of hearts, Steve was sure his son was dead.

But Jake was a fighter, and he survived his first day, then the next, and the next. Because of complications while still in the womb and some difficulties during delivery, he suffered damage to every organ in his body but his heart. At two weeks old while still in the NICU, Jake had a seizure. A subsequent MRI led doctors to discover the extent of the damage to his brain. They told the Roberts that it was likely their son had cerebral palsy.

"What does that mean?" Steve and Alison asked.

The answer was that the doctors wouldn't know Jake's full prognosis, whether he had CP or where he was on its wide spectrum, until he was at least two years old.

Three weeks after his birth, Steve and Alison took Jake home. He had no further seizures, but no matter how often they told themselves that he would be okay, that he would do all the things that Tyler and Zach had done, the facts were undeniable. He couldn't hold his head up on his own. He had trouble locking eyes. He didn't roll over on his own or sit up. At two years of age, it was clear that Jake had a severe case of CP and would likely be in a wheelchair his whole life.

Alison threw herself into caring for her son. It was a round-the-clock job, and she lived with her breath constantly half caught in her chest with worry. They found a new house, in Yorba Linda, which they stretched to buy, but they wanted something single-story and large enough to accommodate wheelchair access. Finding the right care was a struggle, and Alison had to become a medical expert and a tireless fighter to get Jake the therapy and expertise he needed. If he held up his head a second longer than the day before, looking at her with his big blue eyes, it was a Herculean victory. When he turned his head and smiled when he heard her voice as she came in the room, she beamed with pride. When she was out shopping or at a restaurant, she loved the rare person who came up to her and asked about Jake. She loved talking about him.

Steve, though, had trouble making a connection with his youngest son. He couldn't talk with him, and he couldn't imagine what it was like to be trapped inside a body so stiff and rigid. Moreover, he couldn't get past thinking about everything Jake would never do. He would never kick a ball or race across the lawn with his brothers. He would never learn to hit a baseball or drive a car. As much as Steve wanted to find the connection, he was blocked by these thoughts.

Nearing Mile 6 of the marathon, we were moving slowly, almost walking, and we had plenty of time to talk.

"You didn't change my boy," Steve said, explaining why my speech in front of the board had been so inspirational to him. "He'll still struggle to eat. He may never say a word. But your story, what you've achieved . . . it's changed my whole idea of what CP is and what Jake could be. You lifted away the limitations and got me excited about his hitting his next milestones, whatever they are."

By Mile 8, we were both in trouble. Steve was having a hard time. My legs felt numb underneath me, my hips were searing, and I could barely stomach the idea of running another 5 miles.

"I'm in so much pain," I admitted.

"Good thing we're running together then," Steve said with a grimace.

As we continued, he asked me what it was like to live with CP, what the stiffness and pain felt like. He knew that Jake must feel the same in his body, but he had never been able to give voice to it.

We approached the turnoff where I was to head down one way to finish the half marathon and Steve would go down the other one for the full race. Steve asked if I would continue with him on the marathon course.

"It'll be fun," he said, challenging me to go at least to Mile 16, where the foundation's supporters were staffing the water station.

I hadn't known what to say to Steve when he told me his story or, for that matter, how to connect my experience of cerebral palsy with his son's. But Steve's openness and honesty about his own life had made me feel so comfortable that I wanted to do everything I could to help him finish his race. *What's an extra 3 miles on top of the half?* I thought. Like a naive fool.

We kept on. Steve told me that he was sure Jake knew he was running for him. He told me how he had learned to interpret the "noises" his son made to know when he was happy or sad, confused or safe and secure.

"I'm doing this for Jakey," Steve said as he struggled on.

At some point in the fog of exhaustion, we separated from each other. Steve slowed to a walk, I think, but I knew that if I did the same I would collapse. By the time I stumbled into the water station at Mile 16, I was a complete disaster. I sat down on the curb, showered myself with water cups, and tried to understand what I had been *thinking.* Finally, some friends lifted me up and drove me to the finish line, so I was there to cheer Steve on to the very end. Unfolding myself out of the car, I felt like the Tin Man from *The Wizard of Oz,* every joint rusted over and an anguish to move.

Nearly six hours after the marathon's start, as many of the race organizers were already disassembling the pedestrian barriers, Steve hobbled toward the finish. A hundred yards out, Alison lifted Jake, who was wearing the green "Team UCP" T-shirt, out of his push buggy and handed him to her husband. Holding his boy tight to his left shoulder, Steve jogged the last stretch of the race. Jake was bouncing up and down, smiling, laughing, and loving the movement. Everybody clapped, cheered, and wept as father and son crossed the finish line together. Alison and her two older boys were the first ones to greet them, and they held each other for a long time.

Afterward, I stumbled over to introduce myself to Jake, who was now back sitting in his buggy, his parents on either side and his father's marathon medal around his neck. Jake was a big four-year-old boy, probably three feet four inches tall and lean because of the constant involuntary flexing of his muscles. His head was bent sideways. His arms were crooked and rigid, and his fingers knotted. He had flawless pale skin, and his blue-green eyes seemed to take me in with a long glance. As I took his hand and said hello, his face remained expressionless. We were together a minute, maybe two.

As soon as I got home, I took an ice bath and collapsed asleep. The next morning, I lay in bed, unable to move. My body felt encased in concrete. After a while, I had to urinate, but I couldn't even move my legs out over the side of the bed. I rolled out of bed and onto the floor. Then, using my arms, I dragged myself caveman-style to the bathroom and pushed myself to my knees using the washstand. I still made a terrible mess, but I didn't care. Never before had I experienced such terrible pain.

A few hours later, having called in sick to work and now beached on the sofa, I was drifting in and out of sleep when the phone rang.

"I've some sad news," said Paul Pulver as a hello.

"What?" I asked.

"We lost little Jakey last night," Paul replied.

"What?" I repeated, not understanding, not wanting to understand.

"Jake Robert passed away last night in his sleep."

It was a simple thing that killed him: some mucus caught in his lungs. Most kids would easily have cleared it in their sleep. Jake could not, and he had died sometime in the early morning hours. There had been no sign that anything was wrong. The opposite, really. After the race, Jake was happy to be the subject of a bunch of photographs, surrounded by his grandparents, brothers, aunts, uncles, parents, and friends of the family. After a celebratory lunch, the parents and boys went back to their house in Yorba Linda.

Steve kissed him good-night and then tucked his other sons into bed. Eight-year-old Tyler, who considered himself Jake's protector, looked Steve right in the eye and said, "I will always take care of Jake." Alison put their newborn baby, Brady, to sleep, and then went in to ready Jake for bed. She put on his pajamas, brushed his teeth, and tucked the dolphin Tyler and Zach had recently won at the carnival under his arm. She laid out the green UCP T-shirt for him to wear again to school the next day to show his teachers, switched on the humidifier, and kissed him good-night. On his desk were the flash cards she had just made to help him learn how to communicate with his eyes.

The next morning, the family went about its routine. Jake usually slept late, so Alison took Brady with her to drive the older boys to school while Steve stayed in bed, still hurting from the marathon. When she came home, Steve was taking out the garbage for the Monday pickup. Alison went into Jake's room to start his day. He was always a light sleeper, but he didn't stir when she came to his bedside. She went to pick him up, and he still didn't move. Then she saw his still face, and she knew.

A scream erupted from her as she gathered Jake in her arms and ran out of the room. Hearing her, Steve ran inside. Alison was coming down the hallway.

"He's not breathing," she managed.

They put Jake on the carpet. Alison hurried to call 911, as Steve tried to resuscitate their son. He gave him mouth-to-mouth and chest compressions, but the air just came right out of him. Steve knew he was dead, had been for a while.

"He's gone," he kept saying. "He's gone."

The police arrived first, then the paramedics, then their family and their pastor. Steve and Alison held each other, not wanting to let the other go. In the first moment of calm, Alison turned to Steve and said, "We have got to stick together and support each other, because losing a child is one of the fastest ways for a family to break up." Steve never knew how much he loved his wife until that moment: even in her grief, her first thought was their marriage, their family, not herself, not her loss.

Medical personnel from the coroner's office came and examined Jake's body. Already Alison and Steve were torturing themselves over what they did, what they didn't do, what could have caused their son's death. The police wanted to ask Steve and Alison some questions; they had their job to do.

A member of the coroner's staff, a middle-aged woman, came to their side and said, "Unfortunately, we see a lot of this. We see deaths with fragile kids. The hardest thing about it, they're not well taken care of, usually neglected or abused. Your boy was so beautifully taken care of, just seeing his hair, looking at his well-trimmed nails, looking at his whole body. He's perfectly clean and flawless, and I know it's because he had a mom and dad who took wonderful care of him."

It was a small act of kindness in an otherwise uncommonly cruel day.

Much of what occurred that morning I learned only later. On the phone, Paul had few details, but he thought I should know. There would be a funeral in the next few days, he said, and as soon it was set, he promised to tell me the arrangements. The conversation was short.

Sitting on the sofa, I felt the world shatter and fall apart around me. Everything sort of just went dark. I could neither see nor hear anything. I was reeling, truly reeling, for the first time in my life, yet I couldn't grasp why the death of a boy I had met for only a moment hurt so bad.

I wondered if it was survivor's guilt; after all, I had been spared such a severe case of cerebral palsy. Maybe it was because Steve was the first person who had ever told me I was an inspiration. He said I had given him hope for his son; now that hope was gone. Maybe it was the thought of Steve and Alison enjoying such wonderful moments with their son one day, only to find themselves huddled over his body the very next. Their boy was gone from them, and there was nothing they could do but suffer it. Maybe it was all of these things—or none of them. All I knew was that Jake Robert called up a lot of memories in me, and his passing struck too deep to push away.

Pain. Deep, uncompromising, constant physical pain, from the arches of my feet up to my back. Not a single day passed without pain. Pain was part of my nature, who I was, from the time I was born.

Early on in my life—well before there was an explanation for this pain—I learned what to do with it. With no option to live my life without pain, I learned to put it away, to store it in some part of myself, so I could do, and be, in the world. My earliest memories of this doing, this being, centered around banging into things, tripping, and falling. Crossing the family room, I slammed my foot against a table leg, which had not seemed to be anywhere in my vicinity, and broke some toes. Hopping up the front steps to my house, I tripped and chipped a tooth. Running down the sidewalk with our black Labrador, Muffin, I tumbled and sheared off most of the skin on my knees. Climbing up to a treehouse, riding my skateboard, tumbling from a rebound on the basketball court: multiple fractures, a steel plate and screws in my arm. Toes, fingers, wrists, arms, ankles, I broke them all, but there was no stopping me—and, indeed, nobody tried. That was not my family's way.

As far as I can recall, my parents never said, "Be careful," or "Bonner, you shouldn't do that." They knew something was wrong with me, but nothing was said about it to me for years. They treated me the same as they treated my two older brothers, and they expected the same out of me. At the heart of that treatment was tough love. No crying. No whimpering. No complaining. Get out there, try hard, make mistakes, take your lumps, learn from them, and try again.

The master of this school of tough love was my mom's father, my "Bompa," Dexter Paddock. His was a my-way-or-the-highway kind of world. Wobbling lips, fear, hesitation, excuses—they had no place with him. Every morning, rain, shine, winter cold, or stormy swells, he headed out of his house in Laguna Beach, wearing only his red swimming trunks. No towel, no shirt, no sandals. A five-minute walk later, he was swimming north up the coast for a half mile; then he did the half mile back. Every morning, same swim, 365 days a year, all the way to his eightieth birthday.

I was a Paddock, and a Paddock learned at seven years of age how to swim in the ocean and battle those terrible riptides off West Beach. Not long after my birthday, he took me down to the beach, pointed out a riptide, and explained as he had many times before how to escape it. I shouldn't try to swim against the current; rather, I needed to swim parallel to the beach. But this time, he took me in the water with him to actually do it.

Bompa said, "See here. The rip's got us. You'll need to get yourself free." Then he swam away, back to the beach.

Bottom lip out, half in tears, I was scared, but I knew I needed to suck it up and do it. The riptide swirled around me. Caught in it, I felt its power draw me out to sea. I panicked a little, but then remembered his instructions: "Don't swim against the rip. Swim sideways out of it." A few seconds later, I was free, and Bompa congratulated me when I returned to the beach, still shaking.

Usually, though, I didn't need to be forced. Growing up in southern California, we were always outside, and I loved sports: baseball, soccer, basketball, swimming, and tennis—whatever the court or field. My upper body, especially my hand-eye coordination, was the bomb; my lower body, the destruction that followed. Unfortunately, most sports required the two to work together. I chose positions, like soccer goalie and baseball catcher, that best suited my strengths. I thrived on the competition, but spent a lot of my time enraged, kicking goalposts and fences, breaking rackets, punching the ground, cursing my body for what it couldn't do, or do well enough, or fast enough, or for long enough. Whenever teams were picked for a game of soccer or basketball, I was chosen last among my friends, no matter how hard I tried to be as good as they were. The hours of shooting baskets at the playground or kicking the ball against the garage door just didn't seem to do the trick.

Meanwhile, my brothers, Mike (eight years older than me) and Matt (almost three years older), excelled easily at sports. They piled up so many trophies, medals, and ribbons on their shelves that they could have opened their own shop. In particular, Mike was an all-state all-star in just about every sport he played. He had a body like a shovel, with wide shoulders and a narrow waist. The girls loved him. He was on the inside of a world that I feared I would remain outside of forever, my nose flattened to the glass.

My family never treated me any differently, but I knew something was different about me. A master detective didn't need to be on the case. After all, my brothers never wore holes in the toes of their shoes every few months, earning that look from our mother: *Off to the shoe store again.* None of my friends and neither of my brothers were fitted with bright-white fiberglass casts on both legs up to their hips that made them walk like Frankenstein's monster whenever they did go out. One cast might have been fine: anyone could break a leg. But both legs? There was something strange about that, and no way to hide it.

Mike and Matt were not treated like lab rats, off to a new doctor every few months, told to walk here, walk there, prying eyes watching every movement. They were not stuck into this machine and that machine, every part of their body probed, scanned, pricked with needles.

Then there were the plain facts that I looked different and moved oddly. I had these huge, floppy feet (size 11 by sixth grade). My string-bean legs and knobby knees were impossible to hide living in a place where kids wore shorts almost every day of the year. Wherever I went, my ankles flew wide, my knees touched, and my feet made this big slapping sound. There was no creeping up on anybody. "Thumper!" the kids jeered as they heard me coming down the hallway.

Oh, yes. They called me that, and lots of other names besides, in school and at the playground. "DeCalf," the kid without calves—that was one of the clever ones. The most obvious, "Boner" (instead of

Bonner), was the most common. They would shout it while mimicking my gait, slapping their hands against the bottoms of their feet, making sure I could see.

Whenever I fell, the walls and playing fields echoed with laughter. The bullying was painful, like a punch in the gut during kickball. Many of those moments I have blocked out, just as I did the puzzled stares and under-the-breath comments from adults and children alike whenever I crossed the street. I could hear them thinking it, even if they were out of earshot: *Something is different about that boy, but what is it?*

In the days after Jake passed, I thought a lot about my childhood. I felt I was being given a choice. I could dismiss Jake's death and his family's agony by telling myself that bad things only ever happen to other people. Or I could stand with Jake, for him, like the brother I felt I was. For all my falling and breaking bones, for all the doctors' visits and exams, for all the jeering at games or in the hallway, I was lucky. I could walk and run. Not smoothly, but I could walk and run. I had the freedom to go where I wanted, when I wanted—a freedom Jake and Paige Dunning and many other kids with cerebral palsy would never have.

I sat in one of the back rows at Jake's funeral, unknown to most of the mourners in the church that morning. There was lots of music: a drummer, an electric guitarist, and three young women with beautiful voices. One close family friend of the Roberts' read Psalm 23, "The Lord Is My Shepherd," and another quoted William Wordsworth about the death of his own son: "For myself I dare not say in what state of mind I am; I loved the Boy with the utmost love of which my soul is capable, and he is taken from me—yet in the agony of my spirit in surrendering such a treasure I feel a thousand times richer than if I had never possessed it."

One speaker after another approached the pulpit to share their memories of Jake, tears running down their faces. His aunt talked about how handsome he had been and his many nicknames: "Jakey Bear," "Jake-a-bake," "Jacaroni," "Jakarama." Another speaker talked about the glorious day at the marathon and how thankful she felt that Jake's last day had been so full of joy and family. His eight-year-old brother, Tyler, with his spiked hair, brave face, and little trembling voice, spoke of Jake in the present: "Jake is my little brother. He comes to all my games. He watches me play. He smiles when I'm around. I can make him laugh. Even though Jake's body is not with us anymore, I still have three little brothers. I love you, Jakey."

Then it was Jake's grandfather's turn. Jud Robert was an enormous presence, a man who looked as though he had seen a great deal of life, both its ups and its downs. His voice barely shook, but in his words the emotion was clear.

"Our family has been wounded severely. The fact that Jake is no longer with us is incomprehensible. We'll never be the same, and we won't pretend that we are," he said.

The whole church seemed to crumble at this statement, myself included.

"I have a grandfather's bias," he continued. "But, put simply, Jake was perfect. Jake never had a bad thought. He never rejected anyone. He never prejudged. He never hurt anybody. He was never selfish, never jealous. He never sinned. He only loved, and in his essence he was love. Some in the world looked at him, saw his body, and they didn't get him. He was perfect. He taught us all to have faith and never give up despite the odds. He taught us where God meets us in our lives, and he taught us to love at a level far deeper than we've ever known. He taught us what's important and what's not. . . . Jake will live on here. He will live on with the UCP Foundation, and he will live on in all of us with whom he connected. God bless."

Shortly after he sat down, I felt compelled to make my way to the front of the church and say a few unrehearsed words. Through a choked voice, I spoke about how odd it felt to be standing there, as I had known Jake for only a few minutes. Then I explained that I too had cerebral palsy, and that it had taken me thirty years to admit it openly. I got a few laughs by recounting how Steve had cajoled me to run much more of the race than I was able to. I finished by saying, "I ran those last 3 miles for Jake, because he couldn't. I'll continue to run, as long as I live, for him."

Later, when Steve and I had a quiet moment together, I promised him that I would run the marathon the next year, every single long mile of it, for his son.

3

Swimming in the Riptides

No way you have that! What exactly does that mean?"

"How did I not know? Wow!"

These were two of the typical reactions I got when I first started telling people I had cerebral palsy. One uncomfortable conversation followed another—uncomfortable more because of my own hesitation to speak about it than anything else. All I had ever wanted was not to be defined by others by what had happened in the first seconds after my birth. But now, as I geared up for the Orange County Marathon in January 2007, I was forcing myself, no matter how uncomfortable, to be more open.

My fund-raising messages spread the news fast and wide:

> *I have cerebral palsy. I am running the race in honor of a young boy named Jake, who died recently. We shared the same disability. Jake's father said I was an inspiration to him and to his family, and their faith in me drives me to do even more for our community. Please support me.*

Before sending the e-mail, my finger had hovered over the "Send" button for a good minute, perhaps more, but then it was done. Keeping Jake in mind and telling his story first, instead of mine, helped with every conversation after that. Here was this amazing boy. He had the same thing I do. Now I'm giving voice to his struggle and, through it, to my own.

While I prepared for the marathon, training and raising money, I slowly grew more comfortable with this outward stance. At last I was freeing myself from years of hiding and lying to those around me. But it did not come easily, and sometimes I just wanted to take it all back. *No need to look any closer. All is well, perfect, and in order here.*

I couldn't stuff my CP back in the closet, but as far as how I looked at myself, all was still perfectly in order and normal about me. That was how I had always been taught to be, no matter the evidence to the contrary.

Growing up, I was named Bonner Paddock Rinn. My family lived in a nice ranch-style house—one story, three bedrooms, and a stately oak tree in the front yard. Out back there was a swing set, lots of grass to kick a ball around in, and even a treehouse. There were lots of kids in the neighborhood, a middle-class suburb nestled in the hills of Arcadia—the sons and daughters of stay-at-home moms and professional dads (doctors, lawyers, teachers, engineers). My mother drove a Mercedes 240 diesel, which we called the "Slug" because she drove it so slowly, and my dad a big Oldsmobile station wagon. We played soccer, baseball, and tennis and took swimming lessons at the local pool. We went to church every Sunday, all three of us boys in matching outfits, and made frequent visits to our grandparents in Laguna Beach for some time in the sun and surf. Short of the white picket fence, we could not have been more normal: the picture-perfect American family. And any wrinkle there might have been in that picture-perfect picture? That would not have been seen by the outside world.

My mother, Andrea Paddock, was the guardian of the picture-perfect family. She came by the job fairly. Her family was Old California, all the way back to the pioneer and Gold Rush days. They owned lots of land and big houses and had a name that meant something. My given one came from my great-great-grandfather Elmer Bonner who owned a pharmacy in Pasadena back in the early 1900s. When Andrea was fourteen, her grandmother took her on a whirlwind tour of Europe, one followed by the local newspaper. Andrea's father, Dexter (Bompa), was in the navy during World War II, where he helped test and design experimental underwater breathing systems, and after that he had a long, secure career working in the insurance industry.

Bompa was a man of rules and regimens. Apart from the daily swim, he ate the same meals every day almost without fail: cereal with skim milk for breakfast; one slice of bread folded over turkey, gouda, and mayo for lunch; a protein (either meat or fish), a veggie, and a starch (usually rice) for dinner; then a big dessert and a smoke of his pipe in the living room. This discipline and rigidity were counter to Dexter's own father, who was an alcoholic womanizer who liked to bet on horses. Dexter demanded that his two daughters conform to his upstanding, no-nonsense world, even if it meant that they often ran aground on its rocky shore. He loved them, but it was a hard kind of love.

My father, Tom Rinn, was a civil engineer, and a brilliant one at that. Raised in the Midwest, he worked for the Metropolitan Water District of Southern California, the world's largest wholesaler of water. It was his calculations for charging for the volume of water flowing through the state's aqueducts that kept water pumping steadily throughout southern California. But for all his smarts and ability, Tom didn't seem to find much worth in himself. When he was growing up, his family was very much on the outskirts of the community. His father suffered from a severely curved spine and was labeled a "hunchback." As a boy, if Tom was ever asked to a birthday party, his mother would ask why would such-and-such a kid would have invited *him*.

Tom and Andrea met at UC Berkeley in the 1960s. Tom and his best friend and roommate, John McConnell, were introduced at the same time to the tall, athletic psychology student. John, who was six foot nine and brimming with all kinds of confidence, swept Andrea off her feet. Tom? Well, Tom was best man at their wedding. Everything looked to be going perfectly. Andrea gave birth to her first son, Michael. Michael was a healthy, bouncing baby boy. John was a highly sought-after computer engineer, just biding his time before he would pick whatever prime job offer he wanted.

Then John dropped the bomb. He was heading to Menlo Park, California, for a gig with IBM, and Andrea and their son would not be going along with him. John had fallen for the girl who had typed his master's thesis. They had been having an affair for months, even while Andrea was pregnant. After their divorce, Andrea returned to southern California, where Tom was already working at the Metropolitan Water District. Tom wanted to marry her, and she agreed. Just before the wedding, Andrea got cold feet and told Tom that she wasn't sure she could go through with it. He thought she was only nervous and convinced her that they would be good for each other.

To the world, the newlyweds were happy and suited to each other from the start. For the next eleven years (and the first eight years of my life), we were the Rinns of Arcadia. Nice house, nice family, picture-perfect. On Monday, Tom left the house with his suitcase and returned on Friday, after a week of traveling for work. There was little connection between my parents even when they were together. Tom and my oldest brother, Mike, had a very strained relationship, and their fights would echo throughout the house. As for the silences at the dinner table between my parents, the measured jabs, the joylessness of their life together, we all just swallowed it.

Finally, when I was eight, my parents gathered me and my brothers on the blue plaid couch in our living room. They sat in chairs opposite one another across a low table. As I stared at the old oil painting on the wall of a ship crossing the ocean, my mom said that Dad was moving out for a while. I kept repeating, "I don't understand. I don't understand." Months passed, and Dad didn't move back. He never would. "Moving out" eventually turned into a six-year separation and finally divorce.

The spare relationship we had with our father became sparer still. Every other weekend, he came over to the house to fix something or do the yardwork. I used to hang out on the porch steps, waiting for him to finish, so we could throw the ball together. The way I saw it, he would only play if I asked. He never offered. The same with checkers or Connect Four. Now, everything I asked him to do he would do, but it always felt as if he was obliging me, that he didn't really want to be there. The father of the family next door taught me how to ride a bike and how to throw a spiral with a football. On Boy Scout camping trips, I was almost always the only one unaccompanied by his father. During the summer and spring breaks, he took us on long trips, once to Disney World, another time to England and Scotland. We went sightseeing and kept busy, but again rarely interacted. Dad was quiet, rarely venturing more than a few words at a time, and often only if prompted.

If my dad loved me, it was a love that burned too deep inside himself to give off any warmth. My mom only drove the wedge farther between us. Whenever the chance presented itself, she would make subtle swipes. "I'd invite your father to your game," she would say, "but I don't know if he'll come."

Raising three boys, mostly on her own, while working as a substitute teacher at local schools, Andrea could have used the help, but she always seemed to be in control, and she often exerted it through manipulation and blanket punishments. If I wanted to go to the park, she would lay on the guilt trip: "Oh, I *was* hoping to have your help around the house, but, I mean, you go have fun." If I said I was going to have dinner at a friend's house: "Oh, you won't be home? Okay. It was going to be your favorite—meatloaf. That's fine, though." She never came out and said what she wanted or why she wanted it. Same with her punishments. If I didn't want to go to church, then I was grounded and had to stay in my room for the day, no TV, no nothing. If I was crying, I had to go to my room. We never discussed why was I crying. We never talked about what might be wrong: why I might not want to go to church, why I might prefer to have dinner at my friend's house.

The farther Mom's life got from her ideal, the harder she tried to maintain the image that everything was okay, to stay the course. This rigidity was her retreat, a course opposite to the one that her sister, Vicki, took, but incredibly destructive in its own way. Her older sister left southern California for the woods of Oregon. She was the flower child of the 1960s, the one who ate, drank, and smoked when she wanted, however much she wanted. No rules of her own, no adherence to society's rules. In the end, she succumbed to the family curse of alcoholism, drinking herself to death before she turned sixty.

We lived in Mom's house, and we played the roles she expected of us. Do the right activities. Get the right grades. Be the perfect boys. We tried to fit into the mold as long as we could, wanting to please her. Whatever was outside these roles got buried. At fourteen, my brother Mike was struggling with his sexuality. When he watched TV, he always found himself looking at the men, not the women. He told Mom he was gay, and to him, her reaction was clear: "Don't be one of those people." He felt shut down and vulnerable, deciding instead to throw himself into dating the most beautiful girls, playing every sport, and rushing the craziest fraternity.

My cerebral palsy was different in some ways, but the same in others. Mom did what she could to help me, but whatever my issues, it was private business to be put aside everywhere but the doctor's office. The view essentially was: "Bonner has CP, but it does not define him. He is the same as any of us. Period. End of story." We absolutely never spoke about my disability, whether at the dinner table or to the world outside. My middle brother, Matt, didn't have any knowledge of my diagnosis until years later when we had all grown up and moved out. Whatever struggles Matt had of his own, he buried them inside himself, like my dad did.

Throughout these troubled times, my sanctuary was the home of my grandparents, Bompa and Bomma. We spent many weekends and summers at their Laguna Beach house when we lived in Arcadia. Then, when I was thirteen, we moved to Mission Viejo, only a handful of miles away from Laguna Beach, and spent even more time with them. As my dad and I grew apart, Bompa was our father figure and my true north. He was a tough man, hard from his calloused feet and gnarled toenails all the way up. There were no games with him. You told the truth. You didn't show fear. You were on time. You never quit on something. You sucked up defeat, and you kept going. You gave it your best.

Bompa lived by these rules, and he expected us to do the same. I learned many of them while we played on the beach or swam in the ocean with him, hour after hour from dawn till dusk. Retired, he had lots of time for us. Later, I would understand that he was much easier on us than he had ever been with my mom and her sister. There were never any physical punishments from him: Mom had forbidden it.

After high school, I was eager to be free of everyone in my family except Bompa. But my average grades didn't exactly make me a shoo-in at an Ivy League school. We were also cash-poor. With the limited amount set aside by my family and the meager sum I earned slinging burgers at McDonald's and packing groceries at the local market, I couldn't pay for more than a couple of years' tuition at a state university. Instead, I enrolled at the local community college to study business.

The summer after my first year, I played a lot of soccer in an indoor league. As the goalkeeper, I didn't have to run much; plus I had big hands, a long reach, and some pretty good hand-eye coordination. One night after a game, the assistant coach of Concordia University pulled me aside and asked if I wanted to try out to be their goalie. A week later, I had a college scholarship. Yes, an athletic scholarship. Granted it would only cover part of my tuition and it was for the team of a small religious school that had gone winless (a big 0–19) the year before, but for me it was as if I had been chosen to play for Manchester United.

Manchester United we were not. We lost almost every game my freshman year. Still, college athlete? That was better than normal.

I had shot up in height. My body filled out. I was living away from home, no connection to poor old "Boner." Nobody needed to know about my CP or about the shooting pain I experienced after games from my ankles rolling over again and again.

In my sophomore year, Concordia recruited a better goalie. I sat on the bench; we kept losing. I was ready for the big college experience and transferred to San Diego State, joined a fraternity, drank a lot, dated a lot, worked out a lot, and studied very little. I had mastered hiding my awkward stride and putting off answering any questions when it *was* noticed. With a hearty laugh, an easy way with meeting people, and an always-ready-to-go attitude, there was nobody on campus more the quintessential party frat guy than I.

I drifted away from my family and finally had a complete break with my dad the summer leading into my senior year. It started as a fight over his refusing to help me more with the cost of college and ended with my shouting at him for never being there for me when I was a kid. Soon after, I changed my legal name from Rinn to Paddock, giving my grandfather someone to carry on his family name and honoring him for everything he had done for me.

There was never any doubt about what I would do after graduation. My brother Mike said I was tailor-made for sales. The uniform company Cintas hired me right out of college. I rented a house in Pacific Beach, just north of downtown San Diego. Flush with cash, I partied even more than I had in college. My time with Cintas led to a job with the payroll company ADP, then to a small sports marketing company, and finally to the Anaheim Ducks.

From a thousand feet up, I was living a perfect, normal life. It was the one I had been taught to follow. But by then Mike and I had drifted apart as well, so I had separated myself completely from any honest connection with the people closest to me, my family. And

I was lying to myself—and everybody around me—about a funda-mental truth of my daily existence: my cerebral palsy.

It took a nudge from Henry and Susan Samueli and the death of a small boy for me to shift course, but on this new road I still felt lost.

The morning of the 2007 Orange County Marathon was dark and cold, and on the way down to the race, I was terrified. My 16-mile run with Steve the previous year had almost ruined me. I remem-bered how my body had broken down, and now I was asking it to go another 10 miles beyond that. There was no way I would not finish, and that just intensified the fear of what I was about to do to myself.

I met up with the Robert family before the marathon's start. They provided a keen reminder of why I was there in the first place. Steve thought they could honor Jake by running in the race together. Alison had not wanted to come back to the event, but hard as it had been, she had agreed, and she, Steve, Tyler, and Zach (now ten and eight) signed up for the half marathon. When they told their family and friends, a whole bunch of them volunteered to run as well. Over forty people now clustered together at the start, all sporting T-shirts with Jake's smiling face and the words "Team Jake."

In the corral behind the starting gate I met up with my running partners for the day, Karla and Melissa. Friends from San Diego State, they were both in pretty mean shape and promised to run part of the course with me. They calmed me down with cracks like, "Bonehead, why are you making me do this?" followed by laughter.

Finally, the gun banged, and we were off—or were going to be once the thousands of others ahead of us cleared the start. The going was all good up the first hill, but then it had been the year before too. This time I kept the pace nice and slow. I wouldn't be fooled again by the adrenaline. No way. Not me. This was in the bag. Five hours max.

For the past year, I had trained as best as I knew how—or as best as advised by any quick Google search. I followed a training grid and ramped up the miles week after week. Occasionally I hit the gym and lifted weights. Three months out from the marathon, my body began resisting the steady increase in distance. My knees and ankles screamed once I hit the 10-mile runs in the hills around my apartment in Newport Coast. At the end of a 13-miler, I veered off the road into some bushes. Sheer exhaustion. After that, each time I tried to run, I just didn't have the energy. I decided to simply rest for the final eight weeks, hoping that enough strength had been built up in my legs. If not, my commitment to finishing the race would get me the rest of the way.

From my first fund-raising e-mail, the support had been over-whelming. Most started off the conversation with, "No way you have cerebral palsy!" followed quickly by, "It's incredible what you're doing." Relief blended into comfort, then confidence, and finally excitement. I felt proud that I had come clean. I was em-powered to speak more and more about why I was running the race. Contributions rolled in at a far faster rate than I could ever have imagined. My boss and coworkers at the Ducks made dona-tions, and people I didn't even know threw money into the pot. By the day of the marathon, I had raised over $30,000, a huge sum, and a show of faith that I could not disappoint by bowing out of the race early.

Which was easier said than done. Nine miles into the marathon, I was struggling. Running was not a natural movement for my body—or, more accurately, for my brain. The muscles in my legs never worked in sync. Everything in my body was tight and rigid from the start. With each stride, my ankles bowed out while my knees almost touched, making my legs looking like eggbeaters. There was never any balanced strike of the forefoot. Mostly, I landed on the inside of my foot, rolling inward on my big toe. Because of the stiffness in my lower back, I ran hunched over, and because of my equilibrium issues and lack of balance, I had to concentrate on the ground in front of me to keep me from falling. As I tired, these poor mechanics became downright poverty-stricken. Fatigue multiplied, particularly within my large muscles (quads, hamstrings, and calves). This left my smaller, supporting muscles to bear more of the strain, and they weren't up to it. That's a lot of anatomy to state the fact that I was not born to run.

By the race's midway point, this was clearer than ever. Melissa, who was battling knee pain, diverted off to finish her half marathon, while Karla kept at my side, fighting her own fight. We spoke about Jake, about what life must have been like for him, trapped inside a body that simply wouldn't work. He never ran. We had to do it for him, because we were lucky enough to have legs. We were half joking, because right then and there those legs were absolutely killing us.

By Mile 16, way out by the El Toro marine base, I couldn't speak, let alone joke around. I grumbled answers to Karla's questions, and soon she stopped asking them. She had prepared to do only the half, but had kept me company, and she was falling apart. A few miles later, Melissa was waiting to pick her up. I was clearly hurting, and Melissa decided to jump back into the race to help me. She made it another mile before her knees forced her to stop.

By Mile 20, I was on my own, with 6 more miles to go. The physical pain was like nothing I had experienced before. My feet felt as though they were covered by a thousand blisters that had been cut open and rubbed raw. My ankles, knees, and hips felt as if battery acid had been poured into them. My calves were clutched in a pincer grip. With the pain came a strange kind of warmth, a sensation I hadn't felt before. I wondered how much damage—permanent damage—I was inflicting on my body.

I thought about slowing down, pulling up short of the finish, quitting altogether. Such thoughts were quickly replaced with mutterings: "Screw it. Ruin my body? I don't care."

Strangers were cheering from the side of the road, but their words were white noise, lost to me. I almost felt as if I were about to black out. Everything was getting foggy, distant. Still I ran, forcing myself to stare at the pavement ahead of me to keep from crashing. Over and over I thought about Jake, how I couldn't quit on him. I pictured his face. I remembered how Steve carried him across the finish line. Somehow my feet kept moving.

Near the end of the race, I heard the cheers rise to a roar. "Way to do it for Jake!" someone along the sidelines said. My eyes cleared. Ahead, on the right, Tyler and Zach Robert hollered and rooted me onward. I was going to make it.

Crossing the finish line, I seemed to cry and smile at the same time. My whole body went weak. Friends gathered me up and helped me out of the chute. Steve and his family were there. He gave me a big bear hug. "Awesome job," he said. "I love you, man." My dad had showed up as well to congratulate me.

Later, Team Jake visited the hillside cemetery overlooking the marathon course, where Jake was buried next to his grandfather. On the branches of the willow tree beside his grave, Steve, Alison, and their boys hung their medals. Too debilitated to join them, I returned home and curled up in a bed I would barely leave for the next three days. When the exhaustion and agony gripping my whole lower body eased enough to stand without gritting my teeth, I started to think about what came next.

4

The Mountain

ighteen thousand crazed fans waving orange towels? Check. Six hundred bottles of Korbel Champagne on ice? Check. A six-week-old playoff beard, just like the one our players were wearing? Check. The moment had arrived. Now all the Anaheim Ducks had to do was beat the Ottawa Senators to claim the Stanley Cup.

It was June 6, 2007, and I was pacing the tunnel that led to the action on the ice, too crazy with nerves to watch the game or to converse with our sponsors. Four minutes into the third period the fans went wild, screaming loud enough to blow off the roof. I hopped and jumped into the arena as the Ducks players on the ice celebrated their now 5–2 lead over the Senators. This baby was over. Sixteen minutes later, another goal from the Ducks, and we had won the finals. Everyone on the staff hugged and congratulated each other.

The coaches, players, and owners all came out to join us. Henry Samueli raised the Stanley Cup over his head with the captains by his side. "We are Stanley Cup Champions! How cool is that?!" he declared. Following tradition, the players drank from the big silver chalice. But then, breaking with tradition, our owner passed the cup around to everyone who worked for the Ducks. There I was, Stanley Cup in hand, guzzling Champagne. The party lasted all night, and just before dawn a car dropped me off at home. Once inside the front door, I stripped off my Champagne-soaked suit and stumbled upstairs, a big smile on my face.

Grasping the Stanley Cup further fueled this feeling I had after the marathon that nothing was beyond my reach, and I needed to show it by attacking an even greater challenge than running 26.2 miles. The marathon had freed me forever of the need to hide my disability from others and proven a good way to raise awareness about and funds for children with CP who were battling to survive—and thrive—in their own bodies. And although that was certainly *a* motivation for my next adventure—and the one I planned on sharing with others—it was not *the* motivation for wanting to put my body through another torture test, whatever form it took.

There was something else, a need, a dark hunger, that drove me to achieve anything, everything, that others could achieve, no matter how hard I needed to push myself or the risk involved. In a way, it was no different than when I was a sixteen-year-old kid on the basketball court, trying to swoop around my faster, more agile competitors and leaping after impossible rebounds to prove I was every bit as able as they were. Once that had left me rolling in agony on the pavement after snapping in half both bones in my left forearm, but I had blocked that out, along with a lot of other things.

The origins of this hunger—where it came from and how it could be satisfied—were not exactly staring me in the face; that would have taken a lot more self-awareness than I had back then. In truth, I didn't even understand enough to pose the questions. The only one I was asking was *what*. What could I do next? Ultramarathons didn't grab me, particularly after 26 miles had almost shattered my legs to dust. There was no time for a long, cross-country Forrest Gump walk either.

One night during the summer I watched a Discovery documentary on Everest, but I felt that climbing that terrible Himalayan beast was begging for disaster, no matter one's abilities. Still, summiting mountains certainly made for fine drama and a punishing physical test. That might be the right avenue to explore. Then I began quickly researching other peaks. Soon I had mine.

Kilimanjaro. The tallest mountain in Tanzania. The tallest mountain in Africa. And given its volcanic formation, the tallest free-standing mountain in the world. Uhuru Peak rose unimpeded from the surrounding level plain to a height of 19,340 feet. Only about a third of the twenty thousand people who braved the climb every year made it, and a handful died every year in the attempt. A wild goal, yes, but in the realm of possibility, and nobody with cerebral palsy had ever summited the peak by the power of their own two legs. Kilimanjaro was ideal.

Wanting to make a big splash, I waited for the annual UCP-OC fund-raising gala, where I was being honored with an award for my marathon run, to make my Kilimanjaro announcement. Friends and even my whole family, Mom and Dad included, gathered. I concluded my acceptance speech with some unscripted words that seemed to come out of nowhere, up from inside of me.

"We have a choice in our lives. We can be content with where we are, or we can set goals and continue to push ourselves beyond our limits. I'm ready to keep doing that. I want to be the first person with cerebral palsy to climb the tallest free-standing mountain in the world."

Initial shock, then a roar of applause followed.

Afterward, I wanted to escape the stage, but the UCP foundation had arranged for the emcee to help jump-start the fund-raising. He asked me to stand beside him, and then asked the audience, "Who wants to donate for this guy?"

Cheers rang out.

"Let's get this thing rolling," the emcee said, playing the auction-eer in every way except for banging the gavel, and I was the object of the bids.

"Okay, let's start at $25,000. Who wants to kick this off? Anybody? Anybody?"

The first bid was $10,000. By the end of the night, I had raised over $50,000, and there was no turning back.

Up until that time, my only experience with climbing had been the annual church hike up to Sturtevant Falls in my teens. One year, I decided to win the Best Hiker award. I raced up and back down the small state-park mountain, fast as I could. That was more than two decades earlier and, needless to say, Sturtevant Falls was many orders of magnitude smaller than Kilimanjaro. Not that I knew ex-actly how many, since most of my research on the climb was limited to Wikipedia entries and YouTube videos. It was clear, however, that to reach the top of Uhuru Peak would require long days of hiking and steep climbing at high altitudes with low oxygen, confronted by wind and freezing cold at every turn. We would have to carry heavy backpacks, to bunk down at night in tents, and to make for the top of Kilimanjaro in the pitch-dark when the unpredictable weather was at its most predictable (apparently the really bad storms usually hit in the afternoon or early evening).

I would need a team and training. One of the first calls I made was to Paul Flores, a former roommate of mine in San Diego. Paul was Mexican American, with long black hair pulled back in a ponytail, who spoke in "dudes" and "bros." He was born in southern California, but after his older brothers were told they needed to choose between joining either the Crips or the Bloods, their parents moved them to Grantsville, Utah. Grantsville was a middle-of-nowhere kind of town with a thousand people and few Hispanics, so Paul learned to fight at a young age. His father was a Vietnam veteran, but it was his mother who taught him how to box.

Ignored by his teachers at the local public school, Paul managed to reach the eleventh grade without being able to read. A tutor fixed that, and he got straight As thereafter until graduation. Unsure of his future—what to do, how to pay for college—he called up an army recruiter. In April 1994, he started basic training at Fort Benning.

Paul's brother was in the same platoon, and they both ended up in the Rangers. Already tough and fearless from his hardscrabble childhood, Paul became tougher still. He served as an ammo bearer for the gunners in the weapons squad and rightly earned his nickname, the "Iron Horse." It was not unusual for him to hike out on exercises with 120 pounds on his back—everything from the regular kit to tripod mounts, spare barrels, night-vision gear, and 50 pounds of ammunition.

Paul's philosophy was, "If you know somebody is going to hit you, you hit him first." A bad brawl, a bum charge for smoking marijuana off duty, and an independent streak too wide for military life saw Paul back in Utah a few years later. He tried college at Utah State, but got mixed up in drugs. Realizing he was heading down a wrong path, he quit and left for Salt Lake City. He mowed lawns and began rock climbing with a friend. Soon he was hitting the mountains every weekend and during the winter too. He trained to become a massage therapist and found himself working on a few Olympic skaters. A girl led Paul to San Diego. He worked as a bartender, a server, and even a chef and had an apartment next to mine. Soon after we met we ripped down the fence that separated our apartments.

Paul was easy to like. He surfed and partied, he had a mystical calm, and there was never any doubt he had your back. I called Paul one day to see if he wanted to meet up for a drink. At the time, he was working over seventy hours a week just to stay afloat.

Paul told me, "I can't. Don't have any money."

I replied, "Paul, I'm calling to hang out with you. If we sit on my couch, watch TV, that's cool. I just want to spend time with you."

He later told me that I had earned his friendship for life that day.

Paul moved back to Utah, got married, found a job working maintenance at a smelter outside Salt Lake City, and kept up his love of climbing. When I called him about Kilimanjaro, he said immediately, "I'm in." If things went bad for me on the mountain, I knew that Paul would hoist me on his back and carry me down.

Through Paul, I met Tim Geiss, who organized hikes and mountain summits around the world. He volunteered to lead our expedition and set fall 2008 as the date for our climb. When he asked if I needed any special gear or training for the climb because of my CP, I simply said, "I'm fine. I'm good like everybody else." And I believed it.

While Paul began training in Utah in early spring, I hit the hills and canyons around Newport Beach—short hikes during the week, long ones on the weekend, following my own improvised schedule based on the informational packets Tim sent to everyone.

A few times I asked my brother Mike to come along on a weekend hike. Although he lived only 10 miles away, I rarely saw him more than a couple of times a year. I knew he liked to hike, so I hoped it might be a good way to reconnect. Either he never got back to me until it was too late, or he said he would join me and then didn't show up. Finally, I stopped calling. I tried to get my other brother, Matt, to join me for the climb itself, but he begged off because he had a young kid.

Slowly our team filled out, an odder collection of folks than have probably ever made the attempt together. Tim Geiss was team leader. A wiry, youthful forty-five-year-old, he was a flight attendant for Delta, but his sideline was leading these kinds of tours. Jayson "Dilly" Dilworth, my other roommate from San Diego, who now lived in Austin, Texas, was a joker, a Botox salesman, and, as we sometimes joked, the redneck version of me. Nancy Sinclair was the oldest of the group. She was head of marketing for one of the Ducks' sponsors and had climbed Mt. Whitney four decades earlier. Her granddaughter had CP. Rick White was a late addition to the team. He booked a plane ticket to the wrong continent—we called him Magellan. Last but not least, Shirley Ala was a physician's assistant and backcountry skier Paul knew from Utah.

As far as I could see, we were the ideal team. Tim was the expert, Paul the mystical warrior. Dilly was the comic relief, Shirley the healer, Nancy the grandmother. And Rick . . . Well, at least we knew who not to follow on the mountain. I was the rallying point, the reason, I hoped, why the others would keep pushing if they decided they didn't want to do it for themselves.

> *There is the grand dome or crater of Kibo [Uhuru], with its snow-cap glancing and scintillating like burnished silver on its eastern flank. . . . What words can adequately describe this glimpse of majestic grandeur and godlike repose?*

Tim included this dreamy quote from early explorer Joseph Thomson in one of the prep packs he sent out five months before we left for Africa. It sounded fabulous. But he also detailed the dangers involved for us on the mountain. Beyond suffering potential hypothermia and altitude sickness, we faced the possibility of acute mountain sickness, whose symptoms included nausea and vomiting; high-altitude cerebral edema, indicated by profound lethargy and manifest confusion; and—worst of all—high-altitude pulmonary edema, indicated by bluish skin color, shortness of breath, and rapid heart rate, which, if it went on too long and excess fluid filled the lungs, could cause death.

Never once confronting the notion that I might be more susceptible to these risks than anybody else, I put them aside and kept training. When I got to the mountain, I figured I'd be just another climber working to make it to the top. In April, I climbed Mt. Baldy in the San Gabriel Mountains outside Los Angeles. We started fairly high up, and it took four hours to reach the summit at 10,064 feet. The final half hour involved hiking up a steep ridge. I felt my heartbeat in my eardrums and knew I was hitting my body's limits. But I made it up and learned two valuable lessons. First, I needed to use hiking poles on my next climb, because I kept losing my balance on the trail; and, second, I was a long way from ready for Kilimanjaro.

On the upside, my mission to summit one of the "Seven Sisters" was gathering a lot more attention and funds than I could have imagined. Originally, I had hoped to raise $100,000 for UCP. Donations rolled in at a quick and steady pace throughout the summer, everything from big checks to little ones. Some of the smaller ones meant the most, like the one from a boy who sold his bike to give $50 to my campaign. Local magazines and newspapers featured stories about me, accelerating the fund-raising even more. Through my work with the Ducks, I got huge support from my sponsors for the climb. Toyo Tires, Oakley, Herbalife, and Young's Market Company all donated either money or equipment for our team. By late summer, I had raised close to a quarter of a million dollars.

In June, three young filmmakers who had just graduated from Chapman University's film school threw in with our team. They wanted to shoot a documentary about my attempt. It was a haphazard, last-minute addition, but they were committed. The same day we met, two of them, Mitch McIntire and Kent Bassett, borrowed some of my clothes and joined me on a hike. Everything was coming together, by both my intent and chance.

Three weeks before leaving for Africa, I set out on my big training climb: Mt. Whitney, the highest mountain in the lower forty-eight states. Coming with me were Mitch, who was tall and thickly built, and Kent, who was thin and wiry like a long-distance runner. We started out at 3:30 A.M. Even with my new headlamp (and new boots and hiking poles), it was disorienting trying to follow the trail with the small beam of light, a warning signal of what I would face at night on Kilimanjaro.

At 6:15 A.M., the sun rose, casting the Sierra Nevada range in a beautiful yellow and red haze. We crossed a stream by a single-log bridge. I barely managed. Then it was onward and upward. Hour after hour, I dragged my feet up the trail, pushing down hard on my hiking poles to compensate for my weak legs. None of us had brought enough water, and we were desperately thirsty. Wearing new boots was a tragic mistake: my feet blistered, and my ankles hurt. Near the tree line, we stopped at a stunning mountain lake and tried to catch our breath before beginning on the series of ninety-nine switchbacks that would take us to the top at 14,505 feet. The trail turned into a scramble over giant gray rocks. Way up on the ridge, other climbers looked like little ants. Time and again, I thought we were close to the summit, only to realize that we faced yet another switchback.

Clouds rolled across the sky, the wind gusted, and I started to get a chill despite the strenuous effort. Over the last few hundred feet, the bones in my feet felt as if they were breaking.

At the top, we celebrated briefly and ate our lunch on a flat rock. We signed the log book at the stone house at the summit, and then I had to face the fact that now I had to find my way back down. After fifteen hours and over 24 miles of trail, I finally stumbled back to my car. My feet and the tendons in my ankles were shot. My toes, which had been banging into the front of my boots with each step, felt broken. Driving home, my legs stiffening with each passing minute, I worried that I had done myself a serious injury. More than that, I feared how I was going to manage eight days in a row of such hikes on a mountain higher than this one by almost a mile.

The next couple of weeks, I woke up every morning hoping the unusually intense lancing pain in my ankles and feet would have disappeared. Every morning I was disappointed. Finally, I knew I had to see a doctor. Fifteen days before we were scheduled to leave for Africa, I went to see the Ducks' team physician, Dr. Craig Millhouse.

Millhouse was about as unflappable as they come. Working for decades on ice-hockey players has that effect. On the exam table, I told him about my training hike and the mission ahead.

"Why would you do that?" he said, chuckling. "Sounds like quite an adventure."

I shrugged. He wasn't wrong.

Then he rolled his chair over toward me and began feeling around my feet with his fingers and thumbs. Each time he probed too deep, I had to take a sharp breath. My arches, the balls of my feet, my heels, throughout my ankles—all of it stung.

"Well," he said, "you haven't completely snapped the ligaments off the bone, but there's a lot of damage. A lot. You need some ankle braces and physical therapy, but two weeks isn't enough time for you to heal completely."

Now I was scared. There was no way we could postpone the climb. Everything was already set in motion.

The next day, I was fitted with braces to support my ankles as I walked, and I started with the therapist. Stretches. Ankle rotations. Foam rollers. Resistance work with coil bands. She even had me picking walnuts off the ground with my toes. The exercise improved my strength, but I was nowhere near healed. With each hour ticking down to the time we were to leave for Africa, the pressure mounted.

Betraying every instinct to avoid doctors, I also made an appointment with Dr. Afshin Aminian, my neighbor and one of the leading orthopedic specialists in the country. His prognosis was very clear and firm. The tendons in my ankles were injured and would not repair themselves by Kilimanjaro.

Then he said, "With zero physical challenges, climbing mountains is difficult. But with your cerebral palsy, you've got muscles that don't function well. They'll cramp and fatigue far quicker than an able-bodied person's. Your coordination isn't perfect. And given the altitude and the lack of oxygen, we don't know how your brain will respond, particularly as it's been damaged since birth. There are many uncontrollable variables."

"I know. I know." Those were my words. In my head though, I accepted none of what he said about my condition, same as when Dr. Starr had first diagnosed me almost twenty-five years earlier.

"You risk slipping and falling and dying," Dr. Aminian said firmly.

"I'm good," I said, thinking only that Kilimanjaro is dangerous for everyone.

He looked at me as if I was crazy and let me go.

I kept my injury, and his warnings, to myself. Before leaving for Africa, I drove out to see Bompa at his Laguna Beach home. He was ninety-one and, with my grandmother in a care facility, he was living by himself.

Bompa was his usual gruff, tough self, but now with a layer of fragility. His hands shook slightly, and his every move seemed to take some deliberate care. I knew he was only holding on until Bomma passed, not wanting to leave her alone after seven decades together. As we sat down for lunch at his big butcher-block table with its iron legs (a table that once reminded me of Bompa himself, apt since he made it), I considered the fact that this might be the last time I spent with him. As usual, he was dressed in torn jeans, a faded shirt, and no shoes.

"When's your flight? . . . How long's the climb? . . . Who are you going with?" Bompa asked lots of questions. His final question: "Are you ready?"

"Ready as I'll ever be," I said, knowing better than to boast around him.

He gave a worried smile. Then I gave him one of the African stone necklaces I had gotten to give to my supporters in advance of the climb. Bompa fumbled with the screw clasp, but finally I got up and secured it around his neck. I could tell it meant a lot to him, even if he wouldn't say it. We hugged.

"Take care of yourself. I'll tell you all about it when I'm back," I said.

"Come home safe," Bompa said. "Love ya."

Outside, sitting in my car before driving away, I put my hands on the wheel and shook from the emotion of it all.

At home, I finished packing all the gear. My flight to Africa left in sixteen hours. Finally, after all my checklists had been triple-checked, and after I had put it off as long as I could, I went into the kitchen and paged through the will I had prepared in advance of the trip one last time. The documents, all signed and notarized, were a grim reminder that Kilimanjaro was more than an adventure. I was desperate to prove something, to myself and to the world, and I was willing to drive to the edge to do it.

My body had not yet healed. My doctors had warned me against going. But there was a certain peace in knowing that I was willing to give everything to the effort. I sent an e-mail with a scan of the documents to my brother Matt, whom I had declared the executor of my estate.

I sent a second e-mail to my father. Since our break when I was in college, we had mended our relationship with slow and stuttered steps. He had remarried, to a wonderful spitfire of a woman named LaDonna, and although my dad was still very quiet, he was becoming more open about his feelings. Our relationship still needed a lot of work, but dinners together and his showing up at my marathon race and then my announcement about Kilimanjaro were helping.

Before I went to bed, I checked my fund-raising website. There was a message from Steve Robert. He had just committed $1,000 to my fund-raising campaign, the last donation I would receive before I left the next morning. Steve included the message, "I'm proud of you. Know that you will always have a part of Jakey with you."

Sleep did not come easy.

It was August 28, 2008, and we were on our way to Tanzania at last. There was no fanfare at my apartment, no tearful good-byes with my family at the airport. The early morning flight from LAX to Detroit with the documentary film crew was uneventful. At our connection in Detroit, I met up with Dilly. From Detroit to Amsterdam, the plane's entertainment system was stuck on a single movie, *Kung Fu Panda*. I tried to sleep, but planes, where I am stuck in a single position, are brutal on my body. It was hard to know whether I'd dozed off at all, since that furry panda was playing on a *Groundhog Day* loop. Most of the time, Dilly and I joked around with each other, trying to ease the tension.

"I live in Texas. The highest thing to climb there is a barstool," Dilly drawled, stretching out his long legs.

"Are you nervous?" I asked.

"My wife's nervous."

I looked at him. He was nervous. "Hope you gave her a big kiss good-bye."

"How far do we hike each day?"

"I don't know," I said, never having once even examined the trail we would take to the summit. "Tim will tell us."

"And meals?"

I shrugged.

"Who's carrying what? Will we be stopping a lot? Which day's the hardest?" He ran down a list of questions.

Finally, I said, "Dude, I have no idea. We'll learn together."

"Well," he smiled. "Shit howdy, that sounds good."

We both laughed. Dilly had his sayings.

Dilly had grown up in a small town between Austin and San Antonio, where his dad owned a pizza shop. He went to Texas State University and moved to Houston after graduation. Like me, Dilly got a job in sales straight out of college. Two years into his job with ADP, he wanted out of Texas, to see some of the world. His boss thought there might be a position coming available in San Diego, but Dilly would have to wait—maybe for months. That night, Dilly packed his bags, drove for twenty hours, and went straight to the San Diego office of ADP, my office at the time. He talked his way into a job, although he was given one of the toughest spots in the area: from Tijuana to downtown San Diego.

I liked Dilly from the start. He was a born salesman, and though he didn't speak a lick of Spanish and stood out in the predominately Hispanic territory, he killed it. At the office, his was the cubicle next to mine. I took him out for a night on the town, and three days later he moved into the spare bedroom in my beach house. Paul Flores was living right next door. We were three amigos.

After a few years as roommates, Dilly moved back to Texas and married a local girl, but we remained close. In May I had called him to ask him to join me on the climb. I needed somebody who knew me backward and forward, who would tell it to me like it was. More than that, I needed his humor. Dilly asked his wife, Karen, what she thought about it. She said, "Make sure he makes it, and you get back safe."

Dilly had only four months to train and, with his sea-level town and 100-degree summer days, the conditions were not exactly ideal. But he didn't flinch. He swam upstream in a river near his house for two hours at a time to work on his cardio. He hiked up and down the few hills there were in the town to condition his legs. As he traveled a lot for work, he used to stay in the tallest hotel he could find, strap on a thirty-pound backpack, and climb the steps for two to three hours at a time.

"I'm Huckleberrying out here for you," he told me.

Now we were Huckleberrying together.

When the plane landed in Amsterdam, we met up with rest of our crew, who were coming in from various parts of the States. Paul and I hugged, and then he introduced me to Tim, our team leader.

What struck me about Tim was his Buddhalike calm and the fact that there was not an ounce of fat on his body. He gave me a firm handshake and one of those thousand-yard stares. He was definitely measuring me up, both physically and mentally.

It was an uncomfortable few moments, but finally he said, in his typical quiet voice, "Are we ready to do this mad adventure?"

"Absolutely," I said.

Another long flight, and we landed in Tanzania in the middle of the night on August 29. As we taxied from the runway, I thought the airport looked eerily empty. There were only a few lights and no other planes. I was a long way from home now. A pair of vans took us to a motel by the airport. In the lobby we gave a muted group cheer and then went off to our rooms. My bed might as well have been made of concrete. I spread out my sleeping pad on top of it, but that was little help. Eventually exhaustion took over.

When I woke up the next morning, I stretched out my legs and ankles. They were still not 100 percent, but I hoped they would continue to heal over the next two days before we started our climb. We moved into a hotel in downtown Arusha and toured the city. The roads were packed with every kind of vehicle: hand carts, motorcycles, pickups, bicycles, 1980s Toyota vans masquerading as "buses," taxis, and all the rest. Clearly, there were few traffic laws—or police to enforce them—and crossing an intersection was like a game of chicken on steroids. We went to the cultural center, basically a lure to sell tourists souvenirs and trinkets, and snapped photos of ourselves wrestling with a fifteen-foot wooden alligator. I danced and played the drums with some teenagers who had assembled by the entrance. For a moment, it was fun not to think of the mountain that awaited me.

Back at the hotel, over dinner, Dilly informed us that, in his infinite wisdom, he had been taking Cipro for the past week.

"Tell me you haven't," Paul said.

"What do you mean?"

When we reminded him that it was the malaria pills—not the antidiarrhetics—that he was supposed to take in advance, he gave us a sour look. Everybody broke down in laughter.

"You'll need a jackhammer to take a crap," Paul said.

"Well, shit howdy," Dilly said, shrugging. "Why didn't anybody tell me?"

We laughed until our sides hurt, and then Tim gathered us together. He went over every detail of the climb: what we needed to bring, the role of the porters, what we would eat, the distance and elevation we would travel each day.

"There will only be one really hard day," Tim said, and I wondered if he meant hard for him—or for me.

Halfway through his prep talk, Tim asked if we would be willing to pay the extra $10 a day for the porters to carry up a portable outhouse. Someone cracked that Dilly wouldn't need to pay, and again we were overcome. Nothing like a little bathroom humor to break the tension.

The next morning, we piled into our safari vans and drove out of the city. It didn't take long before we were in the middle of the countryside. We passed every kind of ramshackle dwelling—places made out of branches, scrap wood, rusted corrugated sheet metal, rocks, whatever could be found. Usually, there was a scrawny animal tied to the side of the house. Typically a goat, rarely a cow. The poverty was overwhelming, and I felt as though I had fallen into some kind of time warp.

After an hour, we pulled off the road and stopped at the gate to the Usa River School. When Tim and I were organizing the trip, I told him about my interest in meeting Tanzanian children who had cerebral palsy. It took him a month of research to find a place that cared for them. As the school's headmaster led us past the gate and into the grounds, we quickly learned why that was the case.

In Tanzania, as in many African countries, children with disabilities are shunned, mistreated, and even killed. They are not allowed in schools. The government offers no care facilities or programs for them until they are sixteen years old. Prior to that, they have to fend for themselves. It is not uncommon to hear stories of children with cerebral palsy or Down syndrome being locked into closets and cages or being left by their families on the side of the road in the middle of the night. In some remote villages, children are burned alive out of fear they have the Devil inside them.

Waiting for us in the central courtyard were three dozen teenagers, all in matching blue uniforms, their eyes looking us over nervously. Most of them suffered from a physical deformation, such as a club foot or a missing limb, or from a neurological disability like mine.

I went up to a few of them and introduced myself in the pidgin Swahili I had learned, which basically consisted of, "Hi. My name is Bonner."

One girl, who clearly had Down syndrome, shook my hand and tried to say hello in English. She was very shy and stumbled over her words. The headmaster asked her to try again, and with a clear voice she finally said, "Hi. I'm Barbara."

I smiled, and she gave me back the biggest smile I could ever remember.

Afterward, the kids lined up in three rows and sang to us in Swahili. The headmaster translated the lyrics for us, something along the lines of:

Even though life is not perfect,
the sun will come up today,
and the sun will go down tomorrow.
What happens in between is what matters.
Remember to be happy and kind.
Remember, it's all about people.

Most of the words were lost on me, and the song was offpitch and uncoordinated. But none of that mattered. They sang with such hope—you could see it their faces, hear it in their voices—that it left every single one of us uplifted. During their next song, they welcomed me into the circle. I danced about and butchered the chorus. Everyone laughed and had a good time.

Then the headmaster gave us a tour, showing us where the children slept and the classrooms in which they learned to read and write as well as knit, carve wood, and make jewelry. There were several large, well-constructed buildings, but most of the place was empty. Clearly there was room for many more students. From their shop, I bought some necklaces and then thanked the kids for their songs before returning to the bus.

As the headmaster closed the gate after us, a chill went through me. Here I had met thirty to forty teenage kids from the whole of Tanzania, and it was the only place in the country I could find that helped children with disabilities. The obvious question was: Where are all the other kids? There had to be tens of thousands or hundreds of thousands who needed care. How many were instead being abandoned, starved, hidden, locked in cages, or killed? It was a thought that would not leave me.

That same night, after an early dinner and a final briefing from Tim, I returned to the hotel room I shared with Dilly. We were leaving for the mountain early the next morning, and there was a lot to pack. It looked like an REI shop had exploded inside the room. Boots, thermal underwear, hiking poles, dry-wick T-shirts, gloves, hats, Camelbacks, toiletry kits, and dozens of other items littered the beds and the floor.

As I began sorting through everything I needed for the climb, Dilly was battling to roll up his bulky flannel-lined sleeping bag, which was more a square than a rectangle. Dilly was wrestling with it as though it was a crocodile he had by the tail, trying to fold it and cram it into a nylon sack while it continued to wriggle out of his grasp. Fifteen minutes into this skit, I was doubled up with laughter.

"Where'd you get that thing?" I asked, thinking the bag looked like something I wouldn't even take to a sleepover as a kid, let alone a mountain with subzero temperatures.

"Bass Pro Shops."

"Okay."

"I got it in the bargain bin. It was $10, down from $300."

This broke me down ever further. Dilly was always a bit cheap, but there really should be limits.

After a few more hours of packing and watching BBC TV, we crawled into our beds and turned off the lights. For a long while we were both quiet, unmoving.

"Are you awake?" I asked.

"Yeah," Dilly said. "I'm trying to get in my head what we're about to do."

"We're not here to attempt this," I said, trying to convince myself as much as him. "I've *got* to do this. I can't be weak. I've got to do this."

Dilly rolled over and switched on his camera. I wasn't sure what he was doing until he turned the screen toward me and hit play. He had shot a video of the Usa River schoolkids singing. We listened to their song several times. Afterward we were both silent again, back in darkness.

I didn't sleep much, maybe a couple of hours at most, but by the time the sun came up, I was as ready as I would ever be.

5

It's About to Get Real

It was time for the final preparations. Sitting on the edge of the bed, I donned my ankle braces and then drew the letters "J" and "R" on the handles of my hiking poles. I would be thinking of Jake Robert every time they struck the ground. I stuffed a necklace I bought at the Usa River School into the front pocket of my backpack, along with the "comfort cross" of St. Christopher, patron saint of travelers, given to me by a friend, and a small plaque that said "Never, Never, Never Give Up," sent by a young girl with CP named Bridget who had raised $700 for me selling lemonade. The mementoes helped to settle me. After checking my gear one last time, I hoisted my backpack over my shoulder and turned to Dilly.

"Let's do this."

He nodded with the same nervous enthusiasm that I felt. We headed down to the lobby. My ankles and legs were now numb rather than sore, and I took that as a good sign. Outside the hotel, a shuttle van waited. The other members of our team were already loading their bags.

"Good morning, brother," Paul said, giving me a bear hug that almost lifted me off the ground. "Are you ready?"

"Oh, yeah, big-time ready," I said with a half laugh.

Tim gave me a quick hello, but he was busy checking in all the bags. Our whole team, numbering ten including the documentary crew, was shuffling around the van. Occasionally we looked at each other, then away, as if to say, *I know what you're feeling, because I feel the same, but let's just not talk about it.*

We clambered into the van, and I scored the seat on the left-hand side by the door, so I could stretch out as much as possible. It was a three-hour trip to the entrance of Kilimanjaro State Park. From there, it was another hour to where we would begin our climb. The driver shut the door, and the van sputtered to life. The clunker, a former airport shuttle, must have been thirty years old. Its engine sounded about as powerful as a lawnmower's.

The first half of the trip was cheerful, with lots of small conversations going on, but once we cleared Arusha and the sun began to rise, things got quiet. I stared out the window, watching the occasional motorcycle zooming past or Tanzanians emerging from their small roadside shacks. Eventually, the landscape cleared into long stretches of sugarcane fields, and I imagined the climb ahead as Tim had explained it to us.

There were many routes to the summit of Kilimanjaro. Some were short and steep, challenging the hardiest climbers; others followed a relatively gentle slope and were supplied with sleeping huts. Tim had chosen the Shira Route, and although not especially technical (we were told), it was one of the longest, most remote, and most strenuous climbs. Approaching the summit from the west, the Shira Route offered some of the most beautiful scenery, but there were no huts, and we would set out at a high elevation, which meant we would have less time to acclimatize.

For seven days, we would trek across moorlands, ice fields, lava ridges, alpine deserts, and steep barren trails of pulverized volcanic rock. We would hike more than 64 miles from beginning to end and climb over 10,000 vertical feet. The higher altitudes would starve our bodies of oxygen, and temperatures would range from the high 50s during the day to below zero at night. The unpredictable weather on the mountaintop might also bring hurricane winds, rain, and even sleet and snow. No short, quick, and easy for us.

Yet as the bus rumbled down the highway, I felt confident as ever in my ability to summit Kilimanjaro. Tens of thousands of others had. I would do the same. After all, I had always held my own as an athlete (with a lot of determination and stubbornness). With everyone but my brother Mike, I measured stroke by stroke in the ocean. On the basketball court and soccer pitch, I may not have been the best, but I was okay. I had a few dozen trophies and ribbons to prove it. A half marathon—boom, I ran 16 miles instead, on the sparest of training. A marathon—it hurt, but I finished.

Nearing the Londrossi Park Gate, our bus's lawnmower engine was clearly tiring. I doubted its ability to get us up to the Shira Plateau, still a long windy climb up a hole-pocked dirt road. At the gate, we piled out, glad to stretch our legs as we signed into the park and its officials checked our passports and made sure we had the right permits to climb Kilimanjaro. Tim introduced us to our Tanzanian lead guides, Bariki and Moody, both of whom said hello in English, gave us a short smile, and then hurried off to inspect our bags and equipment, which their porters would be taking up the mountain to our campsites.

After a lot of shuffling back and forth, we loaded back onto the bus and headed out. A few minutes away from the gate, we came upon a broken-down jeep with a couple dozen porters sitting on its roof and on the side of the road. A moment later, they were crammed onto our bus, taking up the few free seats or finding spaces in the aisle. There was a lot of joking and bantering in Swahili.

The bus chugged up the steep, bumpy road, sounding as if it was about to quit at any moment. We were moving at barely a crawl. It quickly became hot and stinky, but whenever someone opened a window, the dust from the road would swirl in and choke us.

I was now squashed into my seat, unable to move, and my legs began to hurt. I tried to think of something other than how slow and long this ride to the plateau was going to be, but I was restless and in pain. I tried to stand, but there were so many ruts in the road that I was almost thrown from my feet. Dilly was sitting behind me, looking as though he might hurl his breakfast into his lap. I couldn't have been a much better sight.

"Almost there. Very close, very close," Bariki kept saying, with a bit of a laugh. He was taller and lankier than our other guide, and he seemed to be perpetually amused by us.

After an hour, I knew I had to get off the bus. I would rather walk.

"Stop," I told the driver.

We were going so slow, it was hard to tell if he even needed to put on the brake. The door clattered open, and I staggered off. Paul followed right behind me. I was more certain than ever that he would be my protector throughout the climb.

"Any lions or elephants?" I asked Bariki.

"Not usually," he said, shaking his head.

Paul and I hiked up the side of the road. Moody followed us out, and then the bus clambered on past the three of us in a cloud of dust. It was good to be free and finally hiking. A half mile later, we reached the launch point of the Shira Route. Some of our porters were already there, preparing lunch. The two cooks were wearing tall white chef's hats. Given that we were in the middle of Kilimanjaro National Park, surrounded by thick jungle in one direction and a long stretch of moorland in the other, the hats were one of the most hilarious things I had ever seen.

As we ate, the bus drove away, and the porters departed up the trail to our first campsite. Low clouds hung over the plateau, obscuring any sign of the summit we were aiming to reach. Over the course of our lunch, the wind began to pick up, and we had to keep our hands on our paper plates to keep them from blowing away.

Soon enough, Tim said we should be heading out. Our first day would be an easy three- to four-hour hike of 4 miles, rising little more than 1,000 feet. It would help us acclimatize.

I raised my tin cup and hollered, "Game on! It's about to get real!"

Everyone on the team clanked cups and cheered, then gathered their backpacks. It was almost 50 degrees, and I was hot. I was wearing thin long johns under my black cargo pants and matching Patagonia fleece jacket. Better to be prepared, Tim had warned, as the temperatures could swing at any moment. With Moody in the lead, we set off.

On day one of our climb, spirits were high. We moved in single file across the moorland. The pace was relaxed, the dirt trail was easy to follow, and we were all eager to finally be starting. A half hour into our journey, I definitely could feel that I was breathing more heavily than normal because of the elevation, but it was nothing that slowed me down. My ankles and feet felt the best they had since the

Whitney climb—no doubt, I figured, because of the adrenaline of getting started.

The trail threaded through the moorland, which was blanketed in low brownish-green shrubs. From time to time we passed piles of boulders that looked as though they had been hurled off Kilimanjaro eons before. As we descended into our first valley, a light rain began to fall. Mitch, one of the documentary crew, pulled out an umbrella and rigged it on his backpack to protect the scores of batteries he and Kent had brought. Soon, the wind caught the umbrella and turned it inside out, and Mitch looked as if he was carrying a radar installation on his back. We got a good laugh, one of many that day.

"This thing is no problem," Dilly said, feeling confident in view of the leisurely pace.

"Oh, yeah," I said. "We got this."

We crossed a dry riverbed and then climbed back up a zigzagging trail. Tim and Shirley pointed out various flowering plants and birds to each other, while Moody and Bariki spoke to each other constantly in Swahili.

"They're probably talking about your mom," Dilly joked.

I felt great and kept a steady rhythm. Occasionally the documentary crew ran ahead of me to frame a shot before asking me to slow down and say something. Pretty soon, I tuned them out. The key with my body was to keep moving. Once I stopped, my muscles wanted to tighten and lock up. They quickly understood this and adjusted their way of working.

Only Nancy, our team grandmother, was having problems. From our arrival in Arusha, we were all worried about her level of fitness. Nancy had joked that she only trained while washing dishes and walking around the block in her boots. Now on the trail, she was slowing and stopping repeatedly. Bariki kept at her side, and they gradually fell back in the distance.

"Okay, we go," Moody said at one point, waving us onward when we had paused to wait for her. He was a man of few words, and I figured he would do the same if I were the one lagging behind. Over the next few hours, we made our way up and down a few more ravines, but otherwise the trail seemed almost flat. As the sun waned from the sky, the temperature dropped and the wind picked up. We hiked along the Shira Ridge and finally came to a clearing where the porters had set up our camp. Each of us had a small blue egg-shaped tent, with a low profile to protect it from the wind. Beside these was a larger mess tent.

"All right, that's a wrap," I said.

Dilly, Paul, and I gave each other a chest bump, feeling pretty good about ourselves. We retired to our tents to take off our boots and unload what we needed from our backpacks—toiletries and the like. As I bent down to get inside, I suddenly became light-headed. It was the first time the altitude had really hit me, and it was a sobering moment. I unrolled my sleeping bag and tried to figure out how I was going to stretch out my body in such a small space. Only if I lay diagonally would my feet not stick out of the front of the tent.

While I was working this out, Tim called for us. We gathered beside him near the mess tent, wondering what the problem was. Then he pointed in the distance, away from the setting sun.

"The clouds are clearing at the summit," he said excitedly.

I only saw the same clouds that had been hanging over the mountain the whole day.

"No. Higher," Tim said, tilting my head upward.

I angled my head another 20 degrees, and there it was: the summit. Way, way, way higher and much, much, much farther away than I had ever imagined it would be. Mouth agape, I tried to come to terms with the amount of effort it would take to reach it. It was the first time I fully realized what I was facing in the days ahead. For a moment, those scenes from the Everest documentary I had seen, those scenes that first inspired me to dare a climb, raced through my mind: summiteers gasping for air, fighting through snow, ice, and wind, traversing precipitous cliffs, a single misstep sure death. Kilimanjaro was no Everest, but it was still a dangerous monster, and I was left with a hollow, scared feeling in my chest.

"Whose idea was this anyway?" I joked, trying to find a way out of the tension I felt.

"Climb without limits, right?" Dilly said, making fun of my fundraising motto.

"I'm starting to think there might be limits," I said. "But I guess there's no turning back."

"But it's so far away," somebody on the team marveled.

"Twenty miles until we reach the main part of the mountain," Tim advised.

Now that the sun was down, the temperature plunged below freezing. I bundled up in several layers and then went over to the mess tent, finding my way by the narrow sliver of light cast by my headlamp. The surrounding darkness was impenetrable. The porters had set up a couple of square tables, one with a single sad flower in a glass in the middle of it. The stark scene, with the wind buffeting the blue tent and a couple of lanterns providing the only light, made that flower seem all the more ridiculous.

"How romantic," Paul said.

We all ate together. Starving, I shoveled down the pasta and garlic bread. Tim gave us a breakdown of the next day's climb, then two key tips for the night: one, drink a lot of water, the altitude will dehydrate you; two, never leave your tent to urinate without a headlamp (you risk stepping off a cliff and dying—"It happens, a lot," he said). We took bets on who would freeze to death first, Dilly or Jeff, the documentary crew's cinematographer, who had rented a sleeping bag in Arusha.

Nancy remained quiet throughout dinner, and I worried she might not make it through the next day. She had been last to reach the camp and had struggled to walk steady and straight as she came up the trail.

Back in my tent by 8 P.M., I burrowed down inside my sleeping bag, exhausted but unable to sleep. Overall, I felt good about the day. My legs were in decent shape, the braces were helping my feet, and so far the altitude had not affected me too much. The distant view of the summit had been a reality check, but I told myself that we would chip away at that mountain each day until we were at the top.

The tents were closely clustered, and there was the inevitable banter. Every few minutes, Dilly would chime out, "This sleeping bag sucks," and everybody would laugh. Although I was nice and toasty inside my extreme-weather Marmot bag, it was impossible to get comfortable and be able to breathe at the same time, particularly with the bag's hood drawn over my head to keep out the cold. I flipped from my stomach to my back like a hamburger. My heated breath turned the nylon by my mouth moist, which was kind of gross, and my arm fell asleep. Finally, I drifted off.

Throughout the night, I tossed and turned, and every time I woke up I drank water, as Tim had ordered. There was a disturbing symphony of snores and farts from the other tents; the altitude, I was learning, wreaked havoc on people's systems. Every couple of hours I had to pee. The first time I put on all my clothes, pulled on my boots, and headed out a fair distance from my tent, as Tim had advised. Each time after that, I wore less and less and peed closer and closer. By the fifth time, I was outside in only my long underwear and Crocs, and thank goodness my tent was waterproof. It was freezing cold, and the wind was howling. "Welcome to Kilimanjaro," the mountain was saying to me.

Lying like a mummy inside my sleeping bag, I tracked the rise of the sun by the changing shades of blue of my tent. Soon enough I heard footsteps and a call in broken English, "Good morning." Before I wrestled my way out of my bag, one of the cooks unzipped my tent flap and stuck his head inside. He was holding a metal tray with an empty mug and two pots.

"Maji moto," he said in Swahili, two words that meant "hot water," but terms that I would come to associate with the start of another day of torture. On this particular morning, the start of day two, they were welcome words. I took plain water, no tea or coffee, and used it to clean my toothbrush and warm my hands.

After changing my underwear and socks but wearing the rest of the previous day's clothes, I emerged from my tent. There was a crunch of frost underneath my feet, and the sky was a clear blue with wisps of clouds. Straight ahead in the distance was the summit, reminding me again of the challenge ahead. Tired after a restless night's sleep, I stumbled across to the mess tent. All of us looked exhausted except for Tim, who was all relaxed, calm, and at ease, as if he were on a Tahitian vacation or something. Only Nancy was absent.

Over our breakfast of porridge, bananas, and bread with jam and honey, we spoke mostly of how cold it had been during the night. Finally, Nancy appeared. She looked disheveled, her eyes not quite focusing, and she seemed down. Everybody said good morning, but it clearly wasn't one for Nancy. She remained quiet through the rest of the meal, as Tim went over the day's five-hour hike.

When the others went off to gather their backpacks, Nancy drew me aside. "I had a lot of problems sleeping last night," she said.

"Do you think it was your pad?" I asked.

She shook her head no.

I then suggested how she might better position herself in her bag, but she cut me off.

"I'm having trouble breathing. I'm tired after yesterday, and it was the first day, an easy one." She paused. "I can't continue."

"Are you sure?" I asked, though I agreed it was probably best she stop.

"I was hoping to make it to final base camp to see you off, but I can't."

I gave her a hug. She looked as though she needed one.

"I wish you could be there. But your coming here, supporting me, it's enough."

Soon after, we headed out in the same single line as the day before. A half hour into the hike, Nancy said her farewells and turned down a supply road with one of the porters for a rendezvous with a truck. It was the last time such an option would be available. Any higher, and you would have to stagger off the mountain on your own steam—or be hauled down. As we left Nancy, I did feel relief that I would not have to worry about her higher up on the mountain. But her struggles were a sure sign of this mountain's inability to forgive any weakness.

We continued across the Shira Plateau toward the base of Kilimanjaro, traveling through the same moorlands as the day before. Every hour or so these huge black ravens swooped over us. They were as big as eagles and made this terrifying helicopter "swoosh, swoosh" across the sky. "Crows on 'roids," Dilly called them.

Most of the day I followed behind Moody, watching the heels of his threadbare construction boots instead of the surrounding vistas, so as to keep my balance on the rock-strewn path. My feet began to cramp, and my breathing was strained.

Moody kept repeating, *"Pole, pole,"* which means "Slow, slow." (My first thought was, *I'm using my damn poles!*)

With the sun now bright and high in the sky, it became hot, and for some relief I zipped off the lower half of my cargo pants, revealing the braces on my feet. I felt the eyes of the others on me, same as I had when the doctors put in me casts up to my hips decades before to fix my gait. Back then, I hated the spotlight the casts put on me, and I even mastered ambling around without crutches to support me. Now on the mountain, braces exposed, I acted the same, making sure to straighten my walk and to level my breathing, so that my climbing companions weren't reminded of who they were accompanying up this mountain.

Whenever we stopped for a drink or a snack, Paul came up to me and asked, "How are you feeling, brother?" or "How're the feet?"

Each time I said that everything was fine, and he would give me a fist bump or a "Good to hear."

As we crossed the plateau, we hiked up and down several ravines and canyons—same as the day before. I only knew the time of the day by the position of the sun. I didn't want a watch; I didn't want to know how slowly time was passing. From what Tim had said, we were rising roughly 2,500 feet in elevation over the five-hour hike, but it quickly became clear to me that I had no idea what this meant in terms of the ravines and the valleys in between, in terms of what was ahead. The uncertainty was unsettling, but as with the time element, it was probably for the best. Sometimes knowing too much of what lies ahead makes a challenge doubly difficult.

On the side of the trail at the base of a steep canyon was an old rusted gurney with straps and a single rickety wheel under its center. It looked like a backboard nailed to a unicycle.

"What's that?" I asked.

Tim explained there were several of these gurneys on the mountain, and they were used to carry people down if they couldn't make it on their own. I imagined how it would feel to be locked down onto that torture machine, hurtling down the mountain. The picture in my head was not a pretty one.

We weaved our way through a sloping field of black volcanic rocks and emerged from the canyon, finding ourselves above the clouds at 12,600 feet. Our campsite was on the ridge, just up ahead.

Before we went into our tents, we marked the end of day two with, "That's a wrap!" followed by a clasp of hands, chest bumps, and finally a guttural roar. Silly ritual, I know, but it was ours.

I sat down on a ledge at the edge of the camp, looking out at the valley floor, now far below. As the sun descended, the clouds rose over me and across the mountain. The sky was on fire, with streaks of oranges and reds and yellows that deepened in color with every passing minute. Try as I did to not be too religious, there was a touch of God in that sunset.

In the mess tent, we gobbled down dinner and, seeing that we did not want to head to our lonely beds in the dark just yet, Paul brought out a deck of UNO cards. At first only our team was playing, peering at our cards by the light of our headlamps, but then Moody and

Bariki came over and started following the game over our shoulders. Pretty soon we had a contest in the works; our guides counted in Swahili each card they had to draw and loved sticking each other with Draw Fours, Reverses, and Skips. They thought the game was the greatest thing ever, and the tent was loud with cheers, exasperated sighs, and laughter.

An hour later, I returned to my tent, promising myself not to drink so much water during the night that I had to make twenty grandpa visits to nature's toilet. The fact that we were camped on a bluff and the fact that the night was pitch-black were two reasons for just taking sips from my CamelBak.

I stared up at the dark roof of my tent, thinking of the climb the next day. Tim had advised us it would be the first tough day of our expedition: steep zigzagging trails reaching to over 15,000 feet of elevation. It would be the highest I had ever been in my life, and I wondered how the altitude would hit me. While the scream of the wind coming over the ridge continued, I finally fell into an uneasy sleep.

"*Maji moto.*" Yawns, grumbles, new deodorant slathered onto old deodorant. The rustle of sleeping bags, the stagger of steps to the mess tent. More yawns, a clap on a back here, a "Man, was it bitter cold last night" there, the gathering at the trail head. Grabbing my poles and thinking of Jake, and then Moody setting off. "*Pole, pole.*" The routine was becoming familiar. But this was only day three. There were still many mornings to go.

We set off up a terrible slope that I might have managed better if I had been scrambling on my hands and knees. Instead, I leaned heavily on my poles and forced my feet onward. Just fifty steps into the climb my feet were not feeling good. They were stiff, sensitive, and throbbing. Two days of hiking had slowly taken their toll, mostly because of the uneven ground. Each step was just a bit awkward, my feet rolling inward a little more to the left than usual, a little more to the right, causing flashes of pain in my arches each time. My big flippers couldn't take it—particularly since they were already in recovery because of what had happened on Mt. Whitney.

We were nowhere near the crest of this first challenge of the day, and I was slowing and getting very quiet inside of myself. Dilly and Paul tried to joke with me, but I remained silent. There was no room for distraction or banter. My focus had to be on a single purpose: watching each movement of Moody's boots ahead, following them with my own. The others swept past me on the side of the trail. I didn't care. I needed to keep a slow pace.

A couple of hundred yards up the slope, I came upon a Dutch climber; his backpack sported a flag with the characteristic red, white, and blue horizontal sections on it. He was sitting on a rock, his head between his legs. He was middle-aged and seemed fit, but he was in terrible shape. His face was white, and he struggled to gather enough breath. Two of his teammates hung by his side, speaking quietly in his ear, very worried.

"It's a long, hard way," one of them said as I passed.

We're into big-league stuff now, I thought. The first two days had been easy. Now any of us, no matter how strong, could be struck down by the altitude. The sight of this Dutchman destroyed my confidence.

Keep going. You got this, I told myself again and again as I made my way to the top of this ramp of hell. At one point, I was stopping every ten minutes to rest, gasping for air, my legs leaden. The others had disappeared into the distance. That was fine by me, as they now couldn't see how hard I was struggling. This hill was the first slap in the face, awakening me to how unprepared and ill-trained I was for this climb. The thought stung.

The trail leveled off at last almost two hours later. My ankles felt as though they were being stabbed with icepicks, and I was sapped of energy. Sitting down, I stared ahead at nothing in particular and took little sips of water from my CamelBak.

Moody appeared at my side with a porter whom he introduced as Minja. I had noticed Minja before because of his distinctive beanie hat and the long, rainbow-striped umbrella he kept stuffed in his backpack. He was tall and thin, with huge baseball mitts for hands, and he had one of the most expressionless faces I had ever seen. Happy, sad, impatient, hopeful—nothing registered. He was stone.

"Jambo," I said. ("Hello.")

"Minja will hike with you," Moody said. "If you need anything, he's your guy."

I half smiled. Minja looked at me indifferently and said, in a very deep voice, something in broken English that I couldn't understand. We were off to a great start.

We left behind the moorlands and now looked to be crossing a high desert, the landscape empty but for strange pillars and clumps of lava. For a while I remained in the middle of the pack, but then gradually dropped to the rear again. Minja kept at my heels, going at whatever pace I set, which was never faster than a turtle crawl. Only when the others took a break would I catch up with the group, but by the time I arrived they would be ready to go. Paul offered to carry my backpack, no doubt seeing from the constant grimace on my face how much I was hurting. I thanked him, but said no. I wanted to do this on my own, and he had his own bag to haul.

My legs felt as if they were swelling, and pulses of pain shot from the instep of my right foot. Any help the braces gave me on the first two days had worn off. Worse, the altitude was really kicking into high gear. A slow, relentless headache began to grip the sides of my temples. There was nothing to do about it but suffer, continue, move onward. At one point, Tim stopped me on the trail and asked how I was doing. I simply hung my head. I didn't have the energy for words.

Halfway through the day, the temperature plummeted without warning, and the mist that had clung to the mountain like a blanket began to freeze. Visibility dropped to a dozen feet or less. It was the first time I realized how quickly the weather could change and how easy it would be to get lost on this mountain, to take the wrong step to a very long fall. If it were not for the lava formations, the landscape would have looked as barren as the moon.

In the midst of this desolation and fear, I found my thoughts, almost inexplicably at first, drifting back to the Usa River School. For such a hurried visit, every detail was still vivid. The nightingale voice of the girl without legs sitting in a wheelchair in the front row. The shy *"Jambo"* from Barbara. "There is no other place," the response by the headmaster when I asked where other disabled children were treated. The two teenage girls who sang arm-in-arm together, each wearing one of the other's sandals, so they both had a green and red pair. I remembered looking at one empty half-built building while the headmaster spoke of those who never made it there, those abandoned, locked in cages, set afire. I remembered dancing beside a teenage boy, his elongated face overtaken by the huge toothy smile. The Usa River School was such a retreat for children like him, yet it barely sustained itself on the intermittent government funds, and only those over sixteen were allowed within its gates. It was a tragedy, a crime, that so many were unwelcome in their own bodies and left untreated.

And yet here, in what felt like one of the bleakest places on earth, thinking of the kids at the school gave me hope. The optimism they all shared despite their circumstances reminded me of why I was here in the first place, pushing my legs forward.

And I needed all the help I could get. Day three was living up to its brutal reputation. Whenever I asked Minja a question ("How much longer? Where are the others?"), he would only reply, "Yeah, yeah, yeah," or *"Pole, pole."* I was pretty sure he didn't understand anything I was saying.

Keep going. Survive, I kept telling myself, hour after hour.

At last, cold and wet from the icy mist, crushed with fatigue, and suffering with each step, I reached the Moir Camp in the late afternoon. In my tent, I struggled to take my boots off without passing out from the pain. I knew my feet were a mess. Paul came by to see if there was anything he could do. He helped me over to Shirley's tent. Our team nurse greeted me with her usual cheery smile. I took off my Crocs and socks, and she examined me. A worried look quickly came over her face, particularly when she saw how swollen my legs had become.

Each of her manipulations of my ankles and feet, whether left, right, up, or down, took my breath away. The tendons in my ankles felt frayed into useless strands. Shirley massaged my feet, trying to ease them. There was a large mass of dead skin on the ball of my right foot, caused by my boot rubbing against it, and she wanted to cut it away to ease the pain. I appreciated her good intentions, but I didn't want to risk it. With five days to go before we returned down the mountain, an open cut on the sole of my foot seemed like a bad idea. What if it got infected? Paul offered some advice from his Ranger days on how to reduce the swelling. From the weak sound of his voice, it was clear he wasn't doing so great either.

Returning to my own tent, I lay down on top of my sleeping bag and tried to pull myself together. I couldn't show others how hard this was for me—how tough it was to breath, how much my legs hurt, how worried I was about whether I could continue. *Keep it to yourself. Nobody needs to know.*

The mood at dinner was somber. Nobody was cracking jokes, and nobody was looking for a game of UNO. Instead, we had a short debate about whether or not any of us would use Diamox, the altitude-sickness drug. Our Tanzanian guides advised against taking it, and Tim was in agreement, since one of its side effects was dehydration, a significant danger. Most of the team was struggling so much with the elevation—from upset stomachs to gripping headaches—that a little dehydration (or more frequent trips to the bathroom at night) seemed like a small price to pay. In the end, Tim and I were the only ones who said we didn't want to take any Diamox.

It was pretty quiet in the mess tent that night. The top of Uhuru Peak was still very far away, and there were several days left to go. After such a long, exhausting hike, the thought of more of the same dampened our collective spirit.

After dinner, we all retreated to our tents. I conked out within minutes. What I didn't know was that during the night Paul would be battling a serious case of altitude sickness himself. He had been suffering with a bad cold since he left Utah and was having trouble sleeping. Sometime past midnight, his head suddenly felt as if it was about to implode. He tried to relax, but the pressure in his skull only intensified. He crawled to his knees and then out of his tent to get some fresh air, hoping that would help. A bout of diarrhea overcame him. He paced around for a few steps, and then collapsed on the frozen ground, gasping for air. The pounding in his head was the worst pain he had ever experienced—and Paul had suffered some. He stayed outside the tent, thinking that the cold felt so good, so right, until his survival instinct kicked in, and he realized that he would die if he remained out there much longer. On his hands and knees, he got back into his tent, bundled himself up in his sleeping bag, and focused on his breathing, waiting, hoping for the excruciating headache to disappear. It did not.

Kilimanjaro was merciless that way.

6

The Wall

Paul looked terrible. He squinted in the light, as if the sun was boring into his skull. It was before breakfast, the next morning.

"How are you doing?" I asked.

"Not good at all, brother," he said, a rare admittance. Paul was never anything less than positive.

"It's just . . . My cough's bothering me," he said. He told me a little about his trouble sleeping, but not in much detail.

It wasn't in Paul's nature to complain, but it was clear that the Iron Horse was hurting pretty bad. There was never any doubt in my mind who was the toughest bastard in our group, and if Paul was struggling, I wondered how any of us would make it. It was becoming clear that this mountain made one pay for any weakness. Clearer still was how many of them I had to expose in the first place.

In the mess tent over coffee and a chewy porridge, there were a lot of sunken, weary eyes and listless movements. Everybody was beaten up pretty bad by the altitude. Sleeping on the ground through a night of bitter wind and cold hadn't done much to help with that. Rick said his headache was a hundred times worse than any he had ever experienced. Dilly said that his took his breath away. Mine wasn't as bad, but I was still groggy, and my stomach hurt. I forced down the lukewarm porridge, knowing that I would need the energy.

Taking stock of our team, Tim addressed us. "We're going to head down in elevation some, have a quick, short day, and get to our next camp, so everyone feels a little better. Keep your fluids up."

After breakfast, I hit our portable toilet for the first time. My ass almost froze to the hard seat and, for just a second, I had the twisted thought that I might have to summit Kili with it frozen to my backside. When I came out of the toilet, not feeling much better, the strangest, most incongruous sight struck me.

There was Dilly, sitting in one of the mess-tent chairs, which he had positioned out in the sun. Feet stretched in front of him, jacket unzipped, sunglasses on, he was basking in the sunlight as if he were on the beach instead of surrounded by craggy barren rock 15,000 feet above sea level. Scattered about him were his sleeping bag and clothes.

"Catching my bronze . . ." Dilly said, tipping his Oakley sunglasses down a little on his nose and giving me a big grin, " . . . and feeling sexy." He pushed his sunglasses back into place and tilted his head back to the sun.

For a long moment, I didn't know what to think; then I just laughed. Paul joined me to look at the spectacle, as did the rest of the team.

"Getting my bronze on," Dilly said to the gathering crowd. "I'm defrosting, boys."

It was the brief moment of comic relief we needed before striking out for the day, and I loved Dilly for the gift.

We headed down a ridge opposite the one we had climbed the day before. We moved in a loose band, everyone at a stable, glacial pace. My headache steadily eased, but for some reason I was having a lot of trouble with my balance and coordination. I would see dips and angles in the trail and know that I needed to adjust my steps, yet my brain refused to coordinate. My legs felt strangely disconnected from the rest of my body, and it was tough to maintain any rhythm in my stride. Increasingly I relied on my poles to control the chaos and to keep me upright. Minja remained behind me, but fortunately he never had to catch me to keep me from falling. Although the descent demanded less exertion, it was still tough on my knees, hips, and quads, and my toes kept jamming into the front of my boots, inflicting further damage on my feet, which had started hurting the moment I tightened my bootlaces that morning. At this point, there was nothing I could do about it.

Kilimanjaro had given us a sunny, warm, windless morning, and we took frequent breaks with lots of water. An hour into the day's labors, we saw small pockets of vegetation on the side of the trail, then shrubs, then giant Dr. Seuss–like trees. I had never been so excited to see the color green.

With the lower altitude, my breathing slowed, my headache disappeared, and I felt human again. I knew I would have to climb back up the elevation we were losing, but at that point it was the lesser of two evils. I felt good enough to snap some photographs as we passed a waterfall. However, as we moved from high desert back to moorland, my coordination did not improve, and the assault on my feet did not lessen.

We reached our camp, at 12,700 feet on the side of a valley, so early that the porters had not yet set up our tents. On arrival, we gave a halfhearted cheer, still struggling with morale after the long night before. The sun at its peak, we sat on the ground and ate some sandwiches made with stale bread for lunch. Then most of us crept into the tents, now pitched, and tried to rest.

I was so exhausted that I couldn't sleep. A couple of hours later, while I was staring at the necklace I bought at the Usa River School dangling from the roof of my tent, a chatter of voices passed our camp. I poked my head out to see another team of climbers coming up a different trail. Bored with staring at the blue roof of my tent, I stepped outside. Below the ridge where we were camped, the clouds were rolling into the canyon forming a billowy white carpet under our feet. I walked down to the ridge and stood on an outcropping of rock, feeling as though I could almost step out onto the clouds and walk clear across the canyon. To my right, about a quarter mile in the distance, stood an imposing vertical wall of rock, behind which rose Uhuru Peak. Something about that high fortress of rock left me feeling a little weak.

Soon after, the rest of the team joined me on the ridge. "What's that?" I asked Tim, pointing toward the wall.

"That's what we're climbing tomorrow," Tim answered. "Barranco Wall."

"No!"

"Yes."

"I didn't know that was there," Dilly said.

I stared at the wall. Tim explained that it was not a technical ascent, but it *was* a steep, 1,000-foot-high scramble, and I would not be able to use my poles for balance. For a second, I was angry at myself for not investigating our route thoroughly enough to know that this Barranco Wall existed. Then I was simply scared.

"That's nuts," I said, trying to laugh it off, but that wall was not funny.

Soon enough the clouds rose, and the wall disappeared behind them, but the sight of it was burned deep into my skull. Permanently. *One wrong step, one momentary loss of balance, and . . .* I pushed the thought away.

For the rest of the night, all we talked about was the Barranco Wall. The team had a thousand questions: Were we to pack differently or wear anything different? Would we go up single file? In what order? Was it a continuous climb or would we stop midway? Moody told me that I would be sandwiched between him and Minja. We would try to get to the wall early in the morning to avoid any other teams, and we would take it as slowly as we needed to. Nothing that was said made me feel any better.

After dinner, many of us went straight to bed. Paul took a couple of Tylenol PM from me and conked out within minutes. I played some UNO with Dilly and the guides, but it barely distracted from the thought of the wall, which seemed to get higher and steeper in my mind with each hour that passed. Normally, I would not have let my fears and doubts run amok like that, but I was tired, too tired, to stop them.

Finally, I returned to my tent. I massaged my feet, trying to loosen their stiffness, but even in Crocs they hurt. The balls of them had been in so much pain that day that I had compensated by putting my weight, too much of it, on the outsides. This only compounded my troubles.

Sometime in the middle of the night I woke up. In the dark, the magnitude of my attempt to summit Kilimanjaro and my lack of preparation for it really hit home. Day after day of exertion, the altitude, the cold, my weak legs, my tortured feet, and my lack of coordination and balance. Any of these, or all of them together, could prevent me from reaching the top. Picturing the Barranco Wall for the thousandth time, I added death to the list.

It was day five, and with Dilly and Paul at my side, I stared up at the base of the Barranco Wall. My uneasiness drained the strength from my legs, and I wondered how I could possibly make it up 1,000 feet of vertical rock.

"My God, it's tall," Paul said. He looked better after a long, restful, Tylenol-induced sleep.

"I'm worried about my balance," I said. "If I step left or right at too great an angle . . ." I didn't finish my sentence. "I'm not worried about climbing it, about the effort, but if I fall, it's a big fall."

Paul and Dilly glanced at each other. I was not a small guy. If I really lost my balance, even Minja wouldn't be able to stop me from pitching over, and I might carry him off the mountain with me. Paul tried to reassure me that he would be behind Minja to catch him catching me, but I thought that sounded like a lot of opportunities for dropped balls.

"At least it's a nice day," I said.

The sky overhead was clear and the sun warm on my face. For a long while, we stood at the bottom of the wall, watching two teams, one Swiss and one German, make the ascent. They looked as if they had grown up in the mountains. We studied the track they took, hopping here, reaching there, stopping on this ledge, sidestepping that steep overhang.

"Okay, look at what he's doing." Dilly pointed out one climber who was leaping from one rock to the next.

"Wow. Oh, that part looks hard," Paul said, indicating a Swiss climber stretching for a handhold to scramble up a boulder.

"And I don't want to get stuck there," I said, pointing to a huddle of people waiting on a narrow slip of a ledge for their turn to continue up.

The first climbers had neared the top, and they were so high up they appeared like nothing but ants zigzagging back and forth. None of this watching or waiting did anything for my nerves. In the end, I had to just shut my eyes, to gather myself. *Take it one bit at a time,* I told myself. *Don't get stuck on making it up the whole wall right now. Just climb one part at a time. Let the rest take care of itself.* I slowed down my thoughts, reminded myself that I was there for the challenge, that I could do this, that there was no quitting until I reached the top of Kilimanjaro.

The time came to start. Moody took the lead, I went second, and Minja followed behind. As we scrambled over the first few boulders, Minja stayed very close. Quiet, stoic, and calm, his presence reassured me that he would be there for me if I needed him. I suspected I would.

There was no warm-up on Barranco, no slow rise in the angle of its face to limber up the muscles or acquaint you with technique. It was steep from the word "go." I slowly made my way up the first couple of hundred feet. Gloveless to get a better grip on the wall and pressed flat against the rocks, I tested each foot and handhold before hoisting myself up. Some sections were straight climbing; others had a thin angled trail through boulders, where I could put one foot in front of the other—and barely that.

Moody and Minja talked almost constantly to each other. Well, Moody chatted away in Swahili, and Minja gave limited, toneless responses. They were mapping out the easiest course up the wall. I carefully watched every move Moody made (latching onto a rock, a little jump, a long slide of the feet), and then figured out if I was able to do the same, adjusting the course slightly here and there to my own abilities. Several times, Moody offered his hand to help me up a section, but I refused it. Not only did I want to do this climb on my own, but also, frankly, I didn't trust anybody but myself.

Moody hopped over the rocks, his legs moving naturally under him. Mine couldn't do the same. It had never been more clear to me that climbing was about having faith in your body—in all its parts, hands, fingers, arms, legs, and feet—and having the fluidity, agility, and coordination needed to orchestrate its movements. I had no faith in mine now, and this lack of confidence unsettled me.

At one point, my face pressed to the wall, gathering the courage to take the next leap, I was a kid again—only instead of climbing a mountain, I was trying to drop in on a skateboard ramp on my aqua green Billy Ruff promodel board. I watched as my friends went, one by one, gliding with ease off the edge, moving almost effortlessly down the smooth curve of the ramp's surface. By the time it was finally my turn, I wasn't excited; I was angry. I was angry about how easily all the other kids had made it look. I was angry because I knew that even if I pulled off the same feat, nothing about it would be easy.

I stepped onto my board and moved down over the lip of the ramp. For one brief moment, everything was fine. I heard the turn of the wheels and felt the rush of air as it blew into my face. But then my feet didn't adjust quick enough to the change of balance of my upper body. In one awkward motion, I crashed, tumbled, and slammed my elbow on the ramp, learning, once again, that my body was different. Back then, it had taken faith in my body to drop over that edge, but in the years since I'd been learning that having faith in my body came with a painful price. My body had failed me too many times to trust it.

Now on the climb, the consequences of this lack of trust made things more dangerous for me, and it wasn't until this moment that I realized just how vulnerable this made me. More than the kid on the skateboarding ramp, I had reason to doubt myself, to question whether my limbs would let me down. Awkward sidesteps, crisscrossing feet, little jumps, shimmying up on my hands and knees, getting pushed in the back by Minja—the first half of the ascent was ugly and inglorious. My hands were cut up. My pants and fleece were dirty. My ankles burned from the uneven footholds. But I was still alive.

After another stretch of climbing, Minja spotting me from behind several times, we took a forced break on a ledge while we waited for another team to continue up and clear the way. Five minutes turned into ten, then fifteen. We had stopped before for logjams of climbers to clear, but never for this long. I was facing the wall, close enough to kiss it. I didn't want to move, worried that I might lose my balance. Forced to remain in one position for so long, my legs and ankles began to tighten up badly and to shake.

"Backpack?" Minja asked, extending his hand.

"I'm good," I said, not wanting to make any changes. He kept his hand outstretched, and I shook my head.

I was very skittish now and thought that if I moved, I might pitch over the side of the cliff, 600 feet down.

"How you feeling?" Paul asked. He was standing to my left, just past Minja.

"I'm good," I lied.

Another five minutes passed. Moody and Minja spoke quietly to one another.

"We have to get going," I said, interrupting them. If I had to stay there much longer, there would be nothing I could do to keep my legs from cramping up and collapsing.

"The Barranco Wall," Dilly called out. "My new favorite activity."

I wasn't finding anything funny right then. I was psyching my-self out, letting every worry about my body's inabilities and the pre-cipitous drop off the ledge grow larger and larger in my mind. The strain of the first half of the climb had worn down whatever force of will I had used to push away my fears. I just wanted to be done with this wall, to get off it.

At long last, Moody started moving again. I threaded my way across the ledge. My feet were stiff, and my legs uneasy. Every step was made with hesitation. "You're doing good, bro," Paul encouraged from behind. We were crossing diagonally, from left to right (and up), a stretch of boulders with very little room for error. Minja remained to the outside of me, risking his own safety to keep me on the wall.

I grabbed a handhold, but before I pulled myself up, I lost faith in my choice and hesitated. Moody looked back at me. He knew I needed help.

"There." He pointed to where I should grip the boulder.

It was too far away. There was no way I could trust my body to stretch that far. A little higher up, but closer to me, was a cleft of rock I could reach.

"I'm going for that spot," I said.

"If you feel good," Moody replied.

I reached up, seized the handhold, and pulled myself up. My feet shuffled across the boulder. I followed Moody's next step and hauled myself up some more. On the next maneuver, losing concentration, I didn't reach far enough out to get a hold on the rock. My fingers slipped away from the wall, and for a second I felt my body fall away.

My heart sank. I thought this might be it. A crippling plummet or . . . the end.

Then, just as suddenly, I was pressed back up against the wall. Safe. With one hand, Minja had arrested my slip and shoved me against the boulder. He kept his hand pressed hard into my back until I nodded I was okay. There was no doubt in my mind that he had saved my life. He just looked at me with that stony face of his, not worried, not looking for any thanks. I thanked him anyway.

On we climbed. Minja kept his body close to mine, occasionally pressing his hand hard into my back. It was as if he was playing defense against me in basketball, except the court was on a ledge up a thousand-foot cliff face. A couple more times he kept me from slipping off the Barranco Wall.

It dawned on me that the lack of expression on Minja's face was seriousness, not indifference. He was there not to make friends, but to help me reach the summit in one piece.

As we neared the top of the wall, I began tripping every few minutes. Tired, I was getting lazy about lifting up my feet to clear the next step. Instead, I was kind of dragging them up. Thankfully, the slope had become less steep, and so when I fell, I pitched forward into the wall and only scraped up my hands. An hour or maybe a lifetime later, we finally cleared the wall. I stumbled over to a rock, sat down, and wriggled out from under my backpack.

Dilly and Paul congratulated me on "not dying," and even Minja gave me a high five. Looking down from the top and out across the huge desert valley, I felt a momentary sense of relief and pride. This quickly gave way to exhaustion. I leaned over and tried to recover my breath. My legs trembled uncontrollably. Worse was the mental exhaustion. Someone was talking to me, but I had trouble following. My brain didn't seem to want to work. It couldn't carry one thought to the next, and this distressed me. I knew that if I was anything but completely alert, I would take shortcuts and make mistakes about where I placed my feet.

I wasn't the only one hurting. Mitch looked like death warmed over. His face was empty of color, and he looked dazed. He and the rest of the documentary crew had carried their cameras up the slope, preparing shots and filming as they went. They were not immune to the strain and altitude.

We all stayed where we were, resting, for what seemed like a long time. I had been too nervous to eat much at breakfast; I now devoured a half-frozen Power Bar and sucked up at least a liter of water from my CamelBak. The clouds cleared enough to give us a stunning view of Mt. Meru in the far distance. Then Tim rounded us up, advising that we still had a long way to go—up and down three extensive valleys—before we could set up camp. Already spent, I struggled to fathom how I was going to manage another four hours and another 1,000 feet in elevation before the end of the day.

I told myself yet again not to think of the whole challenge as a single entity. *Take one valley, then the next, then the next. One at a time.* I put out of my mind the thought that there were still two more days of climbing, including the long night hike to the summit. *One hurdle at a time. Focus on that one and on nothing else.*

And so we continued on. We followed a flat trail around the mountain, then went down a long valley, across a riverbed, and then right back up the other side, not gaining any elevation in the hour-long trek. Then came the next valley. Down and up. The mountain was covered in fog, which obscured much of what lay ahead and, thankfully, how far we still needed to go.

Then we reached the third valley. Everything around us was crushed reddish-black volcanic rock. This last valley of the day was a monster: very steep down and so steep up that I could not even use my poles to push myself up. It was largely a scramble straight up, my knees often brushing against the slope. The balls of my feet, taking most of my weight, were being absolutely punished.

To keep my mind off the pain, I tried to speak to Minja about the climb to the summit ahead, but he would only answer, *"Pole, pole."*

When I staggered out of that final valley, I had nothing left in me. I dragged my legs toward the camp, which was set on a sharp slope. Reaching my tent, I took a long deep breath and then half fell through the opening. I peeled off my boots, trying not to pass out from the misery of it all. When I lay down, my head was at least twelve inches above my feet because of our angled position on the hill. I turned my body around so as to elevate my feet, but then all the blood rushed to my head, and I got dizzy. I laughed at the insanity of my situation; then, in a compromise, I wrestled my body sideways to the slope. Outside, I could hear huge birds cawing and swooping overhead. They might have been pterodactyls from the terrifying sound they made.

They can have me, I thought. *Let them pick me up and carry me to the summit in their claws.*

This was my last thought before I passed out, my feet halfway out of my tent. I woke up a couple of hours later, just in time to stumble over to the mess tent. There was a fresh shipment of food, so we dined lavishly on bread that tasted like compressed sawdust and some kind of meat substance.

After dinner, most of us returned to our tents. I massaged my feet, but they were too sensitive, particularly under the arches, to do it for very long. Even moving my toes was painful. They might as well have been stuck in rigor mortis. I decided to leave them alone. It was almost impossible to get comfortable on the slope. I curled up on my side, but felt as if I was about to roll downhill.

"Previously on *Dexter*," Dilly intoned, the little glow of his iPod faintly visible from my tent. His solar-powered battery always had enough charge for one episode a day. He sounded restless, no doubt because his flannel sleeping bag was basically nothing more than an ice blanket. He tried to joke about it, but I knew he was miserable. Last night he hadn't even wanted to go into his tent to sleep.

Eventually everything grew quiet. Once again, I was sure I was the last one awake. I stared at the necklace made by the Usa River School kids hanging from my backpack and thought of how much more courage they had than I did.

We struck camp and got going by 8 A.M. on day six, wanting to arrive at the final base camp by lunchtime, so we could take a long rest before setting out for the summit later that night. There was not much talking; everyone was focused on what lay ahead. It was only fifteen hours until we made our attempt. The countdown had begun.

We trekked across and up several ridges. Uhuru Peak was now staring down at us from above. The rise in elevation was fairly gradual as we rounded the side of the mountain, but at that altitude, close to 16,000 feet above sea level, nothing was easy. My feet and ankles were beyond the repair of an uneasy night of sleep, and I just suffered them.

Throughout the morning's trek, I thought of nothing but the summit and of what kind of commitment it would take to get me there, both physically and mentally. I knew how tired I already was, how much my feet hurt, how cold it would be setting out at night, and how much trouble I had making my way in the dark. All these things, taken together, would make the ascent tough. But in addition to those factors, there was the extreme altitude, the unknown terrain, and the possibility of a storm hitting us midway to the peak. I knew I would keep pushing myself forward, but that might not be enough. I might fall off the trail in the dark, and they would never find me. My legs might give up on me from exhaustion, and I would simply collapse on the slope. My brain might swell from the elevation, and I would pass out or even die.

So many things could go wrong, many of them beyond my control. There was no avoiding the truth: I had never been so confronted by my limitations—or so terrified by them—in my life.

We arrived at our final base camp just before noon. Our tents had been erected among giant slabs of lava rock. Sitting down on one of them, dirty, stinking, and hungry, I realized how much I missed home. I missed hot showers and fresh clothes. I missed the ocean and the warm sandy beach. I missed buffalo wings, pepperoni pizza, In-N-Out burgers . . . the simple things.

Then I thought of my family. Distant as I was from them, I missed them too. I had embarked on this adventure without them, and I wished somehow they could be there to cheer me on, to help me through what I was certain was to come: more moments of terrible weakness and doubt.

Sadness over their absence slowly turned to hurt. For so many years, I felt, they never had my back. First, my father after the divorce. Then my mother, dividing us against him and forcing each of us into her mold, despite the fact that I had a physical condition that made fitting into a mold of any kind impossible. Then Mike, who once always seemed to be the first to my defense, basically disappearing from my life since college and rarely showing up when I needed him. I had hoped he would have been there to train with me. A hike or two, at least. Maybe he could have spurred me to prepare better. With my simmering hurt turning into anger, I finally stood away from the rock and retired to my tent.

After a long rest, I gathered with the others. Moody and Tim, both as serious as I had ever seen them, detailed how we would make the summit attempt. Given that I moved more slowly than other climbers, they wanted us to leave an hour earlier than planned, 11 P.M. instead of midnight. We needed to reach Uhuru Peak just after dawn. That was critical because when the sun came up, the frozen ground would start to loosen and turn into a snowy mush. Getting to the summit would be like trying to climb up a sand dune. Further, the weather patterns during the day were much more unpredictable than at night, and we might get hit by a surprise storm.

Tim and Moody told us to make sure we had batteries in our headlamps, to keep drinking water throughout the night, and to take it slow. *Pole, pole.* There was no prize for first place. Moody then introduced individual guides for each member of the team. I already had Minja, but now we each would have somebody to look out for us. They were the porters who had been hauling up our tents and food throughout the climb. Now they were our guardians, and we were to listen to them without fail.

Moody and Bariki took us outside the mess tent and showed us one of those single-wheel metal gurneys. If something went wrong with one of us, Moody said, that person would be strapped to the gurney and wheeled down to a lower altitude. There was no other way off the mountain.

Tim and the guides then took us on a three-hundred-yard jaunt to a ridge overlooking the summit. Tim told us how important it was to stick with our guide, stay together, and to keep moving. Sitting down for longer than thirty seconds, he warned, would allow the frigid temperatures to really hit home, and we could freeze to death. He encouraged us, telling us that we all had the strength in us to make it. The climb wouldn't be easy, but the important thing was to just keep moving. Again, our lives depended on it.

Then it was back to the mess tent for an early dinner. Paul raised his mug of coffee for a toast: "We're all going to the top."

Everyone clinked mugs and raised a cheer. We had started with ten, but after Nancy dropped out, we were nine.

We returned to our tents before sunset to try to get some sleep before go-time. I put everything I would need for the climb into my backpack, then lined the inside of my sleeping bag with all the clothes I would wear for the ascent: long underwear, red blizzard jacket, sweatshirt, snow pants, beanie, and balaclava. This way, they would be warm when I put them on in the middle of the night. I forgot to include my boots; I didn't even think of it.

As the sun fell, the temperature dropped, and even with my sleeping bag stuffed like a sausage I found myself shivering. The wind began blowing, its gusts buffeting the fabric of my tent. I tried to sleep, but I kept wondering what kind of terrain we were facing, whether it would be scree or hard rock or snow. Mostly, I worried about the first part of the climb: making my way through the dark. I had trouble crossing from my bedroom to the bathroom in the middle of the night, and I remembered Mt. Whitney well, trying to keep my balance on the forest trail without anything for my eyes to focus on so I could get my bearings.

Sleep eluded me. I questioned why I had come to Tanzania, what was it that drove me here. Clearly I was desperate to prove that I was equal to any who had dared this mountain. *Prove to whom? Others? Myself? Was this worth risking my life and enduring such agony, day after day? What would it reveal anyway?* Lying there in my tent, I didn't have any answers. But I needed to find them.

My eyes were heavy from the high altitude, but still sleep did not come, just short restless dozes. No breath was deep enough to draw the oxygen I needed from the air. No matter how tightly I cocooned myself in my sleeping bag, I was still cold.

7

Fire in the Furnace

At 11 P.M., a porter came by to make sure I was awake. I was already up and dressed. I was wearing four layers and was still freezing; my breath looked eerie in the glow of the headlamp. The wind was so strong that the gusts were blowing the side of my tent flat against the ground. It was deadly cold, 15 below or less—without doubt the coldest it had been since we began. Sitting alone in my tent, I was already short of breath, adrenaline racing. My mouth was dry, and my tongue felt twice its normal size. I knew I needed to calm down and relax, but I was unable to slow the parade of fears marching through my head. The wind, the cold, and the darkness outside only made these fears seem worse.

"*Maji moto, maji moto,*" the porter chanted. I drank some hot water, warming my hands on the mug, and then pulled my balaclava back down over my face to keep the biting cold air off my exposed skin. Then I slowly, painfully, strapped on my braces and boots. The moment I slipped my feet into the boots, I knew I had made a mistake—a big mistake—by not putting them into my sleeping bag with the rest of my gear. They were frozen solid. My already stiff feet were now encased in what felt like concrete. They felt numb immediately. *Nothing to do about it now. Got to get going.*

The darkness outside the tent was overwhelming. Even with a headlamp, I could not anticipate how I would find my way through the pitch-black. Then the gusting, frigid wind hit, and my adrenaline spiked even higher. My boots an icebox, I paced back and forth, occasionally stomping my feet.

Minja appeared through the darkness. "Hello, Bonner," he greeted me, in his deep voice.

The others assembled. I gave each one a fist bump, but my mouth was too dry to speak. Sips of water did nothing to help.

Waiting for everybody to gather seemed to take a long time. I was growing colder with every passing second and wanted to get started—anything for a release from my nerves. "All right! Let's get moving!" I kept saying, though my voice was whipped away by the wind. My hands began to burn from the cold, and I loosened my grip on my poles, which helped with my circulation.

At long last, Moody stood at the front of our team and said, "We go." He led us forward, single file, into the darkness. With our hunched backs and solemn faces, we might have been a prison chain gang. Tim was right in front of me and Minja behind. I struggled to settle into a rhythm. My legs were already hurting, and my balance was off. With the spare circle of light cast by my headlamp, I could hardly see where to put my feet. The hood of my jacket limited my peripheral vision and my ability to hear—but I could still hear my breathing, ragged and heavy. Whenever the wind changed direction, it blew my jacket hood down over my headlamp and blocked its light. I'd try to push it away, but with my half-frozen hands it was like trying to swat clumsily at a fly in a windstorm.

Twenty minutes into the climb, I was a wreck. I stared at Tim's boots and tried to follow his footsteps up the steep trail. Even when the headlamp did cast a clear halo of light on the path, it provided little solace. I didn't know where I was or whether there was a cliff to one side or the other. The trail was uneven, and the wind threw me off balance even more. I felt it might flick me off the mountain at any moment.

Terrified, I grew short of breath. My backpack seemed to weigh more and more, and I felt increasingly awkward in my heavy jacket, as if I was some fat mummy trying to stumble his way up a mountain. A half hour into the ascent, Minja put his hand on my shoulder. It was time for a break. Standing there, trying to suck some partially frozen water out of my CamelBak, I was full of doubt and self-criticism. This was the point in the day's climb when I was supposed to be feeling my freshest. How could I possibly handle six more hours of the same at ever-increasing altitudes? Once again, my haphazard approach in preparing for this climb was coming back to haunt me.

Tim asked me if I wanted to sit down for a moment. I did not. I could not. I might never get up again. I tried to eat a PowerBar, but it had frozen solid. I tore at it like a dog, getting only a few bites before my jaw hurt from the chewing. I sucked at the tube on my CamelBak, but it had frozen solid as well. Squeezing the tube didn't break up the ice crystals. Tim and Minja had a go, but didn't have any luck either. Minja took my CamelBak off and poured the water into a metal screw-top bottle, which he put into my backpack.

I began to shiver uncontrollably. I shook my numb hands and beat them against my thighs, hoping to get the blood moving. The only warmth I felt was from the burning pain in my ankles and legs. It was clear to me that, if things did not improve, I would never make it to the summit. Minja asked if I wanted him to take my backpack and, like a fool, I refused.

"I may not do this," I mumbled quietly to myself. I thought about what that would mean for everybody who had supported me, from my coworkers at the Ducks to my friends, to Jake's family, to all those kids who chipped in money from their lemonade stands and the like. I could not let them down. They had faith in my ability to reach the top of Kilimanjaro. They believed in me. And I couldn't betray that belief. There was no way I would let that happen.

No way.

Time to get moving. Time to pull myself together and get myself into a rhythm.

We headed back onto the trail, Tim ahead of me once again. My little internal motivational speech carried me through the next twenty minutes—maybe the next half hour. Then the wind picked up some more. The gusts roaring around me must have been striking at 40–50 miles per hour. Chippings of rock spat into my face, hitting my goggles, pinging off my ski pants. It felt as though I was climbing through a tornado. My hood continued to block my headlamp intermittently, and the wind would sometimes treat my jacket like a sail, yanking me off balance.

On we climbed, the slope unrelenting, one switchback after the next. I lost all sense of my surroundings and of the others on my team. The only thing that mattered was Tim, charting my path. I focused on his heels. *If he could handle this, so could I. So could I.* Exhausted beyond belief by the end of the first hour, I questioned how I would continue for the next ten. But Tim kept trekking upward, and so I followed.

One time, at a hairpin bend, I heard a voice through the howling wind. It was in Swahili, a combination of a hum and a song. It was Minja. The sound broke the monotony of the wind, and as we continued Minja continued to sing. I would hear him whenever I turned my head or when we reached another switchback. The song, which had the softness of an old hymn, reminded me of the Usa River girls' song. The thought of them encouraged me, and I finally found some rhythm in my pace.

When we next took a break, I discovered that the top of the screw-top bottle had come off and my water was gone. Minja didn't carry any water either. The altitude hit home, and I heaved for breath, trying to suck in as much oxygen as possible before we started moving again.

The trail was now littered with large rocks, and I could no longer drag my feet along, one after the next, which is what I had been doing. I needed to lift my legs now, and this moved the effort and the danger to a whole different plane. Time and again, unsettled by the wind and darkness, I almost tripped and fell. Terrified that my lack of balance might see me pitch off the side of this mountain, I slowed even further.

At some point, Tim separated from us, maybe to see how the others on our team were doing. Minja took the lead, and I realized that Dilly was behind me. Mouth shut, eyes wide, he looked as terrified as I felt.

"You doing all right?" he finally managed.

I shook my head no.

We followed Minja, and Dilly's guide took up the rear.

Another hour, maybe more, and my legs were shot. I let myself get lost in the searing pain. It started in my toes, spread across my arches into my ankles, then rose up my calves and into my knees, quads, and hamstrings. Every muscle from my lower back down was in spasm. With no other release, I howled into the wind. Dilly must have been in the same state as he howled along with me.

"Shit worked!" he shouted, nudging me with a smile.

"A war cry," I said.

We kept howling and trekking upward, switchback after switchback. But eventually the howling lost its appeal. We were still hours away from sunrise at 6 A.M., which was when Tim said we should be reaching Stella Point, a ridge several hundred yards below the summit. There was still so far to go, and with each passing step my pace seemed to slow.

At another break—I couldn't tell which one at this point—Moody came up to me. He shined a flashlight into my eyes, then raised three fingers. "How many am I holding up?" he asked. I said the number. He asked my name, then where I was. I must have answered correctly because I got a thumbs-up.

Paul materialized out of the darkness. "I know it's hard," he said. "But you're doing a good job, bro. You're *doing* it."

His eyes were glazed, as if he was drunk, and I imagined mine looked the same. I was certainly feeling similar effects.

Then we were back on the trail once more. The others moved farther ahead, becoming nothing more than the tiny lights of their headlamps on the switchbacks higher up the mountain. I felt all alone in the world but for Minja.

My dry, scratchy throat nagged at me, and I wanted nothing more than a long drink of water, which I could not have. I was struggling to take even a few more steps, with so far still to go, when Minja stopped me again and asked if he could take my backpack. Far past pride, now merely trying to survive, I said yes. The relief from taking off my backpack kept me moving through several more switchbacks. I couldn't imagine being able to continue under its weight.

As we climbed, the wind began playing a maddening game with me. When we were heading straight into the wind, my hood blew back, and my headlamp shone onto the trail. On the downside, this face-on assault blasted pebbles and dust into my face and overwhelmed me with its roar. When the wind was behind us, my hood blew down over my face, blocking my headlamp and leaving me in the dark, unbalanced, and with every step a gamble. Yet it was only then, with the wind at our backs, that I could hear Minja's singing.

The night seemed as though it would last forever. Four hours, five, I had no idea how long we had been at it, but the sky appeared to have no intention of ever growing light. The rest breaks could not come quickly enough.

"Is it time?" I would ask Minja.

He would either shake his head or say, "Close. It's close."

Just keeping going until the next break, I would tell myself. *You don't have to go any farther. Just the next break.* When we stopped, I would lean heavily on my poles, head hanging down, trying to gather my breath. When it was time to move again, Minja would take my arm and pull me back onto the trail.

Somewhere—the hundredth switchback, the thousandth—the pain in my legs blew past anything I had ever known. With each step my feet and ankles sent shock waves of agony. I wanted to cry, to sit down on a rock and weep, but that would mean giving in to the pain. I had known pain my whole life, as far back as I could remember, from the time I woke up each day until I hit the sack. I had adapted to it, but that was not the same as escaping from it. Pain just became something I understood very well. I knew how to handle it. No good came from this physical pain; there was no way to benefit from it. It simply needed to be blocked out.

But now, the longer I continued, the less able I was to shut away the pain and stay positive. I was too tired. The altitude, the wind, the endless night—they had worn me down. The altitude and exhaustion mixed with my own self-doubt to create a bizarre cocktail of emotion. Those questions about why I was here and what was I trying to prove came flooding back, but I had few satisfying answers.

In a haze of frustration, I started to think of everyone who had ever doubted me. Of every jeer and joke. Of every time I was picked last for a team in soccer or basketball. I thought of the unlucky fate that had brought CP to my door. The psychological pain drove me on. The anger drove me on. I pictured a furnace fueled by these feelings. *Throw in some logs.*

I remembered playing kickball during elementary school. This equally supercompetitive kid and I were always battling each other. He thought he tagged me out with a throw, but then lost out on the call. A big shouting match ensued between us. In front of everybody on the playground, he dug into me about my funny walk: "Stomp, stomp, stomp!" My face reddened. I shouted back at him. Then— pow!—he punched me in the stomach, and I went down.

I added it to the furnace.

I remembered all those visits to all those doctors. Walk here, bend there, the stab of needles. I heard "Boner . . . Boner . . . " and the cruel playground giggles that followed. I remembered all the lies I had told when someone asked me why I was walking differently, and all the girls who had probably never liked me because of my stork legs. I remembered those damn casts up to my hips and having to walk

Above: Baby Bonner.

Right: With my chicken legs in all their glory.

Below: My family and a neighborhood friend. *Top row:* Mike, Dad, Mom. *Bottom row:* Me, Matt, and family friend.

Above, left: On the night before his death, Jake with his father Steve's marathon medal. *Photo by Alison Robert.*

Above, right: Giving Bompa the African stone necklace before leaving for Kilimanjaro.

Above: The children of the Usa River School gave me hope during some of the darkest hours of the climb.

Above: Team Kilimanjaro, including documentary crew and guides. My guide, Minja, is on the bottom row, far right. *Photo by Nancy A. Sinclair.*

Above: Base Camp before the daunting Barranco Wall, seen here on the far right of the mountain. *Photo by Shirley "Turtle" Ala.*

Right: Day Five of the climb, with Paul and Dilly behind me, my support team every step of the way.

Above: Dilly "bronzing" in the sun.

Below: Summit morning. Dazed and exhausted before the final push upwards.

Left: After a grueling night, I made it to the rooftop of Africa.

Below: Celebrating after the summit. *Photo by Shirley "Turtle" Ala.*

Above: With Ashley, one of my foundation's leading lights.
Photo by Shane Reichardt.

Above, left: Dr. Aminian *(on right)* has been an invaluable partner in helping spread the OM Foundation's work.

Above, right: With Michael Clarke Duncan, narrator of my documentary

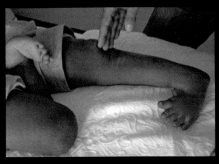

Above: Preoperative exam of Juliana by Dr. Aminian

Left: Juliana before her double amputation surgery. *Photo by Joan Coleman.*

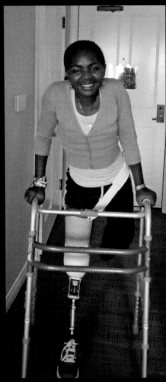

Above: At the center in Africa the foundation helped build, Juliana walks. *Photo by Joan Coleman.*

Left: Juliana getting fitted for her new prosthetics.

Above: My trainer Greg LeFever *(left)* and my Yoda master (Greg Welch).

Above: With Jakey's brothers Brady and Cody and cousin Daly at my final training race for Ironman. *Photo by Alison Robert.*

Right: At Crystal Cove with Mike for my final training swim. This was the same ocean Bompa swam every day. *Photo by Michelle Rodriguez.*

Left: Mike on the day before Ironman race, setting up my gear. Reuniting with my brother got me through two years of arduous training.

Below: Go time. 5 a.m. race day. *Image courtesy of E-PR.*

Below: With Kevin Robson at the start, both nervous and eager. *Image courtesy of E-PR*

Above: Swim done. Now 112 miles on the bike. Preparing. *Photo by Jesse Brewer.*

Left and below: The Blue Hat Army, 125 strong, supported me every step. *Image courtesy of E-PR.*

Left: With Bill Ruddel of Cannondale and 4-time Iron-man World Champion Chrissie Wellington.

Above: My close friend Jesse Brewer urging me onward at the start of the marathon. *Photo by Jesse Brewer.*

Left: A high-ten and hug with Kevin Robson. Many miles still to run. *Photo by Jesse Brewer.*

Above: My jump-dance across the finish line, 22 minutes before the cutoff. *Image courtesy of E-PR.*

Above: Welchy was the first to greet me at the finish. *Image courtesy of E-PR.*

Right: In the medical tent with Ironman race director Diana Bertsch.

Above: With Dad, Mike, and Matt the day after the race.
Image courtesy of E-PR.

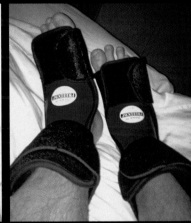

Above left: Welchy and I came back to watch the 2013 Ironman World Championship.

Above, right: My sleep companions for 1.5 years of training and recovery.

Right: At Oakley's headquarters for the launch of my signature eyewear.
Photo by Shane Reichardt.

Above: The children at the Faraja School in Tanzania supported by the foundation.

Above: With Dr. Aminian and a member of the Arpan medical team, meeting with staff at the Faraja School.

Below: Jake's gravesite is adorned with dozens of marathon medals to celebrate his life and lasting inspiration.

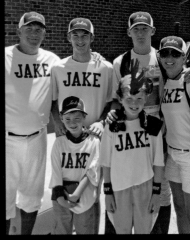

Above: My biggest supporters, the Robert family. *Photo by Alison Robert.*

Below: Jake's family at Orange County marathon supporting the OM Foundation.

around like Frankenstein's monster—and feeling like Frankenstein's monster.

The furnace started to roar.

Each time I crossed a switchback and didn't see any lights ahead, I was sure I was about to reach Stella Point. Then I would get to the turn, and there would be the headlamps again, up ahead, still bobbing up the mountain, still so far for me to go.

With each step, I heaped another log into the flame: the scrapes, bruises, broken bones, clumsy falls—all of them. And I continued. The trail got even steeper. It was still dark, but I thought I saw a hint of blue on the horizon. Digging my poles in, I pushed myself up another step. Then another.

We finally took another break. Unable to stand any longer, I sat on a boulder. I turned to where the sun was supposed to be rising, but any blue I had seen had been in my imagination. It was still pitch-dark.

"This night is endless," I said, marveling at the fact. "Where is the sun? Where is the light?"

There was no answer. The darkness of the night was matched only by the bleakness of my memories.

Then I was on my feet again, heading upward. Each step was slow and made with intent and great exertion. Too tired to lift my feet, I dragged the tip of my boot across the ground. I planted my left pole, then dragged my right foot a few inches forward. Then right pole, left foot, a few inches. They were baby steps, nothing more, and I knew I must have thousands more ahead of me before I reached the summit.

I began to move and think in seconds, in individual moments. One second, I wanted to quit. The next, I urged myself to continue. Each was a battle. Each time I carried on was a victory, bloody and bruised though I was.

At last I saw the horizon start to turn to a dark blue. Dawn was coming. I must be nearing Stella Point. The wind kept buffeting me. The cold bit deep, and the altitude drew away any strength I had left. But dawn was coming.

When I saw the first sliver of sun, I almost wept with joy. But as night lifted, I saw the world as if lost in a fog. The lack of oxygen in my brain was messing with my eyes. Nothing was visibly distinct. Not the summit, not the trail ahead of me. Minja kept humming and trekking forward. I realized that Stella Point was still a long distance away. The realization came like a slow-motion punch to the jaw and knocked me off my feet. I staggered down onto a rock by the side of the path. My hands let go of my poles, and they dangled from my wrists by the straps. I sat, slouched forward, with my arms on my legs, my head hung down almost to my chest. The balls of my feet and my hip flexors stung with such intensity that I didn't dare move. I sucked in a few deep lungfuls of air, but they had no effect.

That whole night through I had told myself, *Make it until the sun comes up, and you'll be good.* And now I had done exactly that, but there was still too far to go. Another hour—more—to Stella Point, then another hour after that to Uhuru Peak, the summit of Kilimanjaro. *Too far. Too far.* My eyes blurred, and the fog around me thickened. I heard voices, but the words meant nothing to me. Someone snapped fingers in my face, but I might have been a statue for all the response I gave.

I pulled my balaclava down off my face and tried to revive myself with a few deep breaths. *It worked before,* I thought dimly. This time, however, I was completely and utterly exhausted. I tried a PowerBar, but it was still like trying to eat a stone. When I finally managed to chew off a bit, my throat was so dry from a lack of water that I could barely swallow. It was no use. I was done, kaput, down for the count.

I stared at the holes worn in the knees of my pants, felt the cold seeping through them. My knees had been knocking so much with every step that they had worn through the fabric.

I heard Swahili and turned my head to see Minja hovering over me. He reached under my arm and tried to lift me to my feet.

"We go," he said. "Let's go. Time go. Weather come."

My legs were as limp as wet rags, and I fell back down onto the rock. Others tried as well, with the same result. It was no use. I lifted up my hand to signal them to leave me be. I felt the sun on my face, and the heat felt so good.

"How are you doing?" Dilly asked. I recognized his voice, but I couldn't answer. He put his hand on my knee. "Just breathe. Breathe."

"We're close," someone else said.

I knew this was a lie, and my spirits sank even lower. Everything around me—the wind, the voices of encouragement, the cold, the tugs at my sleeve to help me up, the mountain, all of it—faded away. I could feel my eyes rolling back in my head and the world slipping away into deep warm blackness. For a second, I was lost to it. *Give up. Stop. You don't belong here. Let them carry you down the mountain on that metal stretcher. That would be easier than any more of this struggle.* Then even those thoughts drifted away. I was nowhere, nobody, nothing.

In the next second, I made a different choice. *Wake up! You can't stay on this rock. Get back on your feet. Who cares how much it hurts?! Fight through it. Never quit. That is who you are. That is who you need to be.*

The fog and the dizziness lifted away. The pain, thirst, cold, wind, and mountain all returned. I was still 1,000 feet, maybe more, from the summit, and there was no way I could stop, not now, not after all this struggle.

I tried to get up, but my legs still did not have the strength. I raised my arm again, this time with my hand outstretched: *Help me up. I need help.*

Minja pulled me up off the rock. I wavered on my legs, but then held steady, my poles supporting me. The others in my team must have gone on ahead again, as it seemed to be just Minja and I against Kilimanjaro once more. I staggered forward. One step followed the next.

The trail zigzagged up a sharp slope of scree toward Stella Point. My boots slipped on the small rocks, doubling the effort required to cover the distance to the ridge. I started to feed the furnace inside me again, this time with more powerful stuff than playground taunts. Harnessing the anger, I confronted haunting memories of my family. Sitting on the couch, my parents telling me that Dad's only moving out for a while, when in fact, he never returned. Having our neighbor's father teach me to ride a bike, since my own wasn't around. My brother Matt doing his own thing. Mike gone altogether, to college, abandoning us. Time and again, he would set a date to hang out, and then he would never show, never even show. There I would sit, stewing, not knowing why he had not come, blaming myself.

And then there was my mom. For my entire childhood she ignored that something was wrong with me, dressing us up like the Partridge family every Sunday for church, while I suffered through a childhood of bruises and broken bones. She never acknowledged what was so painfully obvious: that I was different. That I was not like everyone else. That I had cerebral palsy. The furnace roared again.

Head down, one sluggish foot at a time, I advanced toward Stella Point. No matter how many steps I took, no matter how long I climbed, it felt as though I was getting no closer. The furnace weakened to a flicker, all those hurtful memories having exhausted themselves inside it. The cold and bruising agony in my body returned in force.

Then I heard Minja again, chanting his Swahili prayer. Lulled into a trance, I trudged ahead.

Other voices broke into my reverie, and at first I thought they were some weird trick of the altitude. Just another wicked joke from Kilimanjaro. Then they grew clearer. Some were yelps and cheers in Swahili, and others were calling my name.

"Come on, Bonner! Come on! You got this, Bonner!"

I looked up toward the ridge wall.

Paul came down from the ridge to cheer me on. "You're almost there."

Unable to raise my head, there was nothing I could do but nod and force my feet to take another step, then another, sliding back a few inches on the loose rock each time. It was probably best that I didn't see Paul and the others in our team fight tears at the sight of me so exhausted, struggling so intensely, to make it over those last few feet to Stella Point.

Finally, I crested the ridge. I had reached Stella Point: 18,850 feet above sea level. Tim was straight ahead of me. I stumbled into him, resting my head against his jacket. The others crowded around and patted me on the shoulder. Tim led me over to a boulder and helped me sit down behind it, out of the wind. My legs felt like limp noodles, and I heaved for breath. For several minutes, I remained bent over, spots before my eyes, trying to regain my hold on the world.

Tim brought over a canister of some kind of lemon sugar water that tasted incredible. I had not had anything to drink for hours. At last, I recovered enough to ask Tim how much farther until the summit.

"An hour, that's it," he said. "It's really easy. You did the hard part."

For a long time, I leaned my head against the rock, eyes closed, not wanting to think about taking another step. My breathing eased somewhat, and my vision cleared.

Paul came over and gave me a fist bump. "Love you, brother."

"Oh, man," I said, feeling the first flush of relief that I had reached Stella Point.

"Hardest thing I've ever done," Paul admitted, sitting down beside me.

"Hardest thing by far. You could add up the previous ten hardest things . . . not equal to this." These were the most words I had strung together in hours.

"Most miserable I've been."

"Let's talk about the cold," I said as I shook my head. "I couldn't feel my hands or feet."

Dilly approached.

"Where's my boy?" I called. "Where's Tex?"

"You're the *man!*" Dilly said, giving me a hug.

The three of us rested against the boulder. I looked up at the peak. There was still a long way to go, but for the moment this felt like sweet relief.

"We have to get moving before the weather changes," Tim said and, as if on cue, the wind howled. "Ten minutes."

I nodded. "I'm here. I'm good now."

Paul leaned into me. "If you weren't on this mountain, I'd have been done."

I welled up with feeling. Paul and Dilly were here for me; their friendship meant everything to me.

Moody hovered over us and tapped his wraparound sunglasses. We were so high up that the sun's rays were harmful to our eyes. We put on our sunglasses and rested for a few more minutes. The thought of getting to my feet, climbing higher still, scared me. I didn't know where I would find the strength for the 700 feet to the summit. Every muscle and tendon, from my feet up to my hip flexors, was completely done. Any movement was torture.

Then it was time to hit it. Paul grabbed my arm and lifted me to my feet. My head was swimming, and it felt as if my legs were going to crumple. I settled, and then, following Moody, I trudged back onto the trail.

Any relief I had felt during our break evaporated twenty steps into the final climb. The altitude was wreaking havoc on me. I felt nauseous, spots dancing before my eyes, and unable to trust the ground beneath me. I had the strange sensation that my feet were sinking deeper and deeper into the scree. Soon I would not be able to lift them free.

"Keep pressing on," someone said.

I couldn't respond, couldn't spare the breath or the concentration. Others passed me, but I didn't care that I was falling behind again. The wind whipped around me, and the cold was sheer brutality. I staggered left and right, unable to hold to a straight line. Every few minutes, Minja tapped me on the left shoulder or the right, steering me back onto the path.

One step. Another step. Another.

My world reduced itself to Moody's boots ahead of me and staying on my feet.

It was supposed to be only an hour's trek to Uhuru Peak, but time was now meaningless. My knees were knocking together constantly, rubbing the skin raw, and each step, I was sure, was going to be my last.

I kept asking, "How much farther?" and "Are we close?" I could hear that my words were slurred.

The only answer I got was, "Soon."

Unable to lift my head, I didn't know what to believe.

I tightened my hands on the poles etched with Jake's initials and thought of him, feeding the furnace again. The cruelty of his death, the senselessness of it burned bright and hot. I thought of Steve and Alison Robert at Jake's funeral, the incomparable tragedy of burying your own child.

The trail became very rocky, and I staggered forward in a haze of exhaustion and limitless pain. *When is this going to end? It has to be soon. Keep going.* I heard voices, but the words were garbled. *Just keep moving. Stay on your feet. Nothing else matters.* Someone wrapped his arms around me. Why was he trying to stop me? I trudged ahead, staring down at the hard ground. Somebody else hugged me. The slope had not yet flattened. I wasn't there yet; I couldn't be.

I lifted my head slightly. The team was gathered together ahead of me. I managed to make out the words, "Congratulations! You did it!"

Paul and Dilly pointed to a sign, another 50 feet up on the slope: the mark of the highest point in Africa, Uhuru Peak.

"It's *your* moment," one of them said.

I finally realized what was going on. They were waiting for *me*. They wanted *me* to be the first to the top. I was almost there. This was happening. It was really happening.

My poles bending under all my weight, I dragged myself up the slope. I felt as though I were sleepwalking: my legs stiff, arms out, the world nothing but shapes of gray. Then I was at the sign. I put my fists against it and tapped it a couple of times to make sure it was real. Then I leaned my head against the wood.

I had made it. I had reached Uhuru Peak. I had summited Mt. Kilimanjaro. The fight was over. I had won. A wave of emotion overcame me, and I broke down in tears. I sat at the base of the sign, my hands flat against the rock, unable to stand any longer. For a second I was terrified at the thought of how I would get down off this mountain. I had nothing left. *Nothing.* Then I put that to one side, closed my eyes, and breathed as deeply as I could.

I made it.

Cheers rang out. Paul and Dilly joined me, and we cried together in joy, pride, relief, disbelief, pain, and happiness. With Paul holding me up, I tucked an Anaheim Ducks flag into the sign, and we took a couple of team photos.

The views from up there were amazing: Mt. Meru in the distance, ringed by clouds, a long stretch of fortresslike glaciers, the giant volcano crater, and a clear vista for miles and miles of the flat lands surrounding Kilimanjaro. We were so high up that I could see the curvature of the earth.

"We have to get down," Moody said. The idea of climbing down from 19,340 feet shook my nerves. I took one last look at the view from the summit, rattled by the strange thought that I had only just started something by climbing so high.

8

The Fun-House Mirror

Minja called after me, but he would have had as much luck calling after a ball rolling down the mountain. Legs shot, unable to pick my way down the precipitous trail, I slid down the loose scree. Every 10 feet or so, I crashed onto my backside, but I didn't care. It was the quickest—and probably the only—way I could descend Kili.

On the way, I came upon Mitch, one of the documentary producers, who was sitting on a rock, looking drunk, a pile of bloody puke at his feet. His Tanzanian guide hovered at his shoulder. Altitude sickness had obviously forced Mitch to stop his own summit attempt.

"Did you make it?" Mitch asked, dazed and confused.

I assured him I had. We spoke for a few moments while Minja sharply urged Mitch's guide to get him to a lower altitude. Mitch said he would be okay, and then I continued on my slip and slide down the scree; I needed off this mountain as well.

Eventually, the trail leveled out, and Minja caught up with me long enough to give me a strange look that said, "What the hell were you thinking going down that way?" and I just smiled back. My pants were in shreds, but I had 2,000 fewer feet of Kilimanjaro to climb down.

A few hours later, I reached base camp before many on my team, enjoyed the world's best-tasting Coke, and collapsed in my tent. Every single part of my body hurt. Awakened shortly after by the others coming into the camp, I changed clothes and ate lunch, and then we all trekked farther down together. I managed the descent largely by swinging my hips from one side of the trail to the other, my legs following. It was excruciating, but I rarely took a break, wanting badly to get myself off the mountain.

At 9,900 feet, we reached a permanent campsite, which had a small hut that sold beer and soda. We bought beers for everybody, including the guides and porters, and we finally celebrated. There were lots of high fives and toasts. We broke out into impromptu dances and songs that Dilly said resembled a "bad MC Hammer video." We hoisted each other up on our shoulders and paraded around the campsite. Soaked in beer, breathing air rich in oxygen, and dizzy with the achievement, we were all pretty high, me included.

After a twelve-hour sleep, we trekked down to our van. I hugged Minja and thanked him for being my "guardian angel" on the mountain. Minja clamped me on the shoulder, and then we bundled inside the van for the return journey to Arusha. As we drove back, the others regaling each other with remembered details of the epic adventure, I looked out the window and thought only of how I had narrowly escaped disaster. It took two baths and one shower to wash away eight days of sweat and dirt. Nothing eased my body from hurting with every movement. That night we gorged on barbeque at a Middle Eastern street café that doubled as an auto shop, and the team reveled again in what we had accomplished.

We spent the next few days touring Serengeti National Park by Jeep. We saw giraffes, lions, zebras, elephants, leopards, Cape buffalo, and even a black rhino that charged us across a treeless plain. From there, we traveled to the Ngorongoro Crater, a huge expanse of green inside an imploded volcano. While the others were filled with nothing but celebratory "oohs" and "aahs," I was having trouble enjoying any of it. My body, from my swollen feet upward, was in a lot of pain, and I was crippled with exhaustion. As much as Tanzania was stunning at every turn, it was tough to sit in the Jeep for hours, my legs cramped, bouncing up and down pot-holed dirt roads, when I wanted to do nothing more than eat (my appetite was off the charts), sleep (no amount seemed to be enough), and get back to what I knew (my comfy bed, burger joints, and sandy beaches).

But more than impatience for the familiar, something else was disturbing me, something deeper. One morning, while the others were heading out on an amazing safari inside the crater, I wanted only to remain behind at the lodge by myself. I didn't want another day reveling in our success on Kilimanjaro, because the truth was, I felt none of it.

Everything about the climb unsettled me. Clearly, I had arrived on the mountain ill-informed and unprepared. I had barely survived the summit attempt. Kilimanjaro had exposed my disability—and the limitations it put on me—in a way I had never expected or experienced in my life. Worst of all, though, was how I had drawn on a parade of ugly memories about my cerebral palsy and family—not to mention an anger that I'd never known existed—to push through the darkness to the summit. Now confronted with these memories in the light of day, I found they were not easily stuffed back inside. While my friends still basked in the afterglow of our effort, these raw emotions from my past plagued my thoughts, along with the recognition that the act of climbing a mountain had not been enough to conquer them forever. On the contrary, instead of filling the void, it seemed the climb had dug the hole deeper.

At the same time, I could not shake my memories of the Usa River School either. As I sat in my room, looking out at the beautiful vista of Ngorongoro Crater but seeing none of it, all I could see were the faces of the children, their bare quarters, and the stand where they hawked their simple wares to keep a roof over their heads and food in their mouths. Their resiliency went beyond anything I could find in myself. Time and again while I was climbing, their song had been the only bright light leading me onward. Envisioning those who never made it there, locked in cages or left abandoned on the side of the road to starve, broke me in half. They had a right to live, a right to the best life possible, and it made me feel small to think that shortly I would just hop on a plane and leave them to their fates.

After another day at Ngorongoro, leave I did. From Arusha I boarded a flight to Amsterdam, then took my connection on to LAX. Three weeks had passed since I left, and it seemed like another lifetime. When I drove up to my apartment, I discovered my neighbor's teenage daughters had covered my garage door with butcher paper and painted a mountain and the words: "YOU DID IT! CONGRATULATIONS, BONNER." Much as I appreciated the welcome, I was a long way from being done with anything.

Rest and stay off your feet as much as you can," Dr. Aminian prescribed.

Six weeks after returning to the United States, I was still a mess. My climb had brought a cascade of publicity, and many wanted to know what adventure was next, but I couldn't even fathom the idea.

Because of my CP, my body was slow to repair itself after the punishment I put it through on the mountain. Just prying myself from bed every morning was a struggle. Eight hours. Ten. Twelve. Fourteen. No amount of sleep or downtime could banish the exhaustion that hung over me. It was like mono on steroids. At every meal I wolfed down everything on my plate—and often seconds as well—yet I was still hungry. Those constantly flexing muscles, now trying to recover, burned a lot of fuel. And my feet, my poor feet. Throughout the day, they swelled like balloons inside my shoes, and by closing time at work, I needed to loosen the laces completely or slip the shoes off altogether.

My doctors, Millhouse and Aminian, ran a battery of tests on me. Full physical. Blood work. Pee in the cup. The works. Beyond plantar fasciitis and some strained tendons in my legs, everything, including my hormone levels, was fine. In nonscientific terms, their diagnosis was that I had badly abused my body—I mean really taken it out back and given it a licking—and now it was demanding a long break. So according to doctors' orders, I was to take it easy, stay off my feet, and not exercise anything except patience.

Not so easy for me. I was exhausted, yet restless inside. The weeks that followed my return had been something of a rude awakening, as I gradually realized that my life was not what I wanted it to be. Anyone who's achieved a lofty goal knows the emotional low that sometimes follows in its wake. When the euphoria recedes and you return to your life, you're often left confronting the same problems you had before the journey began. The aftermath of my climb had done little to improve things with my family, and my relationship with them continued to be distant at best. Although I had always envisioned settling down by my thirties, my future wife and I corralling a litter of kids, my love life was going nowhere fast.

I was also beginning to feel ready for something else with work. The Samuelis and the Ducks organization they had built were still great, but the hours were long and there was not much room for advancement, since it was clear nobody above me was leaving any time soon.

As I cast about for direction, the only activity that stirred much passion in me was my volunteer work, but even that proved difficult at times. In December 2008, thanks in part to fund-raising efforts for Kilimanjaro, the UCP-OC opened the Life Without Limits Therapy Center, a one-stop shop providing children with disabilities the specialists they needed in physical, occupational, and speech therapy. The new center offered individual and group therapy rooms and featured a special gym with everything from a simple rock-climbing wall to balance beams, a slide, and a pool of bouncy balls.

As a board member, and since Kilimanjaro a lead spokesperson and fund-raiser for the organization, I spent a lot of time at the center and promoting its benefits. This brought me into touch with more children with cerebral palsy and other disabilities than ever before. Truth be told, these meetings were often uncomfortable for me. It was often difficult to know what to say to the children, some of whom could not speak, and if I was making any connection at all. Then there were the parents, who would often give me what I began to call "the look." Upon introduction, they would stare at me, observe how I walked and moved, and try to connect their child's condition with my own.

Initially, I thought these interactions made me uneasy because I knew their child would likely never reach the level of ability I had. But over time I came to see that my discomfort had more to do with my reluctance to accept my CP and that the two of us were more alike than different. In reality, the distinctions I was making about my level of ability existed only in my head.

Kilimanjaro had jarred loose a lot of things, and in those first months afterward I was still trying to fit the pieces together. The way that my condition had been ignored by my family when I was growing up. The way that I, in turn, had ignored my condition as an adult. Prior to the climb, I had assumed that this pattern had been disrupted once I'd started talking about my CP publicly and sharing my story with others. I had assumed that standing in front of a group and raising money for therapies and CP research meant that my days of pretending to be "normal" were over.

The more I thought about the climb, though, the more I began to see how wrong my assumptions had been. The fact that I had made no special preparations (training or otherwise) for the climb because of my cerebral palsy. The fact that I'd treated myself as though I was just another person trying to conquer a mountain without acknowledging what having CP actually meant. The fact that I'd had to rely on the negative aspects of my history with CP—the taunting, the name-calling—to power myself up the mountain. While I continued to struggle with putting it all together, each piece spoke volumes about how far away I still was from accepting my condition rather than just stating its presence in my life.

What spoke the loudest at that point, however, was the impact the center was making for those who came through its doors. Early in 2009, I witnessed one such moment.

"Hi, Paige. I'm so happy to see you," the therapist said, lifting Paige Dunning out of her wheelchair in the gym. She carried her over to a pommel horse, suspended by ropes from a roof beam. Twelve years old, with brown hair and a severe case of cerebral palsy, Paige was the daughter of one of the board members who had run the marathon with me back in 2006.

"Okay, Paige," the therapist said, positioning herself behind her on the pommel horse so she would not fall. "I know you love to swing. Are you ready to swing?"

Paige offered nothing, her head listless, arms curled, as they swayed back and forth together on the horse. The therapist behind Paige stopped the pommel horse.

"Okay," she said. "Pick your head up this time, and we'll swing. You can do it."

Paige didn't move, head still down. As I watched, I didn't think there was any way she could or would show any reaction.

"I'll rock a little," the therapist said, moving the horse slightly. "But if you want to really swing, you have to lift your head."

A second passed. Nothing.

Then Paige raised her head ever so slightly. The therapist rewarded her by giving the horse a big wide swing. Paige lifted her head more and brightened with a smile.

That short little movement by Paige may not have looked like much, but for her, trapped in a body that fought not to do what she wanted, it was a huge leap forward. Time and again, I was amazed by these kids.

Through Dr. Aminian I also met a seven-year-old named Ashley Arambula. Like Paige's, her cerebral palsy left her unable to control either her arms or her legs. She also had intractable epilepsy, which left her to suffer severe unpredictable seizures that could not be controlled by medication. And yet, whenever I saw her, she had this amazing smile and can-do attitude. There was no retreat or self-pity in Ashley, and she attacked her therapy with a gusto that put me on the floor and gave context to any troubles of my own.

These children were the bright lights in my life. The more time I spent with them, the more inspired they left me, the more I wanted to do for them. Big ideas, big possibilities began to stir within, and soon I was envisioning launching my own foundation and sprouting centers like Life Without Limits across the world. It was an easy next step to know where I would start my work first: Tanzania. There were so many children like those at the Usa River School who needed help.

By the spring of 2009, I was charging ahead with the formation of the OM Foundation. Its motto was "One Man, One Mission . . . Living Beyond the Limits." The mission was to help support children with disabilities, anywhere and everywhere. This would take the form of building centers, funding medical treatments, raising awareness, and promoting acceptance. My days soon became a whirlwind. They were filled with meetings to set up the foundation, my regular work with the Anaheim Ducks, and managing the attention I had received after the Kilimanjaro climb. Between finishing shoots for the documentary and doing interviews for radio, TV, and newspapers, I was, frankly, getting a little tired of hearing myself speak. But I saw what an opportunity all of this interest offered for the foundation, so yap, yap, yap.

The attention only intensified as the documentary premiere approached. We were blown away when Michael Clarke Duncan offered to narrate the documentary for free. An Oscar-nominated actor wanted to be part of what we were doing. The snowball of publicity was amazing, and it grew bigger by the day. I was onto something. I just didn't know where it was leading me next until in late April I sat down to watch the whole documentary for the first time. It so happened to be at its premiere.

———————

Sitting in the dark of the theater in Orange County, with four hundred of my close and not so close friends, I watched myself climb Kilimanjaro. To my right sat Bompa. To my left, my father. During the thirty-nine-minute documentary, the audience moved through emotion after emotion—reflection, laughter, horror, anticipation, triumph—as I made my way to the summit. When the credits rolled, people cheered and applauded. Bompa tapped me several times on the leg as he stared up at the empty white screen, tears in his eyes that never broke. He was proud of me. My dad was proud of me.

Afterward, I smiled and shook hands and laughed and drank and bathed in the limelight. Inside, I was shaken and roiled and, more than anything, spurred to do something about it, something big.

What I had witnessed on the screen was very different from what the others took away. A marathoner friend of mine once told me that endurance events, whether climbing a mountain or running a race, were like looking at oneself in a fun-house mirror: sometimes you liked the exaggerated version of yourself you saw; other times you were horrified. With the documentary, I got a good, long, ugly look in the mirror. All my physical weaknesses were on view: my awkward gait, the stiffness, the clumsiness, the wibble-wobble of it all. Vivid was how vulnerable and undertrained I came to the mountain. So was how far from "normal" I was, though that had been my ill-considered approach to the adventure.

Also on view was my attitude: the glum looks, the despair, the self-pity, the tunnel vision, and the negativity that was only thinly masked. Instantly, I was brought back to the mountain, the dark night before the summit, and it pained me to see myself struggle, knowing that the only thing that had gotten me through it was the shame of my cerebral palsy and family regrets. As I watched it all unfold on screen, my mental failings seemed more pronounced than my physical ones.

Before the lights had even come up, I knew I needed a new adventure, a new test, to try myself against. Jake's death had stirred me to attempt Kilimanjaro, yet now I saw plainly how the climb itself had revealed a mountain of trouble inside me. It wasn't pretty, but at least I had been pushed to see it. The next time I looked into the fun-house mirror, I wanted to like—hell, love—what was reflected back at me.

Watching the documentary again and again through the spring and summer at festivals across the country drove this conviction further home. My body was still a wreck, but once recovered, I was going to do something, something big.

The death of my grandparents solidified this idea, set it in stone. In early September, Bomma passed away first. Afterward, Bompa refused treatment for an infection he had been struggling with, the result of recent knee surgery. As the days passed, he grew weaker and weaker. We tried to get him to go to the hospital, but there was no convincing him. Instead, we hired a nurse to stay with him twenty-four hours a day.

The day before he passed away, my mother, brothers, and I gathered in Bompa's bedroom. He asked us to hold hands and promise to stick together, to be a family. He then let out a howling cry that shook us all to our foundations. None of us had ever seen Bompa show any weakness, let alone cry, and now he just let rip, chest heaving, tears pouring down his face. It is my last memory of him, and though I will never know for sure what provoked the outburst, I suspected he was giving voice to his regrets, to what he didn't do in life or would have done better.

In January 2010, my brothers and I descended the long flight of steps to the beach, as we had done so many times as children. Our mother followed us down. Despite Bompa's wish, the four of us had never been farther apart. Matt was living in northern California, and we only saw each other a few times a year. Although Mike and I only lived a few miles from each other, we barely spoke. Arguments with our mother about how Bompa should have been taken care of and what should now be done with his estate divided us all the more.

We shared a few words that morning, and they were mostly about how cold it was. It was colder still when, after a prayer, said by our mother, Mike and I stripped down to our bathing suits and walked into the ocean. We each had a zip-top bag containing some of our grandparents' ashes. It was their dying wish that they be spread on these waters.

Mike and I swam out past the break line and bobbed in the wintry swells, our teeth chattering. The cold didn't seem to bother the pod of dolphins coursing through the waters 50 yards away. While Mike and I wrestled to open the bags with our numb fingers, we joked that Bompa sure was a tough bastard for swimming in these waters every day until he was eighty. Together we said a final commemoration: "This is where you belong. This is where you always loved to be. We love you both!" We dunked the bags under water until the ashes dissolved into the ocean and then swam in a hurry back to shore.

If I had any chance at living a life without regrets, whether in how I approached my cerebral palsy or embraced the people who should be closest to me, I needed to take another look in the mirror, confront my weaknesses, move past my anger, and accept myself. Given my troubles and how deeply they were woven into the fabric of who I was, this mirror would have to be a real monster to give me the time and the ability I needed to unravel them.

Whatever this adventure, my new foundation would have to be a part of it. With the help of the documentary, I saw my foundation grow and flourish. I wanted to make sure that this next adventure would succeed, but I also wanted to start making a difference immediately—not just in California, but around the world.

In May 2010, I found myself running at full tilt through the Amsterdam airport. Thanks to the fact that the pilot on my late plane out of LAX had radioed ahead, I had been given a chance to make the Arusha flight. It was a sign, I convinced myself, that this journey was meant for great things. Breathless, I rushed onto the plane and took my seat next to Dr. Afshin Aminian. After a side trip to Paris to perform some pediatric surgeries, Afshin was accompanying me on my first mission with the OM Foundation.

Since returning from Kilimanjaro, I had grown closer to this tall, tell-it-like-it-is doctor who was the director of the Children's Orthopedic Center at the Children's Hospital of Orange County. Born in Iran, Afshin attended boarding school in Switzerland and then graduated from Northwestern. He had first studied electrical engineering, but he found that painfully boring and isolating. An adviser suggested that he focus on biomedical engineering, where he could design artificial kidneys, hearts, and the like. As part of the program, he worked in a rehabilitation institute in Chicago and found that he preferred meeting with the patients who needed prosthetics rather than sitting up in the lab on the top floor making their new limbs. The director suggested medical school, and several years later Afshin was a top pediatric orthopedic surgeon. When I launched my foundation, I asked him to be on the board and to be our medical director. He jumped in with both feet.

My emotional connection to Tanzania from the climb made it an obvious choice for our first work outside the United States. When we arrived in Arusha that night, two young Tanzanians welcomed us at the airport, placing garlands of flowers around our necks. They were from a nonprofit relief organization that helped impoverished, sick, and orphaned children in Tanzania. They shook our hands vigorously and ushered us out to a waiting van.

We drove away from Arusha toward Mt. Kilimanjaro along a long dark highway. At last we pulled off onto a side road and then stopped in front of the metal gates. A guard with a machete on his hip opened the gates, and we drove inside the compound of buildings that make up the orphanage. A friend who had visited Tanzania the year before had suggested this organization to me, and Afshin and I had come in order to organize medical treatment for the children, including potential surgeries, and also to assess the possibility of contributing funds for a treatment center.

Because of dueling schedules, we only had forty-eight hours before we needed to return to the airport. It was late, and most of the lights were out in the cluster of buildings. Nevertheless, a number of children and adults were standing about waiting for our arrival. Many of them had come from miles away to be examined by Afshin.

A part of me wanted to get going straightaway, but we were advised against it. They said that the next day would be very busy and that it was time for bed. They led us to a room with two short, narrow beds surrounded with mosquito netting. Both of us were so tall that our feet dangled over the ends of the beds, but it didn't matter. We both conked out in minutes.

In the morning, I woke up to the sound of giggles and children's voices. I emerged from my room to see in the distance the snowy peaks of Kilimanjaro, which I had climbed a year and a half earlier.

As I walked through the compound, kids of every age peered out at me above windowsills and from around corners and trees. I waved and smiled. Some waved back; others shyly ducked for cover. They were as curious about me as I was eager to get to know them.

At the end of the property, I came to an open field on which one day my foundation might build a center. It was a *Field of Dreams* moment—I imagined its walls and roof rising and the children crossing toward it to get the help they needed.

Later, Afshin and I headed over to the kitchen for breakfast. The organization's leaders told us a few of the children's stories. Some had been locked in cages and closets before they came to the orphanage. Some had been abandoned at her doorstep, others left to fend for themselves in the wild. One had been burned to scare the demons out of her. Another, an albino, had been saved from witch doctors who wanted to sever her limbs and sell them as "magic." Many were merely too much of a burden for their parents, whether because they had AIDS or because they cost too much to feed. The conversation was sobering, but it also fired me up to get started.

Afshin set up his exam line under a shady tree, and a score of people gathered. They had come from the neighboring villages, some many miles away. The first patient, a woman, had a deformed foot that Afshin said could be quickly corrected with a special shoe. A translator conveyed this to the woman. Afshin made a note on a pad, and then he was on to the next patient.

Then a man, short as a jockey, approached. His threadbare, dirty clothes looked as if they had been slowly eaten by moths over the course of two decades. In his arms he carried his fourteen-year-old daughter, who was wearing a brand-new pink dress. Her father set her down on the ground a few feet away from us, and she came the rest of the way herself, walking on her knees. It was such a heartbreaking moment that I had to take a seat on the bench. We were introduced to Juliana, and then Afshin took over.

Sitting down next to her, he asked quietly if he could lift up her dress over her knees to examine her legs. Her eyes shifted uneasily, and her hands shook. Nonetheless, she bravely nodded, giving Afshin permission. He examined her lower body, which was in a bad way. One foot grew out the back of her hamstring, just above the knee, and her other leg was bent 90 degrees inward. Afshin asked Juliana and her father a bunch of questions. Every answer was a simple yes or no, rarely delivered with any emotion and never with any detail. From what I understood, Juliana had been using her knees to walk all her life, and her father had carried her on his back for two days "across the bush" to get here.

The orphanage's director, who was watching over the examination, stepped in and asked Juliana if she wanted to live there. She looked to her father, but said nothing. The director then asked the father if he wanted Juliana to live there. After a moment, he said yes. The director then asked Juliana again. She said yes, staring at the ground. The father spit on his hand, then shook the director's. Done. That quickly. In five minutes—less, probably—a child had been given over into the care of another. The conversation left me so overwrought that I had to walk away and catch my breath. No doubt Juliana's father thought that this was his daughter's best chance in life, but to relinquish your child. . . . It was too much for me, particularly since I realized this happened many, many times every month.

After more examinations, we took a break and were given a tour of the whole compound. Some of the children looked perfectly healthy, though their eyes betrayed psychological wounds. Others were pretty severely sick or disabled, lying on mats or shuffling across the room using chairs for balance. One child had burn scars all over her body. I had mixed emotions. The tragedy was heart-wrenching, but then again these children were likely in a better place now than where they had come from.

For the rest of the morning, I played with the children or sat beside Afshin while he performed his exams. He amazed me. He never hesitated as he talked with the patients in line about their sufferings. The younger ones he held as though they were his own children. He calmly gave his diagnosis and then made his notes before moving on to the next patient.

After the clinic, we drove to a remote town called Machame, located in the opposite direction from Arusha. Afshin wanted to check out whether the hospital there had the facilities he needed to perform the surgeries he wanted to do. Juliana came along with us to have X-rays taken of her legs. She was silent and quiet in the back of the van. Afshin and the hospital's head doctor had a long conversation, but it was clear that any surgeries as complicated as the one Juliana needed would require levels of postoperative care that were beyond what she could easily get in Tanzania. We returned to the orphanage, had dinner by lantern light, and hit the sack early.

The next day, we got up before dawn. Outside the kitchen, I passed Juliana's father, who had been given a fresh set of clothes. He had spent the night on the floor and was getting ready to head back to his village. Afshin and I piled into the van and set out for Miryani, a tanzanite-mining town described to us as "the end of hell." Even the police, the orphanage's director said, dared not go there. They ran another orphanage in the town and operated a couple of food dispensaries. A few hours later, we arrived at a ragtag collection of huts on dirt streets. The director advised us to keep our eyes to ourselves until we were safe inside the walls of the food kitchen and to not venture away from that building. We would be leaving before dark, no arguments. Seeing the tough-looking bunch who stared at us as we approached, I quickly understood why.

Even given the town's tough reputation, I was not prepared for the line of half-starved children, barefoot and in rags, who gathered for food. One boy, a seven-year-old, came to the front and took away three bowls of food. He huddled down next to two younger children, who must have been his sister and brother. Neither of them was older than three. He fed them both before shoveling his own food into his mouth as if it was the last meal he would ever have. Afshin and I couldn't help but watch them. The misery of the scene was acute, and we were both brought to tears. They were probably the kids of a miner killed while burrowing into the earth for tanzanite or wasted away by the scourge of AIDS. Either way, I knew I would never forget that little boy and his two siblings; the sight of them was burned deep inside me.

We headed back to the Miryani orphanage and met some albino children who had run away from home. While we were there, two older men carrying a young child arrived at the gate. They were a tribal elder and the chief of a nearby village, and they wanted to hand over the girl to the orphanage. No mention was made of her parents. Afshin examined her. It was clear from her movements that she likely had cerebral palsy. The director suggested we take her back to the main orphanage. So they had welcomed two children in as many days.

As planned, we headed back before dark. Almost as soon as we returned, we had to leave for the airport. There was no doubt that the OM Foundation wanted to build a center for the disabled children or that we would be bringing Juliana to the States for her surgery (and perhaps others too).

While we waited to board our plane, Afshin and I sat across from each other in the airport restaurant, trying to wrap our heads around everything we had witnessed in the past two days. We talked a lot about our next steps in Tanzania and how much we could do. Afshin wanted to take his whole team there each year to do surgeries. We also wanted to train doctors and empower others in Tanzania to help their own people. So much needed to be done.

On our journey back, I also thought a lot about the children I had met, especially Juliana. The memory of her first crossing toward Afshin on her knees almost brought tears to my eyes. Yet the more I considered the moment, the more I was struck by how much bravery and resilience she showed. Here was a young girl who took the worst that life had given her and made do with it the best way she could. There was a lesson there that I needed to learn for myself, and I was more eager than ever to begin.

In fall 2010, two years after reaching Uhuru Peak, I finally began to feel well enough physically to think about moving ahead with plans for my next mountain. I tried working out, seeing how my body handled short jogs along the coast and time at the gym. All was good.

The next adventure was not literally about picking another actual mountain. Nobody knew I had already been thinking about my next project, so almost everyone was ready with helpful suggestions. A favorite was Everest. To that, my answer was always an instant no. It would have been a death sentence, and I had no interest in being stuck on the side of a mountain freezing cold and starved of oxygen ever again.

Since the documentary premiere, however, I had considered a bunch of other crazy ideas: swimming across the English Channel, an ultradistance run of 50 miles or more, Forrest Gumping my way across the United States—something that tested me as never before.

The Ironman triathlon in Kona.

No apple needed to fall on my head to make me arrive at the idea. A triathlon was always in the running, but the Kona Ironman was the only one that kept coming back to me. As kids, my brother Matt and I used to sit in front of the TV for hours every year watching the world's greatest triathlon on ABC's *Wide World of Sports*. I could recite the promo by heart: "The thrill of victory . . . the agony of defeat." We oohed and aahed and gasped as racers chopped through the crystal-blue waters, struggled by bike across the barren volcanic tundra, and stumbled, fell, and at times crawled across the finish line. In particular, the story of the Hoyt men fascinated me. Seeing Dick Hoyt tow and push his son, Rick, who had cerebral palsy, was always an arrow to the heart. Before Kilimanjaro, I had even sent the Hoyts a note about my adventure, saying that as a kid they had inspired me to push myself. They sent back a signed picture with their tagline: "Yes, you can."

The more I thought about the Kona Ironman, the greater sense it made. An Ironman triathlon was the pinnacle of endurance events: a 2.4-mile swim, a 112-mile bike ride, and a marathon run. Nothing could be tougher on the body. The Kona Ironman, otherwise known as the Ironman World Championship, was the pinnacle of the sport. The best of the best competed in the race, and it was a brutal trial of will, body, and heart. A real monster, and the perfect fun-house mirror.

Still feeling good at the start of 2011, I visited Dr. Millhouse. I didn't tell him about the Ironman, but said that I was tired of lying around like a blob and wanted to get exercising again. He examined me, said that everything looked good, and advised me to ramp up my efforts gradually; if I listened to what my body was telling me, I'd be fine. I wonder if he would have said the same if I had told him the truth.

By chance, I was having lunch with some folks at Oakley that same day. (Oakley, a sports eyewear and performance gear maker, had donated equipment for my Kilimanjaro climb, and the CEO, Colin Baden, had turned the screening of the documentary into a big event at its global headquarters.) Somewhere during the usual chit-chat, they asked me how I was feeling.

"Funny," I said, "my doctor just cleared me to exercise."

"What's next then?" Dane Howell asked. Howell worked in Oakley's military division, supplying all kinds of gear to the United States military, including Special Forces, and allies around the world. His nickname was "Guns" because of his ripped arms, and he was big: six foot seven, 240 pounds.

"Do you know any triathletes?" I asked.

"Don't even tell me you're thinking about doing Ironman!" Dane said.

"Well . . ." I sheepishly smiled, jumping in farther than I had planned to.

"You're crazy," said Erick Poston, Dane's boss at the time and a former motocross champion who knew crazy from crazy. Then he asked, "You know who works for Oakley?"

I shook my head.

"Greg Welch."

"The Ironman champion, dude," Dane added.

"I know. He's an absolute beast," I replied.

"I'll go see him and give him your documentary," Poston promised.

Leaving lunch, I felt overwhelmed. Until that point, Ironman was still only an idea, one that I would commit to only if it were physically possible for me to do it—and I didn't know that yet. Now I was announcing my intentions about competing at the Kona Ironman—and potentially meeting Greg Welch to talk about them.

The Greg Welch. By far one of the most accomplished Ironman triathletes in history, the Australian was once known as the "world's fittest man." In the early 1990s, he was the dominant triathlete, winning race after race, including the Ironman World Championship at Kona in 1994. "Sir Plucky" was his nickname, for his madman will and persistence. A couple of miles into the swim leg of the 1999 championship, Welch grew light-headed and short of breath, his heart beating like mad. He stopped for five minutes, thinking he was having an asthma attack. Unwilling to quit, he forged ahead. Over the course of the race, through the bike ride and run, he had fifteen separate such episodes, yet still managed to finish in eleventh place. It was only afterward that he learned his "asthma attacks" were actually heart attacks caused by ventricular tachycardia, a condition that subsequently forced him from the sport. Welch was a legend among triathletes, and besides his gig at Oakley he still announced many of the key triathlons, including the World Championship every year. Some of this I knew from watching Welch compete. The rest I researched, hoping that I might get to meet him.

A couple of weeks after my impromptu declaration to the folks at Oakley, I was sitting in a booth at Wahoo's, a Mexican restaurant near Oakley headquarters, waiting for Welch to arrive. I was nervous and had a laundry list of questions in my notebook. Welch entered, a short fireplug of a man, his face tanned and creased from years in the sun. *What a presence,* I thought, as he waved at a few people in the restaurant before shaking my hand vigorously and giving me a "Howdy, mate" with a wide grin. With all that he had done, he sat down unpretentiously.

I thanked him for meeting me, and he said he was impressed with my documentary, which Erik Poston had given him. Then we huddled over the table and got to it. I peppered him with my list: How long would I need to train? How do I ramp up? What kind of races would I need to do in advance of the World Championship? How much did he know about cerebral palsy? What impact would the CP have? Did he think it was possible?

Welch was straight up from the start. "Finishing will be very hard," he said, with a short laugh. "It's much more than simply running, biking, and swimming."

"Can I do it?" I asked.

"You don't know how many able-bodied people try to do this. There are so many unknowns, and many people underestimate what it takes to get there and what it takes to finish the race. Some of the best athletes in the world struggle even to finish at Kona."

"Okay," I said, mentally wiping away the cold water Welch had figuratively just thrown in my face.

"You'd be nuts to try." Welch smiled. "But it's possible."

He wasn't worried about my mental strength, he remarked. I had that in spades. It was clear to him from the documentary that I had hit my body's limit on the morning of my Kilimanjaro summit attempt.

"You were bonking bad, mate," he said. There was that smile again.

Yet I still managed to get up, he pointed out, and push through to get to the top. He told me that most triathletes who bonk at a race are carried out on stretchers.

Preparing for Ironman would demand much more than mental strength. There was nutrition, conditioning, strength training, proper technique, and an enormous commitment of time and energy and focus to consider. The more we spoke, the more answers I got about how many months of all-consuming training would be required. And the more answers I got, the more I wanted to do the Ironman—and I wanted Greg Welch to coach me. He was everything you could wish for in a coach: smart, honest, strategic, ice cool but intense, humble yet confident.

He asked how much experience I had as a swimmer, a runner, and a cyclist. He asked even more questions about my cerebral palsy and, unlike before Kilimanjaro, I did not skirt the answers. I wanted to come to the race prepared for every inch of ocean and road, and if I was going to do this, then I needed to be honest about my limitations.

Welch absorbed everything I said—no judgments, just "Oh, yeah . . . That makes sense . . . Yeah." An hour later when we left the restaurant, Greg followed me to my car. I could tell he was checking out how I walked, how my legs buckled and my knees knocked. I made no effort to mask my gait. Those days were over for me.

"If I have any other questions, do you mind if I call you?" I asked.

"Sure," Greg said. He paused briefly before adding, "One more thing, though. You had better be damn sure this is something you want to do, mate, because it will take a commitment beyond anything it took to climb the mountain."

"I'll think on it," I said, then shook his hand and thanked him. Driving home, I knew for sure I was going to do it. Now I needed to convince Welch to train me.

Before reaching out to him again, I spoke to my new boss, Chris Underwood, CEO of Young's Market, a major spirits and wine distributor. Earlier that year I had made the tough decision to leave the Ducks when Chris offered me the opportunity to create from scratch a marketing platform for Young's. Further, the folks at Young's were big supporters of my foundation work. They had sponsored my

Kilimanjaro climb, and Chris promised to give me the time I needed for the Kona Ironman; he was all for it.

With his support, I reached out to Welch a few days later. I had prepared a whole pitch on why he should train me.

"I need to do this, but there's no chance I can do it on my own," I began.

Little did I know he had already decided to take me on after first watching the documentary and then meeting me for lunch. Since his retirement from competition, Welch had undergone almost a dozen heart procedures in his battle against ventricular tachycardia. A pacemaker-like device now sent jolts of electricity to his heart whenever it was needed to counter an abnormal rhythm. He knew what it was to struggle against a body that would simply not cooperate. As for his coyness at our lunch about how willing he was to help me with my Ironman ambition—he just wanted to make sure I really wanted it. He was devious that way.

Before I could continue with my pitch, Welch said, "I'll coach you."

9

Swim. Bike. Run.

The Oakley headquarters looked like a cross between a spaceship and a medieval fortress. Passing through its cathedral-sized steel entrance was both inspiring and intimidating. At reception I asked for Greg Welch and waited for him in one of the fighter-pilot ejection seats in the lobby. He came out to meet me, then led me down a corridor of dark mysterious rooms into his office.

"So, we're really going to do this?" he asked.

"Yep."

"You're crazy." He laughed.

"Yep."

"I'm busy. Okay, mate?" Welchy (as I quickly came to call him) started. "I'll write you out a schedule every week, but *you* need to follow it. I can't teach you how to work out, the proper way to run or swim, or how to ride a bike. You need to figure that out on your own, get the right people. You need to join a swim program. You need a trainer. I'll coach, but I can't be there every second to wipe your bum. You have to become your own coach, your own doctor, and your own nutritionist. I'm here to set the guidelines, but you have to know everything yourself. Okay?"

I nodded, and he continued.

"We will work you up in stages. If you got a job in a bank, you wouldn't start as the big manager, right, mate? No. You'd start as a bank teller, and you'd climb the ladder from there."

The first part of my training, Welchy explained, would simply be to get my body and muscles familiar with the three disciplines (swimming, running, biking) and to see how they handled the pressure. If there was something I couldn't do because of my cerebral palsy, he wanted to know right away.

"Don't mistake tired or lazy for inability," he said. "Because I know the difference." He gave me a look and another laugh.

On his computer, he showed me a training schedule he had drawn up for my first week.

"S is for swim," he explained, really getting down to the basics. "B is bike. R is run. W is for weights, meaning core and plyometrics."

There were a lot of workouts, two to three a day, but it all seemed to make sense, and it seemed very doable. Then he punched through a list of notes he'd made brainstorming.

First: Consistency was everything. I couldn't do the same quantity of training that a normal person could do. I had basically been walking around with the equivalent of an injury my whole life, so we had to go for a slow, steady build, allowing time for my muscles to recover.

Second: My posture was terrible. I needed custom orthotics for my shoes and a bike suited to the way I held my body. For equipment, Welchy needed my sizes (shoe, shirt, waist, and height) and ten copies of my documentary to set me up with sponsors and to get the best gear (free of charge).

Third: Nutrition would be key. A major part of succeeding in any endurance event is figuring out the right combination of calories to keep you energized throughout the race, but at Kona getting the nutrition right was essential. This was survival of the toughest, and unless I had fuel in my tank, I was going to be lost. In Kona, perspiration was an issue. I'd be losing nutrients and minerals by the bucket. Everybody was different, but given the spasticity of my muscles, I would be burning through fuel faster than most. We had to experiment to figure out what food regimen would work best for me during the race.

Fourth: An able-bodied person might train for a year in preparation for Kona. I was going to need two years. This meant that my big race would be in October 2012. As it was now early February 2011, I had twenty months of intensive, all-consuming training ahead of me. It would make my prep work for Kilimanjaro seem like a hike up an anthill. I'm sure Welchy heard me swallow hard at this point.

Fifth: Since I took much longer to heal than a typical athlete, we simply had to avoid injuries. Full stop. If I was hurting, he needed to know why and how much.

Sixth: I had to do races. Welchy wanted me in everything from a sprint-distance triathlon to a half Ironman to a full Ironman before Kona. (Another audible swallow from me.)

Seventh: I had chicken legs. We had to fight that muscle tightening and cramping big-time.

Eighth: We were going to build up my stomach and trunk. In swimming, a strong core would help keep my legs up so they could do their job. In biking, it would enable my legs to rotate optimally, supplying the maximum energy to my bike. And, while we were on the subject of the bike, because I had balance and equilibrium issues,

I would start on a stationary bike for a few months, to keep the focus on building up the muscles I would need for the bike.

Finally, ninth: Since the run would be the hardest for me, we were going to focus on fast times for the swim and bike ride, so that I would have enough of a buffer to make it across those 26.2 miles within the time allowed.

For almost an hour, Welchy talked, fast, and I listened, occasionally breaking in with a short answer to a question or a nod of the head. Mostly, I absorbed the information, took hurried notes, and wondered in awe at how lucky I was to have Greg Welch as my Yoda. He clearly had done his research on cerebral palsy and was designing a program based on it. It was like night and day from my training for Kilimanjaro.

More than anything, I sensed that Welchy believed in me, that this Ironman mission of mine was actually possible. This was exactly what I needed.

That Saturday, a hulking black Oakley truck, one of those designed for off-road races, thundered into my driveway, and Dane Howell jumped down from the driver's seat. His cargo was the LeMond RevMaster, a stationary bike that looked more like a lemon-colored tank. It took Dane's enormous guns and my straining back—along with much cursing and grunting—to haul this ton of steel into my garage.

"Have fun with that," Dane said laughing, before driving away.

Looking at this beast crouched between my car and my washing machine, knowing that Welchy wanted me on it at least three times a week for the next four months before advancing to a bike that actually moved, I knew it was going to be a long winter.

Later the same day, Welchy sent me my first week's training schedule. There was a session of either swimming, cycling, running, or lifting weights every day—and often more than one each day. He had included short notes on what I should aim to do and how.

On Monday, February 14, 2011, Valentine's Day, my Ironman training began. I weighed 218 pounds and was likely in the worst shape I had been in years.

"Let patience be your friend," Welch wrote of the half-hour swim, which I was going to do at the local Newport Coast pool. "You will find that fatigue will set in quickly, so just do what you can. Don't rush it."

Swimming, I thought. *No problemo.* Thanks to Bompa, I was raised in the Pacific Ocean, flippers for feet and all that. With the Ironman, it would be my big strength. It was 6 A.M., dark, and frigid cold for southern California when I walked across the empty deck of the open-air pool in sweats and a hoodie. Steam rose over the heated water. There was nobody else foolish enough to be there that early in midwinter, but if I was going to make this Ironman schedule work *and* hold down a full-time job, there would be a lot of early mornings and late nights in my future, no matter the weather.

After shaking for a few moments at the edge of the pool, I hopped into the shallow end, an awkward maneuver at the best of times. The water was warm and felt good. I stretched and took a long pull on my sports drink before finally donning my goggles and pushing off. I glided a couple of body lengths, happy and comfortable in the water, before setting off. My freestyle stroke felt good and clean. The pool was 25 yards long, half that of an Olympic lap, so I was quickly at the wall. I liked the idea of performing a flip turn, but I knew it would throw off my equilibrium.

By the second lap, I was already tiring and breathing heavily. It was clear that I was swimming too fast and not taking enough breaths. Further, I was all over my lane, swimming damn near in a zigzag, and my stroke was far from smooth. *Okay, settle down*, I told myself. At the wall, I stopped, took off my goggles, had a drink, and then started again more slowly. After four more lengths of the pool, my shoulders were tiring, my neck was stiff, and there was no rhythm to my breaths. I had to stop again.

Swimming long straight miles was going to be a very different game from the quick bursts of strokes you needed to escape riptides in the ocean. As much as I loved being in the water, I hated following that little black line on the bottom of the pool, lap after lap. Twenty minutes into my "little splash around," as Welchy called it, I was done, and I pulled myself out.

That same evening, after a long day at work, I hit the streets for my prescribed forty-five-minute walk—to get my legs to where they were "strong enough to sustain running" and to "enjoy the fresh air." Almost from the start, I lacked the concentration required to keep my ankles from rolling to the inside. Near the end of the uphill climb to my house, my back was stiff and rigid. I almost tripped when the big toe of one foot caught the inside of my other shoe. By 9 P.M., I was out cold.

The next morning, I stepped into my garage, cracked the door open for some fresh air, and then climbed onto the RevMaster. It had been years since I had done any biking, evidenced by the fact that I didn't even own a bike. My experience was limited to riding around with a gang of kids on BMXs. Forty-five minutes on the bike, those were my orders: "We need to alternate muscle groups to allow consistency throughout training and recovery. . . . Sit on that bloody thing for forty-five minutes. Wear a heart-rate monitor and record the numbers. Just an easy-to-medium effort, and try and get those legs moving at 70 RPMs."

The RevMaster was old-school. No buzzers or bells or cool displays simulating hills, no electricity at all. It didn't even have straps on its pedals. When I was getting started, my feet slipped off and I nearly cut up my shins. Not an auspicious beginning. Using the little mechanical hand dial, I cranked up the resistance on the wheels and started again. The handlebars were high and close to my chest, and five minutes into my warm-up I was growing uncomfortable. My lower back and hips tightened and cramped. Ten minutes in, the lower half of my body felt completely numb. I stood up to get the blood flowing, but there was not enough tension on the pedals and, again, I almost slipped off. *This is not pretty,* I thought. I adjusted the dial to increase the resistance. Fifteen minutes in, alternating between sitting and standing, I was already tired. Sweat poured off me and puddled at my feet. My back really began to sting, and my quads were telling me they wouldn't be able to last much longer.

I tried to take a drink from my water bottle, but even on the stationary bike I nearly lost my balance. Facing the blank white garage door, no headphones, no TV, I struggled to continue, thinking of how much I hurt, how bored I already was, and how much torture it was going to be to ride this machine for the next four months. Easy-to-medium effort at 70 RPMs? No way, no how.

After forty-five minutes on that "bloody thing," I climbed down, a shell of the man I had been getting into the saddle, my back crooked and the underside of my crotch rubbed raw. I staggered into the house to get ready for a day at the office.

Wednesday morning, day three of my Ironman training, and I was back at the pool, this time at the Aquatics Center at UC Irvine. They ran a master's swimming program where noncollege (read:

"old") men and women like me could come out and hit the pool under the watchful guidance of student coaches. "Do the master's," Welchy wrote in his notes to my schedule. "Learn something new every day. Swimming is *all* technique. You may be the strongest man out there, but unless you have good technique, you'll sink. And let's not do that!"

On my arrival at 5:30 A.M., I was barely awake and pretty lethargic after two straight days of exercise. It was clear from my first splash around at the Newport pool that I needed some help. I approached one of the coaches, a young student named Brianna, and told her of my Ironman ambition—and the fact that I had cerebral palsy. Admitting this was no longer a big deal to me. Brianna pointed me to the far left lane, reserved for the slowest in the pool, and said she wanted to watch my stroke for a few laps.

Feeling under the microscope, I jumped into the pool without my goggles on, only to realize that it was too deep to stand. For the next minute, I put on a show of trying to don my goggles while staying afloat; eventually I ended up crooking one arm over the side while I did an awkward eggbeater kick to tread water. It wasn't pretty, and I dared not look at Brianna for fear she was in hysterics.

Finally, I got started. Into my first lap, I realized that this pool was Olympic length and that I was winded just getting to the far end. I wanted to stop, but pride is a dangerous thing. I turned around and did another length back to where Brianna was waiting for me. Hanging on the edge of the pool, goggles pushed up on my forehead, I gasped for breath like someone who had just swum fifty laps, not a meager one.

"You looked good at the start, but then you really fell apart," Brianna said. "You're dragging your legs like a rudder."

I would have replied, but I didn't have enough air.

"Let's do a couple more laps and see what happens. Can you bilateral breathe?"

"Not sure," I muttered.

Then I was off. The next two laps were even worse than the first one. I had trouble breathing on alternate sides, and I felt as if I were dragging a stone behind me in the water. By the time I finished, and I barely managed even that, my temples were thumping, a sure sign I was pushing it too hard.

On the pool deck, Brianna showed me how I was coming across my body with each stroke, multiplying the amount of work I needed to do to move through the water. She wanted me to keep my head down, level my body out, straighten my legs, reach ahead with my hands, and concentrate on keeping my feet from falling behind me. Everything she said was a consequence of having a strong upper body, but a weaker lower one.

"These are easy fixes. Do them, and you'll be swimming great," she said encouragingly. "Let's see how you do over the next ten laps."

Ten laps! I thought. *They'll have to carry me out of here if I try ten more laps.* But I nodded and then set off. I focused on Brianna's instructions, and she walked along on the deck with me as I made my way down the pool, reminding me of what to do. With my reshaped stroke there was much less effort, and for the next three or four laps it seemed I was gliding through the water. By the tenth, however, I was struggling hard again, so tired that it took all my attention to simply make it forward in the water, let alone worry about how I was doing it.

At the poolside, Brianna congratulated me and then gave me some exercises to improve my stroke, particularly how I rolled my body, so I could pull through the water more strongly with my arms. In one of the exercises I alternated three strokes on one side of my body, then three more on the other. To work my legs properly, she also had me do a bunch of laps with a kickboard and no fins. That was a real breath-buster.

After an hour, I stepped out of the pool, almost losing my balance when I hit the level deck. Knowing that I now had to go do sixty minutes of "W" work almost made me cry.

"Our goal here," Welchy wrote of my weight training, "is to gain enough strength to allow you to sit over your bike with great posture, so that your core muscle group doesn't fail." I slumped down in the seat of my car and drove over to the park near my house. A wise man would have had a snack between the two workouts. I had a drink from the water fountain.

Waiting for me at the basketball park by the parking lot was Greg LeFever. Built like a square block, Greg was a personal trainer in his early forties. We had met as neighbors. Greg was making a mint working for Jaguar Land Rover when one day he got up and quit his job to follow his passion for fitness. When I was training for Kilimanjaro, Greg had offered to help me get in shape, but I hadn't felt I needed it (how wrong I was).

He now ran boot camps out of the park, with a lot of whole-body circuits and core work, and I had attended a few of them since Dr. Millhouse had given me the go-ahead to exercise again. Greg loved using your own body weight and stretch bands to exercise, believing that they allowed you to work both the dominant muscles and the smaller supporting ones. At each class he had handed my ass to me, and now that we were working one-on-one, I was in real trouble.

I was already exhausted when I stepped onto the court. Greg passed me a stretch band to warm up. He had a whole rainbow of colors, each one a different level of resistance. Green was the easiest. Dark orange was like trying to stretch a tire. We started with green. I stretched out my arms and shoulders, then did some "birthday cakes." These entailed standing on the band with bent knees, one end in each hand, and then straightening up, working the lower body.

We followed these with some mat work. Lying on my back, I pedaled my legs as if on a bike. Then Greg had me hold myself in a plank position, forearms and toes pressing into the ground. Within thirty seconds, my whole body shook from the effort. Next, I ran through a set of pushups; then I jumped rope. Five swings of the rope, and I was out of breath and hurting bad.

"You got this," Greg said.

I definitely did not have it, but I forced myself to continue, trusting that he knew my limit better than I did.

We went on to throw a weighted ball back and forth. Then Greg had me balance on a BOSU ball—or, more to the point, he had me fall off the BOSU ball several times. The more fatigued I was, the less coordinated I became. A half hour into the session, I was failing miserably at each exercise and becoming increasingly frustrated. At some point, Greg tied a stretch band to the basketball pole and had me try to do sidesteps away from it. When I lost my balance, the band almost flung me back into the pole—and it was only a green band. By the time I staggered back to my car, I was feeling muscles in my body that I hadn't known existed.

At home, I made myself a bowl of cereal and sat down on the couch. The next thing I knew it was two hours later, drool was running from the side of my mouth, and I was late for work. I rushed into the shower, fell on the way out, hobbled into my suit pants, and drove like a madman to the office. That night I skipped the forty-five-minute walk during which I was to "stand up tall and use good posture."

On Thursday, I eased my sore body onto the RevMaster and did my sixty minutes as Welchy advised: "at your own pace, however you know how." It was quickly becoming obvious to me that my biggest challenge with the bike was maintaining the same position for a long time. My spastic muscles fought against it, and the pain spread from my lower back through my whole body with increasing intensity.

Friday. Another swim session at the master's program and another session with Greg. Somehow I managed that evening's brisk walk without staggering into oncoming traffic. Saturday. A torturous ride on the Yellow Beast, as I now called the stationary bike. Sunday. An hour's walk with a few jogs (well, a slightly faster walk) in between. "A good week," Welchy wrote in advance on his note. "A great way to get started." By the end of my first week, I wasn't so sure.

Actually, I felt as though someone had hit me in the face with a shovel. I wandered about in a daze, unable to concentrate on anything and wanting only to sleep. My stomach was constantly upset. I barely had the energy to shower. On the way to work, I had to shake my head every few minutes just to stay awake. In the office, my eyelids felt as if they had thousand-pound weights attached to them, and a couple of times I dozed off at my desk.

To keep myself from crawling under my desk to sleep, I took frequent short breaks outside to refresh myself. Each night, I conked out at 7 P.M. on the couch while watching *SportsCenter*. A few hours later, I would stumble upstairs and crash into bed, but then I would wake up around 4 A.M., not quite sure of where I was and feeling weaker than when I first went to bed.

Friends asked me to go out on the weekends, but I said I was too tired. Only a few people knew about my Ironman intentions, and fewer still knew that I had started training. I wanted to see how my body responded to the training before I made any kind of announcement. Well, now I knew, and the reality of what I was facing hit home.

This was the first of eighty such weeks before my Ironman, and each one would be progressively more intense than the one before. If I was to become a Kona Ironman, I would have to become a monk, devoted to my training above and beyond everything else in my life. This left me in a pretty dark place. I was already lonely. I had no girlfriend. Besides occasional visits with my father, I didn't really see my family. My brothers and I spoke infrequently, and my mother and I had stopped speaking altogether after the poisonous battle over my grandparents' estate (spurred, in part, by unresolved feelings about how she treated me, my brothers, and my dad over the years).

In truth, I had nobody close enough to me to share my doubts and fears with about committing to such an ambitious undertaking. Even if I'd had someone to confide in, the idea of admitting weakness or insecurity ran counter to the image I was trying to project; in trying to convince others that I was capable of living my life without limits, I couldn't be fully honest with myself about my own fears. This was exactly how I'd faced Kilimanjaro, and it was something I did not want to repeat. Still, I wasn't sure how to resolve it.

On Sunday night, Welchy called me, eager to see how everything had gone over the course of the week. In my mind I heard, *I'm tired, scared, sore. I fell asleep at work. I skipped a workout, and I'm not sure I can do this day after day, week after week, month after month.* But there was no way I was actually going to admit the truth to Welchy. He might lose faith in me and back out of coaching me.

So instead I joked about how I wouldn't be having any children if the RevMaster had any say in it. Welchy suggested adjusting the seat.

"The swimming was pretty hard," I admitted. He seemed happy about that. It meant, apparently, that I was learning.

"I'm a little more tired than I expected," I sugarcoated. "And my bedtime's moving up a little more."

Welchy chuckled before saying, "It's okay if you don't do every workout. You have to listen to your body, and that's most important. Remember, don't get an injury."

Then he asked me what I was eating, and I told him I was eating three square meals a day. He laughed at me and then in so many words said I was an idiot for starving myself. He suggested snacks before and between workouts—"Try a PB&J on long sessions on the RevMaster"—as well as a few more meals throughout the day. "See what foods work to keep your energy up," he said, "but no matter what, increase your calorie intake. Your body can't work out properly if you don't give it enough fuel."

"Okay," I said, properly admonished.

"We'll get it right, mate."

After three more weeks, I felt sure of two things: my body had not completely disassembled itself during the first bout of training—and was actually beginning to accustom itself to all these new movements; and, second, realizing my triathlete ambitions would demand everything I had—and more.

A visit to Dr. Aminian confirmed this beyond a shadow of a doubt. As with Kilimanjaro, he tried to talk me out of the endeavor.

"I got hooked up with a coach," I said.

"That's great," he answered deadpan. "No matter what you do, what diet, even if you have the world's best exercise physiologist, nothing will fix your brain. You'll always be the guy who starts the race at best with half a tank." He then went on to explain how my joints didn't move well, how my coordination was off, how my spasticity wouldn't allow my muscles to develop the needed endurance and strength.

"Yes," I said. "But this time I recognize all that. I'm training smarter now."

He didn't give his blessing, but I think we both knew that I wasn't going to be talked out of this.

Days afterward, I stood in front of a huge assembly of people gathered at Young's Market and announced my intention to be the first person with cerebral palsy to compete in and finish the Kona Ironman under his own power. There was a huge roar of support.

A number of friends, including Paul, committed to racing beside me in Hawaii. (Dilly bowed out, saying bluntly, "It'd kill me to try.") But each morning, whether on the pool deck or stepping into my shoebox of a garage with the hulking RevMaster, I knew it was up to me alone.

My brother Mike wanted to catch up. It was a couple of days before Easter, and he invited me to dinner at an old-school sushi spot in Laguna. We had not spoken in months—and, to be frank, it had been years since we had spoken in any meaningful way. We took a table in the back. Mike was one of the few people I knew who was as tall as I was. He still had the rounded shoulders of a swimmer, but he looked older than his forty-three years.

He asked about my Ironman training, particularly about my swimming. I said there was a lot to learn and, having spent an hour in the pool that morning, I admitted that it was hard. Mike nodded. I asked him how he was making out day trading. He said it was all right. I asked about his boyfriend, whom he had been living with for over fifteen years. Mike said he was okay, but I knew he was lying. My family called his boyfriend German Mike the "Cyborg" for what we felt was his lack of warmth, and my brother seemed the same whenever he was around him. At least in my view, their relationship centered on what German Mike wanted—and my brother's own needs were left to take second place.

We ordered some sushi rolls. Mike fidgeted, and his eyes kept widening. He had something to say, and he was stalling. Finally, after a long lull in an already pretty quiet conversation, Mike got to it.

"My drinking . . . got out of hand, and it got the best of me. It overtook my life."

"Okay," I said, a thousand thoughts and feelings rushing through my head at once. I had seen Mike at family events over the past couple of years where he had been a little out of hand, drinking a lot of wine. At the premiere of my documentary, when I finally found him in the back of the auditorium, sitting by himself, he seemed out of sorts, as if he had been drinking before he arrived. Then there was, of course, the strain of alcoholism that ran through our family: an aunt, a great-grandfather.

Still, none of this had been enough to raise a red flag—until now. Looking at him across the table, I remembered his coming out to me during a visit while I was in college. The prelude to the conversation had felt a lot like this evening, and his eyes had been as wide and expressive (and avoiding my gaze) as they were tonight. I had just turned twenty-one, and Mike called to invite me to a movie. I met him at his apartment.

"We need to talk," he said, at that time twenty-nine years old.

I jumped the gun, saying what suddenly was obvious: "You're gay."

The way he looked at me, I might have been a ghost.

"How'd you know?" he asked.

Well, there had been that young German guy I kept seeing him with—and other hints here and there. I told him that I loved him and only wanted him to be happy.

Mike had struggled through so much in his life. His birth father, John, basically abandoned him when he was still a baby. Growing up, Mike saw him once a year, when John usually took him on some crazy trip. Mike was less a companion on these journeys than a piece of luggage his father felt obliged to bring along. Yet Mike always wanted to be like John and craved his approval. This contributed to the wars he had with Tom, his stepfather and my dad.

Still, when I was younger, Mike had always been there for me. Mike had been the one who had bribed me with the promise of a visit to his college Animal House, so that I would go do my tests with Dr. Starr and visit the physical therapist. It was Mike who had advised me on my career path, who always took me out to dinner or bought me groceries in my early twenties when I didn't have two nickels to rub together.

We had been so close back then, which was why it hurt so badly when he wasn't there to help with my preparations for Kilimanjaro. Though I'd seen him off and on during the two and half years since my climb, I continued to feel slighted by his detachment and couldn't understand his absence from something that had become such an important part of my life. And now, sitting across from him at this sushi restaurant as he tried to share his personal struggle, I was struck by just how far apart we were.

"I'm sober now," Mike said, interrupting the swirl in my head. "I have some people I talk with. They help me stay on course, and I'd love it if you came to one of our meetings, maybe at Easter. I go every day."

"Absolutely," I said, a big part of me hoping that this meant Mike would find something he loved to do again and, more important, end the relationship that was causing him so much suffering.

"Part of the process is going back to people in my life, those I've wronged, and making peace. It's not easy."

"I'm here for you, Mike," I said, choking up. "Tell me whatever I need to do, and I'll do it. I love you, brother. I've missed you." I gave him a hug.

Two days later, I was there at his meeting with him to hear him admit, "I am an alcoholic." After the meeting, I told him how proud I was of him. He admitted to me that one of his biggest regrets was not being there to help me train for Kilimanjaro.

Listening to those words, I felt myself beginning to let go of the anger that I'd been carrying around toward him since those dark moments of my climb. As it turned out, his apology was just the start.

"I'm here if you need me for Ironman," he said.

10

Brothers

"You have to learn to walk before you run," Welchy said, before describing what he considered to be a slow ramping up of my training. *To walk?!* Five months into his schedules and already I felt I was in a full-out, howling sprint and that my body couldn't handle any more pressure.

Monday was the best day, because I had the benefit of a weekend of late-morning sleep. But by Monday evening, after a swim, core work and plyometrics with LeFever, and a walk or jog, any reserve I had built up over the weekend was gone.

Then, on Tuesdays, it was a case of, "On yer bike, mate!" My bike—that dreaded machine. Every morning on the RevMaster was slow death. I strapped on the heart-rate monitor, mounted the seat, and then pedaled away, clocking up mile after mile but going no-where. There was nothing to do but ponder the sweat pooling by the front wheel and check my watch to see if my forty-five-, then sixty-, then ninety-minute sessions were nearing their end.

The bike was ripping apart my legs and shredding my lower back. As I pedaled, I tried to keep my knees pointed straight ahead, but as

I fatigued they followed their natural tendency to lean inward. This tightened my grip on the saddle, numbing my groin until there was no feeling at all. Often, Welchy had me doing intervals, two minutes easy, ten medium, two easy, five flat out hard. "This should hurt a little today," he wrote in his notes. "But I know you like it." By July, I was riding 150 miles per week, double what I had started with in February. I wasn't so sure I liked it.

Contrary to the bike, my swimming was coming along nicely. Once a week, I hit the master's program, learning to bilateral breathe (a struggle at first with my equilibrium issues), to kick with a slightly bent knee (against my unnatural, stiff, straight-leg technique), and to rotate in a balanced way with each stroke (versus favoring my dominant right side—again a result of my CP). As Welchy said, a big part of mastering swimming for me was ingraining the muscle memory. At the start, my head was dizzy trying to coordinate everything I was being instructed to do (bend arm, reach, kick, turn neck, breathe every third stroke, pull arm through, cup hands). My brain was never good at orchestrating multiple movements with multiple limbs. Endless repetition was the solution, so after my Monday master's session I spent the other two swim workouts alone at my Newport Coast pool: repeat, repeat, repeat. Come summer, at 12,000 yards a week, I had done a lot of repeating. Welchy came out to see me one day, and he gave my technique a thumbs-up—"You are *Michael Phelps!*"—but with the caveat that there was much still to improve.

At my private training sessions with LeFever, I was slowly increasing the time I could balance on the BOSU ball and jump rope without coughing up a lung. My walks developed into partial jogs, and I focused on maintaining my body upright, eyes ahead, feet landing straight instead of pigeon-toed.

Part of my improvement, I was sure, had to do with better—but by no means, perfect—eating habits. In the mornings, I had a big bowl of oatmeal straightaway. Then after my workout, I downed a vanilla protein shake with fresh fruit. Lunch was usually something with chicken, and then in the afternoon I had a snack. By dinner, however, no matter what I ate during the day, I was starving. On the way back from work, I usually stopped off for a burrito at the Mexican restaurant by my place. In sum, I was eating roughly 2,000–3,000 calories, which I thought was enough.

In my weekly schedule, the one workout I tended to skip or shorten more than any Welchy had assigned me was the walk/jog/run. Often, I couldn't do it because of work or because of full-on exhaustion. I was at the office fifty hours a week and traveling on average ten thousand air miles a month, not to mention my commitments with the foundation.

"It's the least important," Welchy advised after my admission that I hadn't done all my homework. "After all, mate, if you can't finish the swim and bike, then who needs the run anyway?"

In August, I geared up for my first race, the Pacific Coast Triathlon. It was a sprint-distance race, the easiest of the triathlons. It didn't sound so easy to me: a 0.5-mile swim, 16-mile bike, and 5K run. A few weeks before the race, Welchy finally told me I was ready for a real bike and gave me the address of Billy Ruddell, the Cannondale marketing director in the West. Cannondale was sponsoring me, thanks to Welchy's efforts on my behalf.

The next day, I drove up to Billy's house in Los Angeles, keen to avoid another session on the RevMaster. A former motocross rider, Billy radiated fearlessness through every inch of his five-foot-five frame. In his garage he pointed to two Cannondale road-racing bikes. To me, they looked roughly the same.

Billy pointed to one: "That's the Ferrari," he said. "And that's the Honda Accord, but it'll be more comfortable for you."

On each bike he showed me how to shift the gears and adjust the seat height. Both had clip pedals, but I was wearing flip-flops. Billy wanted me to give them a try anyway.

"If you crash, you crash."

I climbed onto the Ferrari first. It weighed almost nothing, and as I rolled down Billy's driveway and onto the street, I felt every bump in the pavement.

"There's movement now," I cheered, so happy to be on a real bike that actually rolled.

I struggled to change the gears and to balance my flip-flops on the clips, but it was a thrill. I tried the Honda Accord next. It felt more solid underneath me, and the fit, Billy advised, was better for me.

"Learn on this," he smiled. "Then we'll go with the Ferrari."

That night, I shuffled out to my garage in my clip-on shoes, excited to get out there on the road and a little scared to be locked into the pedals with the clips. Welchy had told me, "There are only two types of people who ride bikes. Those who have crashed, and those who are about to crash." There was a lesson in life in that statement somewhere, but I was too focused on staying upright on my bike to get it.

Outside, I straddled my new Cannondale Synapse, slipped the sole of my left shoe into the left clip, and then pushed off the pavement a couple of times with my right foot before securing it as well. Now attached to the bike, I pedaled forward and shot down the street like an arrow, the wind rushing past. I promised myself I would never get back on the Yellow Beast again.

I did what Billy suggested for my first outing and stayed in my neighborhood. It was good advice, particularly since my stability on the bike was tentative at best. I had enough trouble looking behind me to see if traffic was coming, never mind taking a hand off the bars to scratch my nose without losing my balance. I was nervous about stopping, because then I would have to pull the balls of my feet out of the clips before I tipped over onto the pavement. This would be a challenge for any able-bodied new rider. With me, with my equilibrium issues and pigeon toes, it was an ordeal. Nonetheless, I returned to my garage unscathed.

A couple of days later, on my first ride outside my neighborhood, I almost crashed headlong into a $200,000 Bentley that cut me off on a turn. Coming to an abrupt stop, I locked up my back tire and barely managed to free one foot from its clip before falling over. Maybe the RevMaster wasn't so bad.

While I was mastering the bike, I also needed to prepare for my half-mile ocean swim. "Get out there in the Pacific," Welchy told me. It was one thing to body surf and tread around in the water by the shore. It was another to swim far outside the break line for long distances.

I definitely didn't want to be out there by myself, so I did something I hadn't done in a long time: I called my older brother and asked for his help.

"Will you swim with me?" I asked Mike.

"When?"

In late August, two weeks before the sprint-distance triathlon, my brother and I parked on the Pacific Coast Highway and headed down the steps to West Beach—Bompa's beach. I was nervous, both about the swim ahead and about having Mike beside me for it. It was not because of his ability as a swimmer. Mike was a beast in the water, and there was nobody I trusted more in the ocean. We had met several times since Easter, but I was not yet confident that the "old Mike"—the one who didn't show for my Kilimanjaro training, the one who disappeared for long stretches without a warning or call—was really gone for good.

On the beach—me in my spanking new TYR wet suit, Mike in casual board shorts—we went over the plan. It was just as Bompa had taught us: we would swim north first, against the current, so that when we were coming back, tired, we would have the current with us. Mike, who had once been a lifeguard on this very beach, told me that the key to ocean swimming was orienting yourself to a point along the coast. Every ten strokes, he wanted me to raise my head, to make sure I was on the right line. He advised me to stay relaxed. The tighter I was, the more uncomfortable I felt, the harder I would need to work.

"Surreal that we're here," I said. "On this beach."

"Bompa taught us here," Mike replied.

With a lump in our throats, we pulled on our goggles, waited on the edge of the surf for a calm stretch of waves, and then swam out past the break. For a minute, we bobbed in the water. I pointed out Camel Point cliff, about a half mile away.

"Try to maintain the same distance between us and the beach," Mike said. "Who do you want to lead?"

"You."

"I'll swim slightly ahead and to the side of you. Okay?"

On my nod, Mike took off like a torpedo.

Not two minutes into the swim, I was struggling. My goggles had fogged up. I couldn't see anything but the bubbles from Mike's wake, and with no little black lines to follow, the ocean swells tossed me back and forth, and the current pushed back against me. Soon I was breathing heavily. I felt absolutely rigid in the water.

Finally, I slowed to a halt, and Mike and I treaded water as I tried to clear my goggles. During the thousands of times I had been in the ocean, the ocean I loved, I had never felt so uncomfortable. First, we were far out past the break, where I usually stayed to body surf, and this left me on edge. Second, there was no way to orient myself unless I looked up, and each time I did that I lost my rhythm and balance in the water. As it was with my CP, rhythm and balance were not my strong suit. Then add in the rolls of the waves, the ocean current, the salty water, and the fogged goggles. All this—and I was trying to concentrate on each element of my stroke, pushing my brain (which, given my faulty wiring, was never good at multitasking) into overload. I was in deep trouble.

"Settle down," Mike said, his voice calm, easy. He sounded as if he was taking a dip in the baby pool.

I grunted.

"Relax."

We set off again. I kept reminding myself to ease up, to relax, and this helped for the first few strokes. But then when I next raised my head to spot Camel Point, the waves were too high to see it. I kept swimming, my goggles fogging up yet again. A swell rolled me over while I was taking a breath, and I swallowed some seawater. Frustrated, tiring, I fought my way ahead. My hand hit something in the water, and I freaked. It was only some floating kelp, but it heightened my awareness of how vulnerable I was out in the ocean. Finally, we reached the halfway point and stopped for a break. As we bobbed in the water, I tried to pull myself together. This wasn't some lane in the pool. This was the real deal.

"How do you feel?" Mike asked.

"Not good."

"You're kind of weaving back and forth like a big snake."

"Okay."

"Pick a spot to track to for the way back."

"Table Rock," I said, pointing to a stretch of coast to the south.

"Try to relax more, and you lead," Mike said.

I gave him a thumbs-up and then began. Swimming with the current now, I felt my body gliding easily through the water, and my stroke eased. Then Mike caught up with me.

"You're way off," he said.

I looked toward Table Rock Point, then toward the beach. I had veered off course big-time. My zigzagging was adding a lot of distance to the swim.

"If you go off course, I'll tap you on one foot or the other, depending," Mike said.

"Let's go."

Every couple of minutes or so, Mike tapped me on the foot, usually my left one, as my dominant side was pulling me toward the shore. It was reassuring to know that he was leading me in the right direction, but I grew frustrated at being unable to keep a line. With a third of the way to go before we were at the beach, we stopped yet again.

"Follow my feet, close," Mike said. He promised that, over time, I would get a feel for what was straight. My body would know it.

An hour after starting, we emerged from the water and toweled off. I was mad at myself, and Mike was quiet. After hiking back up to our cars, we settled on a place to have lunch and rehash the swim. As I stared at my food, my frustration with the swim felt palpable. Swimming had been the one thing I thought I would be the most comfortable with in the Ironman, but my inability to relax, stick to a straight line, orient myself, keep my balance, and maintain a good rhythm—all of it was deeply unsettling.

Finally Mike spoke, saying he wished he had the secret answer for me to become a better ocean swimmer, but there wasn't one. It would take time.

Looking up at him, I could see how much he wanted to help, and for the first time since I'd emerged from the ocean, my body started to relax.

For a while we talked about his life, mostly about his unhappy relationship and the intensity and isolation of his day trading. He wanted a new direction in both his love life and career, but felt stuck in both.

After we paid the check, I asked him. "Are you free next weekend?"

"Yeah, definitely."

"Do this again? A swim and lunch?"

"Yes. I'm here for you on this. Anything you need."

There was such determination in the way he said it—particularly compared to all the other uncertainty in his life—that I knew he would be true to the promise.

First time?" asked the stocky triathlete next to me. It was September 11, 2011, and I was struggling in the dark to get my bike in the rack before the start of the Pacific Coast Triathlon.

"What made you guess?" I asked.

He laughed.

It didn't take a genius, given that I was the only one out there without a headlamp, bumbling around, not sure where to put anything, and carrying a Macy's paper bag for my bike shoes, running shoes, goggles, towel, wet suit, and BodyGlide.

"Nice suit," remarked another racer.

"Thanks," I said, feeling a little embarrassed about my TYR Cat 5 Hurricane wet suit.

"New bike!" whistled another, checking out my Cannondale Synapse road bike. Welchy had done a fine job of setting me up with some amazing sponsors who had supplied me with top-of-the-line gear.

Everybody around me was talking about other races they had competed in recently. None of them ever spoke about winning or losing. Rather, it was all talk about target times and personal bests/records (PRs). A lot of it sounded foreign to me. I was definitely the rookie. A few of the guys helped me set up my bike, commenting again on the high-end gear. I tried to explain.

"It's my first triathlon. I'm shooting to do Kona Ironman in 2012."

"Really?" one asked, in disbelief.

"That's the goal. This stuff is from my sponsors."

"Your sponsors?"

Now I had them confused. "I want to be the first person with cerebral palsy to do Kona Ironman."

"Oh!" was the collective response.

They were nice guys. One of them helped me zip up the back of my wet suit after I finally squirmed my way into it. The suit felt three sizes too small.

We walked down the hill to Crystal Cove Beach in Newport Coast, and as I looked at the triathletes around me, it was hard not to get swept up into thinking about how I'd fare in comparison. Ever since I was a little kid, I had been supercompetitive, but it was clear from looking at the trim, hardened bodies around me that I was outclassed in every way. My original goal had been to finish the sprint triathlon in less than two hours, but now, my nerves intensifying with every second, I just wanted to finish.

Sand cold on my feet, I pulled my swim cap over my head. It felt so tight that I thought it was going to squeeze my brains out of my ears. Certainly, it made me a little light-headed. *Maybe I should have eaten more than a PowerBar for breakfast,* I thought. *Amateur.*

Easy, Bonner. Easy.

With the others in my age group, I headed to the shoreline and up to the water for the start. Then the gun blasted, and we were off. The first hundred yards was a thrashing, ugly mess of arms and legs. I kept bumping into people. They kept hitting my feet and sides. I felt as though I was in a moshpit, hurled back and forth. Finally, I freed myself from the mass of swimmers and found some rhythm with my stroke. I swam near the outside, nice and calm, and began picking people off on my right, my competitive drive kicking in hard. The two outings with Mike, particularly the one in this same cove the previous week, helped with my orientation.

I finished the half mile in twelve minutes, feeling strong. Striding up the hill from the beach, I tried to pull down the string on my wetsuit's zipper, but the sucker wouldn't budge. When I managed to get it down, the wetsuit itself wouldn't come off. Once again, I twisted, yanked, and squirmed to free myself. Racer after racer jogged past me up the hill, and the sight of them made me try even harder to get moving onto the bike course. At the top of the hill, I finally got the wet suit down to my waist. In the transition area, I tossed it into my paper bag, which quickly fell apart, dropping my gear out the bottom. *Brilliant move, Bonner. Paper? Seriously?*

I sat down to put on my shoes and realized I didn't have any water to wash my feet free of the sand from the beach. My fellow triathletes had plastic containers full of water for that purpose. When I stood in my clip-on shoes, I felt off balance and suddenly very tired. After another couple of minutes trying to put my bike jersey on over wet skin, I was exhausted. Finally a guy from a later wave pulled it down for me. *Ugh!*

Although I had finished the swim in good time, the transition area was almost empty when I finally climbed onto my bike. At this point, the stress and strain had worn me out. I hit the first hill in the lowest gear, barely moving as my feet spun on the pedals. Anybody who had been behind me now seemed far ahead on the section of the Pacific Coast Highway that was closed off for the race. Any rhythm I did find was constantly broken by the up-and-down course. The hills were killing me, and I would have summited faster on all fours. Over an hour later, legs weak, shoulders tight, I entered the transition area again. This time I only needed to change my shoes, thank God, since I was in no shape for another wrestling match with my gear.

Now for the 5K run—or jog, or walk. As I settled into my stride, I was surprised to discover that I felt okay. Sure I was tired and hungry, but I wasn't crawling. My fifteen-minute miles were nothing to boast about, but they were forward progress. Approaching the finish, I high-fived Greg LeFever, who had come out to support me, and then I kicked it into high gear. Exhausting everything I had left in the tank, I crossed the line in one hour, fifty-three minutes—seven minutes under my target goal.

Sure, I had bumbled my way through the transition areas. Sure, I needed to do a lot more hill training on my bike, as I had really struggled on the ascents, my legs burning, my balance uneven. Sure, I should have eaten more before—and during—the race. Sure, there was still a long way to go, but all in all it was a great first race. Later that night, on the phone, Welchy congratulated me. The time had come, he told me, to head to Hawaii for the 2011 Kona Ironman.

A week before flying out to Kona, Mike and I met for another swim in the ocean and lunch afterward. I was telling him about the upcoming trip and about how Welchy wanted me to train on every part of the course while there for ten days.

"Who's going with you?" Mike asked.

"Solo," I said.

"Really? Don't you think you'll need help? Are you going to swim alone? How are you going to get your bike from place to place? What if something happens?"

To be honest, I hadn't even thought about those things.

Mike gave me a look and laughed.

He was right. I would need help. A lot of it.

"I could come," Mike said. "I need a break."

A week later, October 1, we were struggling to roll my hard-plastic bike case to the check-in desk at LAX. The sucker was big enough to hold a pair of dead bodies, and its four wheels rolled like thunder across the terminal floor. I realized already how much I was going to need Mike. We arrived at Kailua-Kona airport on the Big Island of Hawaii and faced another battle with the same bike case when we tried to maneuver it into our rental Jeep. Thank goodness it was so dark that nobody could see what a pair of bumbling fools we were.

The next morning, we had a meeting with Welchy. We left our kitschy 1980s rental house a couple of miles south of the Kona town center and drove along the coast to the Oakley house. On the way we saw a number of swimmers cutting through the water beyond the surf. We also passed scores of triathletes biking and running on the side of the road, having arrived far in advance of the race to acclimatize themselves to the heat. They were all corded muscle, tanned skin, and flawless technique. Over the next ten days, there was probably no place on earth with a higher concentration of fit and trim human beings. And this included their supporters—wives and husbands, children, and friends—and the assembly of people who made their living from the competition.

In the late 1970s, on the neighboring island of Oahu, some road runners and swimmers were having a heated debate over which group was the fitter. A navy commander, one John Collins, suggested that a renowned cyclist had been found to have the highest level of oxygen uptake of any elite endurance athlete. From there, the conversation advanced, perhaps fueled by a mix of bravado and pride, to the idea of staging a contest that combined Hawaii's three long-distance competitions: the Waikiki Roughwater Swim, the Around-Oahu Bike Race, and the Honolulu Marathon.

On a pad of paper, Collins drew a rough map of Oahu. He scribbled, "Swim 2.4 miles! Bike 112 miles! Run 26.2 miles! Brag for the rest of your life!" The name of the race came from a local marathoner who was known for his punishing training regime. "Whoever finishes first," Collins said, "we'll call him the Iron Man."

Fifteen people showed up for the inaugural race in 1978. Celebrated *Sports Illustrated* writer Barry McDermott later chronicled the outcome of that first race:

> *Twelve people finished. . . . Three did not. One fellow turned delirious and quit. Another inexplicably said that he would run only 14 miles in the marathon. And the third wrecked his bike. He was unhurt, naturally, being an Iron Man, but his fretful father persuaded him to retire. All finishers received five-inch-high trophies made of nuts and bolts, each with a hole in the top, for, you might say, the head.*

It would seem not much of an award for so great an effort, but the significance of the event is that there is no apparent significance. No prize money is involved, and little fame.

In 1981, when the race moved to the Big Island, news of the Ironman and of the demands it put on its competitors was spreading throughout the world. The following year, the leading athlete for the women's title crumbled from fatigue several yards from the line, then crawled on her hands and knees just to finish the race. The legend of this greatest of triathlons was firmly set in place.

Now the Big Island was the setting for the Ironman World Championship, and an entrance spot was a coveted prize among triathletes. Of the 1,800-plus competitors in 2011, most got there by qualifying in the top percentile of their age and gender brackets in other races. There were also several spots reserved for Kona Inspired Athletes, and it was one of these that I hoped to claim. As Welchy told me, there were no guarantees, and I would have to prove in advance that I was capable of the effort.

A shirtless Welchy met us at the Oakley house, a multimillion-dollar spread on the beach that the company had rented for the competition. Sitting at a table on the veranda, he detailed a daily schedule of workouts for me—in the ocean as well as on the bike and the run course.

"Are you going to be doing any of the training with Bonner?" Welchy asked Mike.

"Some," he answered.

"Once you feel the heat and humidity, you might want to stay in the car with the AC on," Welchy said, then laughed.

Two hours later, Welchy finished his methodical breakdown of preparations. He even advised Mike on where to park, so he could catch a beautiful view while waiting to hand me fresh water and food.

"That's for you," he said, "because Bonner will be pedaling his ass off."

Straight after lunch, the sun high in the sky, Mike dropped me off at the side of Queen Ka'ahumanu Highway for my first training run. As kids, we had visited the Big Island, and I remembered the sulfurous smell from the lava fields and how I'd poured black sand into a plastic bag to bring home with me. The hot sand had melted through the plastic and seeped away. Both memories were linked to how hot it was there; however, as I started off down the road, I realized that my recollection didn't do the heat justice.

Ten minutes into my jog, sweat burst through my skin, drenching my shirt and shorts and coursing down my legs. The midday sun hit my neck like a blowtorch, and the surface I was running on felt like hot coals. All in all, it was miserable, and the hour's jog felt like a marathon.

From there, we drove into Kona, to the pier by the King Kamehameha Hotel, where the Ironman race started. The narrow inlet was packed with swimmers heading in or out from the 2.4-mile course, which was marked by red buoys. We waded into the water, and Mike said he would lead until the first buoy, so as to shelter me from any collisions. For the first stretch, the ocean was a cool balm from the heat of the day, and with the crystal-clear water, it was like swimming in an aquarium of beautiful fish. At the first buoy, when I took the lead, however, I found that I had very little left in me after the run. Mike kept tapping me on my legs, encouraging me to bring them up and to stop using them as a rudder.

Past the second buoy, my whole body began to cramp up, and I was weaving back and forth. Mike stopped me and asked if I was okay.

"I'm tired," I said.

"Do you want me to lead?"

I shook my head. We had barely swum half a mile. I needed to keep going. After a few more minutes, with the saltwater drying out my mouth and my stroke unsettled by the 8-foot swells, I started to have real trouble. The cramping worsened in my legs, and I couldn't go on. Bobbing in the ocean, which was too deep to see the bottom, I was in trouble. We were at least a twenty-minute swim to the closest point on shore, but that meant nothing, since most of the coastline was razor-sharp lava rock. Any approach would see me caught in the surf and thrashed against the rocks, my skin cut to ribbons.

"What's going on?" Mike asked.

"My legs are cramping," I said.

Mike kept a safe distance. He knew enough from his life-guarding days that if I panicked I might draw him down with me.

"Do you want me to tow you in?" he asked.

The closest beach was at least thirty minutes away. As good a swimmer as he was, it would have been tough to haul me that far. I shook my head.

"You can float if you need to," Mike said in a deliberately steady voice. "Relax, stretch out, and massage your legs."

The tightness in my legs wouldn't release, and I quickly became more worried. Mike kept telling me to take it easy, to give it time. For fifteen minutes I floated on my back in the water, rubbing my legs with my hands; finally my muscles released. We turned back to the pier and slowly, the current with us, made it back to where we started.

"That was gnarly," Mike said, emerging from the water.

"Hope that doesn't happen again," I said.

I had only covered half the course at best, and I had barely made even that. From the look on Mike's face, he felt the same.

Late the next morning, after peeling ourselves out of bed, we made our way up the Queen K Highway, my bike in the back of the Jeep. The trade winds coming off the coast were shoving our Jeep all over the place, and I wondered what they would do to me. Welchy wanted me to hit a quarter of the bike course, roughly 28 miles, on my second full day.

"Good luck," Mike offered, as I rode away, still fiddling with the new bike computer on my handlebars that logged my speed and distance. Soon Mike passed me in the Jeep. He would stop 1 mile ahead on the uphills and 2 miles ahead on the downhills to give me water if needed and to make sure I was doing okay.

Almost instantly, I was not doing okay. Sweat and sunscreen burned my eyes, and as soon as I cleared the protection of a cutout made by the highway into the lava hills, the winds almost threw me off my bike. The RevMaster in my garage was looking pretty good that first stretch. After a few hills, I settled down, making sure I braced for the winds when I came out into the open. Everyone else out for training rides roared past me, but I didn't care. Well, I might have cared a little bit, but there was nothing to be done about it.

The first few times I came across Mike I gave him the thumbs-up, but an hour into the three-hour ride I was toast—almost literally. The sun was relentless, and the heat radiating off the black lava fields was intense. I left a trail of sweat on the road behind me that I could have sworn sizzled when it hit the pavement. My palms were so slick I had trouble holding onto my handlebars.

"Good job, bro," Mike said at the rest stops as he gave me fresh water bottles.

"I'm not comfortable," was my constant response. My stomach hurt, my back hurt, my legs hurt, and I'd give snails a bad rap to say

I was going as fast as they did. I barely finished. Afterward, sitting in the Jeep, I knew beyond doubt that the bike course would make or break me. Somehow I had to ride all those miles and still have enough for the marathon.

At that moment, it seemed impossible, particularly because of the intense heat. It was like riding through a kiln. The sun and dense humidity sapped the strength from my muscles, and no matter how much water I drank, my body didn't seem to be getting enough. The spasticity of my muscles made it very hard to absorb the fluids I needed. I didn't just risk cramping and overheating; I risked spontaneously combusting.

Spurred by my commitment to Welchy and the support of my brother as my training partner, I pushed through—and kept pushing. Over the next six days, I lived and breathed Ironman. Every morning and afternoon, except on the day of the actual race, I trained on the course, getting to know every inch of it. One day, I finished the whole 2.4-mile swim course. Another, I rode up to Hawi, the turnaround point on the bike course. On another, I ran the desolate Energy Lab stretch of the marathon course.

We joined Welchy a couple of times for dinner, and Mike and I found ourselves sitting with World Champion triathletes, among them Chrissie Wellington, the thirty-four-year-old Brit who had conquered Kona three times already. Two weeks before the race, she had taken a nasty spill on her bike and was in real peril of backing out. Everybody was superfriendly, but I couldn't help but think were they asking, "Who is this guy?" I didn't exactly look or walk like these paragons of fitness and athleticism.

Most nights, though, Mike and I ate alone and hung out back at our house, dissecting what had happened during training. There was a lot of joking, like "Wow, that was an easy ride," and so on, but

I was daunted by how tough the course was and by how much work I would need to get in shape for it.

"Oh, I've got a year more of training. . . . It'll come together," I kept saying, but I wasn't sure that any amount of time would do it.

The only thing I did know for sure was that there was no way I could have done that trip without Mike, and although we didn't talk about it, the big divide between us was beginning to heal. For the first time in a long time, we both had someone we could rely on. In my case, he had seen me growing up at my worst, my most awkward. He'd seen me struggle my whole life, and whether it was in the water, on the bike, or on my feet, this shared history allowed me to be honest with him in a way that I couldn't be with others. With Mike, I didn't hold back. I didn't always have to be upbeat and positive, didn't have to pretend that the struggle to train my body was anything other than what it was: the hardest thing I'd ever had to do.

Race day came. In my lifetime, I have been fortunate to attend many major sporting competitions: the Super Bowl, the NBA Finals, and the Stanley Cup Championship as well big-time golf, tennis, and race-car events. Nothing compared to the Ironman World Championship. Participants came from all over the world, men and women of every size, age, and ability. Their families, friends, complete strangers, and everyone in between lined the course. Everybody cheered for everybody. Sure, some fans hooted and hollered a little louder for their particular elite athlete to win, but for 99 percent of the competitors this race was, at most, about realizing a personal best time. And for many, many competitors, it was simply about finishing.

That fact hit home near the seventeen-hour cutoff, which struck at midnight. The last several hundred yards of the run course was packed ten deep with spectators, all of them shouting at the top of their lungs for the racers to finish in time. They cheered more loudly for the slowest of the bunch than for the elite athletes who had crossed the line at blistering speeds many hours before (including Chrissie Wellington, who, despite her injuries, conquered Kona a fourth time that year). What other sporting event, I thought, reveled in the value of competing over winning. People hugged, cried, and screamed as racers pushed themselves to finish before midnight. It was complete, utter pandemonium, all in celebration of the triumph of the human spirit.

But it was not all triumph. A minute before the cutoff, a woman in her fifties stumbled and staggered down the chute. She was doing "the lean," as that half-sideways, half-forward move was called. She was only 10 feet from the finish line when the clock struck midnight, and her hopes of being an "Ironman" were crushed. There was a collective groan throughout the crowd, followed by applause for her attempt. At that moment, I could think only of the groan, realizing that this might well be me next year.

I texted Welchy from the airport before we left, thanking him for the amazing trip and telling him I was ready to do whatever it took to get myself ready for the Kona Ironman 2012.

"It'll be the craziest year of your life," he wrote back. "Get ready, mate."

From my window seat, I watched the Big Island diminish in size as my plane rose into the sky. *I'll see you again soon.*

11

I Told You This Wasn't
Going to be Easy

A Saturday in December 2011. A Saturday in January 2012. A Saturday in February 2012. The week, the month, it didn't make a difference. The alarm rang at 5:30 A.M. I turned over in bed to hit the snooze button, and I already felt spent, done, exhausted. Because it was the weekend, I slept an hour later than during the week. I hoped the extra seven minutes each time I hit snooze would buy me a bit more energy, but it never worked. *Come on now, Bonner. Got to get moving.*

With every week, the training schedule increased in length and intensity. It was like climbing a mountain without end, with a muddy slope that I kept slipping backward on. There was no way to see if I was making any progress, because I was always exhausted beyond measure. It was not as if I finished a comparatively short workout and was then bounding with extra energy. Plus, I never managed to complete every part of Welchy's schedule, so I continually felt like a failure. Maybe Dr. Aminian was right from the start: my CP presented too big an obstacle to my Ironman ambitions. *Don't think of that now. Get out of bed.*

I thought of Jake. I thought of the kids I knew who didn't have the option of rising from bed on their own power. I thought of all the people who had already donated to my Ironman campaign, all the people who expected me to compete. I thought of how disappointed I would be in myself if I didn't finish the race. I thought of all the kids the OM Foundation was helping in Orange County at the Life Without Limits Therapy Center and in Tanzania, where we had donated tens of thousands for a center. I couldn't lie here just because I was tired. *Get out of bed, you lazy ass.*

Sitting up, I drew my legs toward me and unfastened the Velcro straps on the special boots that Afshin had prescribed for me in November, when I had shredded my feet by training in a new pair of running shoes. The boots were essentially glorified splints that kept my feet in the right position while I slept. Diagnosed with severe plantar fasciitis (inflammation of the feet, a common injury of mine), I hadn't been able to walk without pain, let alone jog or ride a bike, for almost two months. For a stretch, I had worried whether my Ironman hopes were crushed, but Welchy told me to rest, to wait, and to let the body do what the body will do. As usual, mine did everything slowly, and it took forever for my feet to heal. Although the boots tore up my sheets, I still wore them to prevent any reinjury.

Finally, I swung my legs out of bed and took my first step. I made myself a bowl of oatmeal and prepared my gear. By 6:30 A.M., the sky was beginning to lighten as I drove south from Newport Coast to just north of Camp Pendleton. The Marine Corps base had a bike trail that ran down the Pacific coast for over dozens of miles. I rode for hour after hour. I enjoyed the beautiful scenery for about all of ten minutes, then I focused only on pumping my legs at eighty to ninety rotations of the pedal crank per minute, the rate that Welchy wanted.

Every so often, I stopped on the side of the trail to stretch my body and to keep the terrible cramps away from my back and legs. Most triathletes, Welchy told me, were able to drive their pedals with almost twice the amount of energy I was able to create. Not only did they push on the pedals in the downward rotation like every amateur cyclist (using the quads), but with their feet clipped into the pedals, they were able to pull up on them in the upward rotation (using the hamstrings and glutes).

With my chicken legs, Welchy only wanted me to push (partly so that I had strength left for the run, partly because my CP left my glutes and hamstrings the weakest). Given the lack of power I was delivering, he calculated that it would take me almost eight hours on the bike to finish the 112-mile Ironman course. That meant I had to train at long lengths to acclimatize my body to that duration of time, and it was a slog that took everything out of me.

After I returned home, I made myself a protein shake and brought it into the shower, where I let the hot water pour over me until my skin turned bright red. Later, I spread out on the sofa and fell asleep. That was it for my Saturday.

Day after day: train, train, train.

Here was a typical mid-February week, 2012:

> *Monday:* 90-minute master's swim; 75-minute brisk walk; 60 minutes with LeFever

> *Tuesday:* 180-minute bike ride on hills; 45 minutes with LeFever

> *Wednesday:* 90-minute master's swim; 90-minute brisk walk

Thursday: 180-minute bike ride on the coast; 30-minute brisk walk

Friday: 90-minute master's swim; 60-minute medium-paced walk

Saturday: 300-minute bike ride (5 hours, ouch!)

Sunday: 90-minute hike or slow walk

"Bon-Bon, here is the torture of the week," Welchy sometimes wrote when he sent me a new schedule. One year into the training, and I didn't yet have the base set—Welchy told me that I was now only just "coming on a time where the base is being laid."

It was not just my body that was suffering from the continuous assault. At work, I was a shell of the go-go, hungry type I had once been. There were no nights out on the town, no parties. I was dating a wonderful woman named Michelle, but I didn't have the energy—or the time, frankly—to treat her to fine dinners and romantic weekends away. At best, I mustered up movie nights at my house, falling asleep long before the credits rolled. Throughout it all, I felt guilty about what I was *not* contributing to work, my friends, Michelle, and my foundation, and this only made the schedule twice as hard to handle.

At the end of February, I went splat against the wall. I didn't want any more pain. I felt as if I had completely plateaued and wasn't seeing any improvement in my performance. I was too tired, too drained, to continue. Everyone, including most recently Paul, who had volunteered at the beginning of my training to compete at Kona with me, had now dropped out. Perhaps I should join them. On a rare night out for dinner with Mike, I sat slumped in my chair, almost too weary to muster up the strength to order and eat.

"What have I gotten myself into?" I asked, thankful at last that I had someone I could open up to, and thankful even more that it was my brother. "How can I do everything?"

"You're making progress," Mike said. "You're doing the best you can."

Not long after returning from Hawaii, Mike had left his boyfriend, and in early January he had been in a car crash that had put him in the hospital. He hadn't had a drink, but I knew he was battling his alcoholism. More and more, we were leaning on each other. Mike told me that the rest of the family was worried about how I was doing.

"You need to figure out a way to recharge, to get your Bonner time," he said.

"I've made commitments," I said, unable to see beyond that wall. "I mean, I'm not even in the race yet. I hope I can pull all of this off."

For a long time, we just sat quietly and ate our dinner. I knew I needed to get some balance back in my life, to find a way to do Ironman, but still have an existence beyond it.

Soon after, I went to see Welchy at Oakley. Although he had undergone yet another heart surgery earlier in the year, he seemed his usual boisterous self when we sat down in the conference room near his office. On the other hand, I slouched in my chair, numb to the world.

"I'm really struggling," I said, masking the truth no more. "I don't have any energy. I'm not recovering well. I'm constantly tired. I don't seem to be improving from the workouts. I'm not sure what to do."

He looked at me for a long moment. I thought he might cut down on some miles, give me a window of rest. I mean, he had to understand, show some pity.

"You're at about phase three of five in your training. There are still a couple more to go, so we need to find you more energy."

I nodded. Maybe this was a kind way of introducing the idea that I needed a vacation. Maybe Tahiti. Bali. Heck, I'd even take a week on my couch, shades drawn.

"Okay, let's go over your diet," he then said, listing what I shouldn't eat. Hydrogenated oils. Anything with high-fructose corn syrup. This was no problem.

"Cut out the booze too."

"Okay," I said, a little less sure, but still, fine. At most I was drinking a couple of drinks two or three nights a week.

"Alrighty, mate. What else takes it out of you?"

I hesitated, knowing the answer, though not the medical reason why the act left me exhausted for a day afterward. "Sex."

"Then you'll stop having sex."

This conversation was veering in a very wrong direction.

"Uh-huh," I think I said. "And my training schedule?"

Welchy did not pull back on that either. He did not give me a month off. He asked for more, said to hit the schedule harder. I was to remember why I was doing this. Remember Jake. Remember who I was fighting for and why. Remember I was fighting for myself. I had to dig deeper, to go all the way, if I wanted to be an Ironman. And even that level of commitment might still not be enough.

I was at a loss for words.

"I told you this wasn't going to be easy, mate. You'll get through this, but you'll have to make more sacrifices."

Welchy gave me a hug, and I walked out to my car a little stunned. I'd gone in wanting a break, and instead he'd told me to work harder. As I sat with my hands on the steering wheel, the enormity of what I'd tasked myself with sank in. I couldn't fake my way through this, couldn't realize in the middle that I wasn't prepared enough, yet still force my way to the summit. If I was going to succeed, if I was going to complete this race in spite of my CP, it would require everything I had—not just on race day, but during all the days leading up it. And I couldn't fight it anymore; I couldn't pretend that I could have a normal life and still pull this off. For better or for worse, I had to embrace it all or run the very real risk of failure.

And so I became a monk, faithful to only one thing: Ironman 2012. Everything else fell aside. Funnily enough, there was some comfort when I stopped trying to balance everything else in my life. I had climbed Kilimanjaro almost in rebellion against my cerebral palsy, as if it were the opponent. I wanted to prove there was nothing I couldn't do. That wouldn't work with Ironman, and Welchy had known it from the start. More than a year into my Kona quest, I was only beginning to accept the fact that to finish the race I needed to embrace all my weaknesses—every single one of them—and find a way through them.

An able-bodied, "normal" person probably only needed a year to train for Kona. Not me. Because of my cerebral palsy, I needed two. So it goes. Others may not need to watch every single thing they eat or drink; others may be able to have sex, to go out, to enjoy themselves. Not me. I needed to save every ounce of energy. Others may experience much greater improvement in their fitness from devoting that number of hours to their training. Not me. My body and my brain were simply not working on the same level. Fine.

More than simply understanding how to train around my weaknesses or limitations, this Ironman demanded I accept my cerebral palsy as part of who I was. I was not, by definition, normal. I would never be. I needed to stop resisting the idea that I should be able to do things exactly as normal people do. Different did not mean impossible. I could still achieve whatever I wanted in life, but I needed to embrace the fact that I had to do it my way, harder though it may be. For years I'd been talking about limits, but for the first time I was beginning to understand how to work with mine, instead of against them.

"Biggest week yet," Welchy wrote for the first week of March. Yup. Thirty-five hundred yards in the pool. Done. Two-hour hilly ride during the hottest part of the day. Gotcha. Weights with LeFever until my arms went numb. Alrighty then. It was a whole new level of commitment, and I rose to it. It was not as if I made a conscious decision to accept my cerebral palsy completely (there was no switch to flip), but each day that I finished what my training schedule demanded, another measure of acceptance came with it.

Before the 2012 race season began, I rode in a charity event outside San Diego with Billy Ruddell from Cannondale and Chrissie Wellington. Prior to battling through her injuries to win at the 2011 Ironman, Chrissie had watched my Kilimanjaro documentary, and it reminded her that sometimes you just need to show up at the starting line and give it your all, even if you're not at your best.

It was great to see her again, and we rode side by side for a long stretch. I gave her a rough breakdown on my training, and she asked about my nutrition. I rattled off what I was eating and not eating.

"Where's the bloody coffee?!"

I told her I didn't drink coffee. Chrissie simply laughed and told me that I need to drink coffee after eating my first meal in the morning at the least. She also promised to set me up with her nutritionist.

The coffee certainly helped me to bring it in the mornings, and over the weeks that followed I tinkered more and more with my diet, particularly with what I ingested during workouts, trying to consume the 275 calories an hour that Welchy wanted me to maintain (any fewer calories, I wouldn't have enough fuel to maintain energy; any more calories, and I was risking diarrhea and the like). I turned into a bit of a mad scientist, mixing powders, gels, and sports drinks of various quantities and tastes during training to see what worked for me.

Welchy had told me that no two people were the same with regard to the nutrition they needed to operate at the highest level. Endurance events like Ironman often come down to making sure you have enough gas in the tank—if you don't fuel properly during the race, finishing becomes nearly impossible. Through experiments, I found that I powered through workouts easier with GU Roctane than plain GU. The addition of caffeine in the carbo-rich energy gel made the difference. To stay hydrated, the C5 powder by Carbo Pro, which has a mix of electrolytes, sodium, and other things, worked best. And, for instance, I discovered after many rigorous tests that chocolate-flavored GU tasted better on the bike than on the run.

In April, I got ready for the Bonelli Sprint Triathlon, in San Dimas, California, the first of four events before the big one. Had the months of training made a difference? I couldn't say for sure, but at least this time I brought a waterproof bag and some water in a plastic container to wash the sand off my feet before putting on my clip-on shoes.

I didn't exactly crush Bonelli. I pushed very hard on the swim, passing people left and right in the water, and posted a good time of ten minutes, twenty-four seconds, but my shoulders were worn out. The bike was better—much better—in spite of my struggles on the steep hills, and I finished in fifty-four minutes, seventeen seconds. However, I made the mistake of guzzling too much of my water mix (C5, salt tabs, and glutamine) before the run. Feeling sick, I had a sluggish 5K at thirty-one minutes, nineteen seconds and finished wiped out. Overall, my time of one hour and forty-five minutes was slightly better than my first sprint triathlon. More important, I could now identify my weak areas and where and how I needed to improve: better shoulder strength, more practice working the hills on the bike, better nutritional awareness, more muscling through the run.

In May, at the ITU World Championship in San Diego, I knocked the Olympic-distance triathlon (basically a quarter of a full Ironman) out of the park. My time in the 0.9-mile swim was slow, the result of some serious snaking from side to side, but it was the most comfortable I had felt in the ocean. The 26-mile bike course was solid. And I ran what was for me a blistering 10K. I tried to look as strong as I could at the finish—Welchy was the announcer. With my transitions between the swim and bike and the bike and run improving as well, I completed the race in three hours, thirty-three minutes—beating my target time by almost half an hour.

Welchy was impressed. That alone sent me moonward.

These were all warm-ups for the Ironman 70.3, a half Ironman, nicknamed Honu, on Hawaii's Big Island. This one would decide whether the Ironman organizers would allow me to compete at Kona. Some of the bike course was the same as for the big race, but the swim and run courses were in different locations. But the conditions made this the best dress rehearsal out there: the heat, the humidity, and the hurricane-like winds were all the same as what I'd face on Kona race day.

Welchy was clear about my target time: eight hours or less. I needed to hit this mark or it was unlikely the organizers would grant me a special spot for the World Championship. They needed to know I had a chance of finishing the full Ironman before the midnight cutoff.

There was never any question about Mike joining me in Hawaii. He was my pit crew, my training partner, my moral support, my nurse, my cook, my driver, and my right hand. We were a team now, and I would have been helpless without him. We had a practice swim in Hapuna Bay, with its long crescent beach and sapphire-blue waters. I kept up with him stroke for stroke and had never felt more comfortable in the water. Mike gave me a huge smile and said, "Just do it like that on race day, no faster, no slower, and you got this."

The next day, after a practice ride on the Queen K Highway, he told me, "Bro, it's night and day. You're not the same person on that bike. So comfortable. No wobbling. You're looking good."

Mike's praise aside, I was heart-in-my-shoes nervous. This was it. I needed to hit my times or all the training and all the pain and effort would have been for nothing. This thought ran through my mind again and again in the days approaching the race.

For almost forty-eight hours before the start of Honu, Mike and I holed up in our rental house, watching *Whale Wars*. There was something about the show's mayhem and cliffhangers that kept my mind off what was ahead.

Race day saw the Big Island walloped by an advancing storm. The ocean swells were much larger than normal. The trade winds were howling, gusts bending the trees that bordered the Queen K almost horizontal. Hitting my goal time was going to be a challenge.

"Wow, we have some winds today," the race announcer said, moments before I hit the water. With all the bodies, legs, and arms chopping the water at once, it looked like a bunch of people were getting eaten by sharks, Mike told me. Given the swells, the densely packed waters, and a thousand swimmers all angling for position, I had trouble taking a breath without getting slugged in the side or swallowing some water. I steered out of the scrum, though I knew it would make for a longer swim. The wind blew one of the outer buoys farther out to sea, making the race longer still.

Overall, it was a very tough swim. I came out of the water tired, and with the race clock reading forty-two minutes, I knew I needed to keep moving fast. I moved so fast, in fact, trying to keep up with the others rushing through the transition area that I neglected to slather myself with sunblock before hopping onto my bike.

We headed south toward Kona and then made a turnaround toward Hawi. It was then that the 40–50 mile-per-hour winds hit. I could barely remain upright. Other riders were literally blown off the road. I bore down on the handlebars and fought my way through it. Halfway through the 56-mile ride, ascending the steep road to Hawi, the wind roared so hard that it almost brought me to a standstill.

On the downhill return, I was propelled by the wind at my back. It was like being shot out of a cannon. At times, I had to brake to keep from being slung into the black lava fields. I finished the bike course in three hours, forty-seven minutes, which left me three and a half hours within which to reach my goal time.

I tried to jog the run course, but ended up walking for most of it. At times I was forced to do so by the gale-force gusts. For the stretches when there was nobody else on the road, I felt as though I were in an old western movie, leaning into the wind as tumbleweeds crossed in front of me. I picked up the pace for the last couple of miles and finished with a total time of seven hours, fifty-three minutes, right under the mark.

My neck and back were scorched red—"like a rotisserie chicken," Mike said, with horror in his voice. I should have cut my shirt off with scissors rather than lift it off over my head—the pain was excruciating.

That night, when we had a celebration dinner on the beach with Welchy and his wife, Sian, I still wasn't able to lean back in my chair. He told me that they had only seen worse winds one other time in the thirty years the Ironman had taken place on the Big Island. Excited as he was about how I had done, he was also brutally honest about my chances of finishing the Kona Ironman.

"We have our work cut out to make this all happen."

Even so, I got the feeling that, for the first time, he actually thought I could do it.

When I got back from Hawaii, I received word that the Kona Ironman organizers had granted me a spot in the 2012 race. With that, any vestige of the life I had known disappeared. I became a machine, built to train. Michelle and I broke up. My friends I never saw. Work only got leftovers. Weekends of fun were a thing of the past.

One day I did a six-hour bike ride on the Santa Ana River trail. The trail, along a concrete river basin, starts at the Pacific and runs almost due east away from the coast, between Huntington Beach and Newport. My plan was to do two loops of three hours, so I could restock with water and food at the halfway point.

I got there at dawn. As I did every time before settling onto my bike, I closed my eyes and accepted the agony that was to come. The ride would be awful. Over the hours, the tightness in my legs, hip flexors, and lower back would sear and burn. I would have to put a Great Wall of China around the pain. And that was okay now. The suffering was the price I had grown willing to pay. It would not stop me.

There were only a few other joggers and cyclists about. I rode through one neighborhood after another. Because it was so early, the parks were all empty, the lots barren. Then farther east I finally got into some wooded hills. After an hour and a half, I turned around and cycled back. By now, a bunch of cars had gathered outside Angel Stadium in Anaheim to tailgate before the game. The neighborhood playing fields had also begun to rumble with activity.

Three hours into the ride, I refueled at my parked car. My muscles were on fire. So be it. I closed my eyes again, rebuilt that wall, and got back on my bike. Others may have moments of exultation on their rides, the cyclist's version of a runner's high. With my CP, those moments never came. It was a start-to-finish panorama of pain, and there was no reward in paying attention to it.

Instead, I focused on little goals, reaching the top of the next hill, crossing the next bridge, pedaling through the next underpass. On the loop this time I heard the screams and laughter of children playing soccer in the park. Angel Stadium was surrounded with tailgaters, music blaring, a real party going on. On my way back (hurting, hurting, hurting after more than five hours on my bike), the parking lots outside the stadium were still full of cars, but the people were all inside, cheering at what sounded like a great game. The neighborhood parks remained crowded—different kids, different families. And there I was too, still fighting to maintain the wall, still pedaling those wheels.

The effort was showing a return. My swims, bikes, and runs were all faster and longer, and my body was recovering from the workouts much better as well. Now weighing 200 pounds (down 20 pounds from when I started), I was almost showing a bit of a six-pack, in the right lighting.

Every Sunday, Mike and I headed out to Crystal Cove, which, compared to Bompa's beach, was much easier to access and had better navigation points to sight. My orientation and balance in the water were better than they had ever been, and although Mike was still and always would be a stronger swimmer, I was starting to push him. When we came back up on the beach, he would be breathing heavily, which was very satisfying. I was not exactly performing a Karate Kid one-legged balancing act on the BOSU ball, but I wasn't too far off. More important, I was using LeFever's orange stretchy band during workouts, the one that was as tough as a tire.

In the midst of this training mania, when I was constantly questioning whether I was pushing myself hard enough, for long enough, came a big reminder of why I was doing the Ironman in the first place. In August, Juliana arrived at LAX. Almost fifteen months had passed since I met her in Tanzania. She would have come sooner for her surgery, but arranging a passport for a sixteen-year-old without a birth certificate (not to mention all the rest of the red tape) delayed her arrival.

On the drive to the Ronald McDonald House in Orange County, where we had arranged for her to stay, Juliana was quiet, her eyes wide as saucers at all the lights and cars. Over the coming days, she bravely sat through a number of tests and examinations by Afshin at the Children's Hospital of Orange County.

Time and again, she asked to see the photographs of people with prosthetics dancing ballet, playing soccer, and running. She never said it, but I knew she was imagining herself doing the same. On the day of her surgery, I worried that she would be nervous, maybe even fighting the doctors as they put in the intravenous lines. Instead, she had a huge smile on her face. The double amputation went fine, and although there were some minor complications in the healing process, Juliana was out of the hospital a week later. In the coming weeks, she started her rehabilitation and was on her way to wearing prosthetic legs and walking for the first time.

Before Juliana left for Africa, I showed her a YouTube video of an athlete racing down a track on bladelike prosthetics.

"That can be you one day," I told her. "That can be you."

She soaked it in and seemed mesmerized by the idea.

Juliana continued her treatment back home in Tanzania, in our new center at the orphanage that Dr. Aminian and I visited. Called Tumaini ("Hope" in Swahili), it was funded by my foundation. With the hundreds of thousands raised for Kilimanjaro and my goal of a million dollars for Ironman, it was my hope that the OM Foundation would help many more children like Juliana.

Spending time with Juliana left me inspired. She showed so much courage, both in her daily struggle to make the best of it despite her disability and in her willingness to put her trust in others to better her life.

It was the same during the moments I had with Ashley, the girl who suffered from both CP and epilepsy, at UCP-OC's Life Without Limits center. She continued to thrive with her therapy, was now able to steer her wheelchair by the movements of her head, and could even navigate on her own two feet with the assistance of a special walker. At the Orange County Marathon earlier that year, I pushed her for the 5K, and we were so slow that there was nobody left near us at the finish line. "First Place!" she cheered. A spark plug, always with a one-liner, she attended my foundation's last board meeting and, like Donald Trump, she gave us all a look and said, "You're fired."

These moments were the few breaks from training that I allowed myself. I felt guilty if I shirked any part of the schedule that arrived every Sunday night from Welchy. The schedule ruled everything. Master's swim. Plyometrics. Up the ante on the bike. Master's again—hard. Walk, brisk. Jog, downhill. Weights, every muscle. Five ten-minute intervals on the bike. Master's swim. Five hours on the bike. All with Welchy's inimitable notes: "You must really love me by now." "You will thank me later!" The more punishment Welchy heaped on me, the greater my ability to take it. I knew there was an end in sight, but I no longer watched out for it. I was in the zone, in the moment.

At the end of August, Welchy sent me a note that was almost a page long. This was a lot of words for my coach. He praised me for being an "incredible guy" (questionable) and apologized for "not being the world's greatest coach" (plain wrong). He told me that he was writing the same workouts for me that had brought him success in his career. Besides the daily routine, he promised, there would be only three more key push-it-to-the-hilt workouts. "You have answered your call to the start line," Welchy concluded. "Almost there, mate. Almost there."

I kept reading and rereading the note. To think that this great champion was devoting so much time to my mission gave me a tremendous boost of confidence. What was more, he seemed to feel I was on the right track. I tried to parse his every word to see if there was any worry, any concern on his part, but I found nothing. *Keep working. You're on the home stretch. You got this.*

The next weekend, I flew down to Austin, Texas, for the TriRock Triathlon. Steve Robert had moved there with his family a year after Jake's death, and I was going to be racing with a Team Jake logo on my jersey. Before the race, we held a concert headlined by country-music star Josh Turner to raise money for my foundation. We were in the opening stages of planning a center in Austin for children with disabilities similar to the one in Orange County. It was a wonderful reunion, and since my whole journey had started with the Roberts, it was the perfect send-off for Hawaii. An added bonus was that Dilly lived near Austin.

On the day of the race, Steve and Dilly walked me down to the swim start. They ribbed me that there were some pretty fit dudes in the same grouping I was in. It was 100 degrees, without a breath of wind, and the TriRock sprint triathlon was a hot sweaty bear that taxed me much more than it should have. Steve and Alison cheered along the sidelines, and their sons Tyler and Zach ran with me for a stretch of the 5K. Their presence meant so much and helped keep away any worries that I would face the same temperatures—or worse—in Hawaii, over a much more grueling course and many, many, many more miles.

Mike and I were standing in our swim trunks, ankle-deep in the Pacific. We were there for my last ocean-training swim. Fifteen-foot waves curled and pounded Crystal Cove Beach, and a fierce undertow muddied the water in their retreat. Unlike at West Beach, we didn't know every rock and drop-off on this stretch of coast.

"Bompa wouldn't want us going in," I said. " 'If you don't know the topography of the area,' he always said, 'don't be stupid and go in.' "

We laughed, still staring out at the surf.

"Easier getting out there than getting back in," Mike said. "Especially when we're tired."

The same could have been said of my whole Ironman adventure. Easier to say you're going to do the Kona Ironman than cross the finish line at the end.

"Should we do it?" I asked.

Only a couple of days before, on my way back from a long bike ride along Newport Coast Drive, I came upon a female cyclist who, seconds before, had been hit by a truck, which then took off. She lay on the roadside, her helmet cracked open, her bike mangled. As her husband cradled her in his arms, I directed traffic away while somebody else called 911.

I later learned that she had died from her injuries. I sat on the edge of my sofa, reminded of how anything can happen, at any time. I didn't want to tempt fate by swimming in these waters.

"Let's not go," Mike finally said. "You put in the work. You've come on in leaps and bounds as a swimmer. Why risk it?"

"You don't need to convince me," I smiled. If this had occurred a year earlier, I would have gone into the water over my best judgment just to prove that I could. Now, I only had one thing left to prove to myself or to anyone. "Next time we see each other, we'll be on our way to Kona. We're going to do that big bad boy."

"You're ready, bro."

12

Me Against the Island

On October 3, 2012, I watched the Big Island growing closer again through the window of my puddle jumper from Honolulu. The rounded cone of the Mauna Kea volcano, long extinct, rose majestically over the clouds. The plane headed down the island's northwestern coast to Kailua-Kona airport, following much the same course I would take on my bike. From the sky, I got a good view of the mix of white-sand beaches, pockets of tropical green, and long fields of rugged black and red lava rock that I would pass on my way to and from the turnaround town of Hawi. On the day of the race I was unlikely to see any of this. My vision would be too distorted by sweat, and I would be suffering from fatigue and in mortal fear of crosswinds hurling me from my bike.

"What's your goal? Have you thought of what it would be like to come down the finishing chute? What's the hardest part of the race? What do you hope to accomplish? What's your target time? What's next?" I had fielded these questions, and many more, during press events in Hawaii's capital and fund-raisers over the two previous days.

"The goal is to finish. I want to high-five everybody coming down the chute. The bike, for sure, the bike will be hardest. I'm here to raise funds for my foundation, to remind children with cerebral palsy or other disabilities not to put limitations on themselves. Sixteen hours, thirty minutes would be a great time for me. The next adventure? Nothing. I think this will do it." Indeed. Now I actually had to go ahead and do it.

Upon landing, I had ten days before the race. The next morning, Mike and I went over to the pier to do a ninety-minute Welchy "splasharound" on the swim course. The small beach, shoehorned between the pier and the stone wall that curved around Kona Bay, was crowded with athletes. Mike went into the water first, but then let me lead the way ahead.

"This is your race," he said, "so show me what you can do compared to last year at this time."

I started slow, warming up and getting into my rhythm on the way to the first buoy. There were some nagging aches and pains, but nothing out of the ordinary. Overall, I felt incredible. After almost two years of fine-tuning my stroke, I was a much stronger swimmer than I had ever been. Working on the angle of my arms, the position of my legs, my bilateral breathing, a smooth kick, the roll of my body, and my equilibrium in the water, I was motoring through the swells.

About halfway to the second buoy, I felt a little twinge in my right shoulder, but I kept swimming. I probably still needed to warm up some, maybe relax my stroke a bit. A few minutes later, though, the twinge had turned into discomfort, then it turned into pain, and with each stroke it got worse. As I neared the second buoy, I was having trouble maintaining a straight line. Finally, I stopped completely, and Mike came alongside me.

"Everything okay?" he asked.

"No. It's my shoulder. Something's not right."

"Let's tread water a bit. See if it loosens up."

I nodded.

After a couple of minutes, the dull pain was still present, but wasn't getting worse. I decided to give it another go. With each stroke, I felt the tendons yanking in my shoulder. I could barely pull my arm through the water. I stopped again. I was worried, very worried.

Mike asked me a bunch of questions, trying to pinpoint what was wrong. The only thing that was clear was that we needed to head back to the pier.

"Do you want a tow?"

I shook my head.

If I needed a tow, how was I going to race 2.4 miles nine days from now? Mike started back, and I followed. I felt like a bird trying to fly with a wounded wing. I could flutter and make a little progress, but ultimately I would never take flight. I grew more and more frustrated with every second that passed. This part of the course was supposed to be my strong suit, where I could win a little cushion of time for the bike and the run. If I had to swim the course with only one arm—and I would, if I had to—then I was in big trouble.

After stopping several more times, we finally made it back to the beach. Back on the pier, I tried to lift my right arm above my shoulder, but I couldn't. The pain was screw-up-your-face intense. I was straight on the phone to Welchy, who was at the Oakley house. From the sound of my voice, he knew immediately that something was very wrong. I explained what had happened on the swim.

"We'll get you in shape for the race, mate," Welchy said calmly. "No worries, all right?"

By the time I had showered and changed, he had set up an appointment with David Darbyshire, an Australian sports massage therapist who worked on a lot of the elite triathletes. Operating from a beach apartment a mile south of downtown Kona, "Darbs," as I quickly learned to call him, gave me a thorough working over, bending my arm at every angle and digging through my armpit into my shoulder. After the treatment, shoulder throbbing, my right arm held close to my chest, I headed back to our rented SUV, where Mike was waiting for me. We didn't speak much on the way back to the small condo where we were staying the first few days, neither of us wanting to give voice to the fear that my Ironman ambitions might well be over.

On October 8, five days away from the race, I drove over to the Oakley house. My shoulder continued to feel as though someone had driven a metal stake through it. Earlier that morning I had another session with Darbs, at which I almost passed out from his workover. The consensus was that the pain was essentially caused by overuse and that I needed to rest the limb. In the meantime I had been able to get out on my bike and to do some light jogging. Welchy greeted me with a hug and asked briefly about my shoulder, but that was all he had to say about it. I figured he didn't want to dwell on the subject or make it loom even larger in my mind than it already did.

It was blisteringly hot and humid, but he found a pair of lawn chairs in the shade by the water. A breeze blew off the water. Welchy leaned forward, elbows on his knees, and started. "Okay, let's go over everything."

Then followed what I can only describe as a master class in taking part in the Ironman World Championship. Everything Welchy had learned in his years as a triathlete, particularly from his races in Kona, he shared with me.

"Prerace, you're going to need to start taking in your calories an hour and a half before the start, because your body's already gearing up. . . . One of the big mistakes people make is to warm up too much, all kinds of stretches and stuff, exhausting their energy. This is made worse by not eating anything. . . . Don't get into the water until you have to. Start the swim in the back, find a sweet spot, and go smooth. . . . Use BodyGlide—everywhere. . . . When you get out of the ocean, drink some of your water mix right away. . . .

"When on your bike, stay as low as possible in the wind. Watch those cutouts: you come out from behind a hill, and the wind hits you in the side of the head, there you go, crash. . . . Two hands on the bike. Cadence eighty to ninety rotations. . . . If your heart rate's running wild, you don't have to stop. Mate, most people think they have to! But it's not true. Back down a gear. If you're in fifth, go to fourth. If that doesn't work, drop a couple more gears. . . . In your transition, don't rush, take your time. . . . If you need to pee, just piss yourself—everybody does it. . . . On the run, walk the uphills and jog the flats and downhills. . . . At every aid station I want you to pour ice down your crotch and into your bike helmet: cool yourself down."

Every once in a while, I nodded and said, "Okay, got it," but mostly I just sat there and soaked up the information. When Welchy had finished, he gave me my next scheduled workout (a two-hour bike ride north out of town) and told me to report in on how it went. Again, no mention of my shoulder.

"You can do this, mate," he said in farewell.

Over the next week, I continued to train on every part of the bike and run courses. There was a clear method to Welchy's madness, because I was now acquainted with every turn, hill, and straightaway on the course. There would be no surprises on race day, which gave me no small measure of comfort. I stayed out of the ocean and continued with massage therapy every day. The pain eased, and I could raise my arm level with my shoulder without pulling a face. Still, after spending years worrying about how my legs would hold up in an endurance event this intense, there was something unsettling about suddenly having to worry about my upper body. It made me realize just how unpredictable this whole thing was.

On one of my training days, Mike got sidetracked and missed picking me up at our prearranged spot. I stood on the edge of the highway, baking in the midday sun, my feet almost melting onto the asphalt. What was worse, I was out of my water mix. Fifteen minutes later Mike finally arrived, sporting a new baseball cap, with some empty food wrappers in the backseat.

I yelled at him for his selfishness; he tried to explain. I yelled some more.

I was still fuming as we drove off. I suppose it was a case of venting the stress before the race. We were soon back on speaking terms. Apart from that one fight, Mike and I were a smoothly functioning team.

My father and his wife, LaDonna, flew in four days before the race. Sadly, I hadn't yet reconciled with my mom, and she would not be coming. An absolute herd of friends, foundation supporters, and coworkers—including Dilly, Greg LeFever, and the whole Robert family—came to cheer me on, though. Michelle, who had remained a friend despite our breakup, joined me on the Big Island as well. Paul, whose wife was about to have a baby, was one of my few friends who couldn't make it. The outpouring of support was tremendous— and such a different experience from Kilimanjaro, when I felt at such a distance from everybody in my life.

On Thursday, October 11, forty-eight hours before the race, I found myself on Alii Drive in Kona's town center wearing nothing but running shoes, underwear, chaps that a friend had bedazzled to the nines, and a huge blue foam "Go Bonner" cowboy hat. I was just one of thousands, everyone in boxers, briefs, tighty-whities, panties, sports bras, and a host of revealing outfits for the annual charity Underpants Run. The emcee, some guy in an Arnold Schwarzenegger costume, boomed over the PA that we were all to take an oath to never wear Speedos, banana hammocks, or any other inappropriate swimwear in public, and then we were off. As I ran the mile or so through downtown Kona, all thoughts and worry about the race disappeared. It was pure fun—exactly what I needed.

Post Undie Run, I met Welchy for the last time before the big day. Much as I wanted to test out my arm in the ocean, he told me to wait until the following day, the day before the race—and then to do only a few strokes in the swimming pool. He was adamant. Then he gave me his final advice for the race.

For the swim: "Most efficient stroke you can do. Don't waste any unnecessary energy. Nice and smooth." For the bike: "Keep to a eighty-to-ninety cadence, whatever the gear. It's key that your muscles aren't overstrained or underutilized. You want the sweet spot. Eighty-to-ninety cadence." And for the run: "Run. Jog. Walk. Crawl. Use whatever you have left to finish." Regarding nutrition: "Stick to it. No matter how bad you feel, you have to eat and drink your nutrition. It's the only way to slow down the destruction the race wreaks on your body. You won't finish the race if you don't fuel up throughout."

Then Welchy looked me in the eye and said, with the intensity of a man who had been world champion of the hardest race on earth, "This isn't a race against anybody but yourself. You're not here to win. It's you against the island. Don't try to keep up with any other swimmer or runner or biker. This is about you coming across the line in less than seventeen hours. Got it, mate?"

"I got it," I said.

He put a hand on my shoulder. "Run your race."

His words made me pause and, with a click of recognition, smile. For the first time, I understood exactly what he way saying, what in fact he'd been saying all along: my ability to fight my own fight was the only thing that would separate defeat from triumph.

Don't worry about chasing after the pack. Don't compare your swim, bike, run to others'. Don't dwell on the differences between your performance and others'. Don't get down on yourself when you see what the other competitors are doing.

Run your race.

You have cerebral palsy, Bonner, but this race, like your life, belongs to you and you alone. Your race is what you make of it—you have a choice. You choose what you want this to be. You choose how to work within your limits to push past them. You choose to maintain a steady, slow pace and grind it out, mile after mile. You choose. Cerebral palsy does not get a vote.

From my Yoda session at the Oakley house, I headed over to the grand Royal Kona Resort to speak to the more than three hundred physicians and medical personnel who would staff the first-aid tents and roam the course to tend to competitors. The doctors also held the power to remove athletes from the race if they deemed it best. Dr. Bob Laird, the gray-haired, preternaturally calm Ironman medical director, who had overseen every race since 1981, introduced me. Over the next ten minutes, I spoke of my journey with cerebral palsy and how I wanted to remove the limitations people put on those with disabilities. I also highlighted the physical challenges I would face during the competition, from cramping and spasming muscles to difficulty retaining fluids, to low energy reserves ("I start with half a tank"), to an elevated heart rate, to difficulties with balance and eye–feet coordination.

Before I wrapped up with a rah-rah promotional video for my Ironman mission, I said, "Say hi to me out on the course. I'd love that. But please, *do not* make me stop or pull me from the race. I came here to finish, not to try."

Afterward, Mike and I drove out to the Energy Lab before the sun fell. It was the part of the marathon course where I would be farthest away from the finish. In the daytime, the research center was eerie, with its enormous pipes that pumped water out of the ocean and white windowless buildings with names on the side like "Biosphere" this and "Hydro" that. I would be coming through at night, which I was dreading. We parked the SUV and walked down to the beach.

"I'm not looking forward to this part," I said.

"Pretty brutal," Mike replied.

"'Where triathletes go to die,' Welchy says." I tried not to think of all the gnarly stories my coach had told me about the lab—about elite athletes entering in the lead only to exit far behind.

"It's just another part of your race," Mike said, though I was pretty sure he thought it would be where I would hit my wall.

Mike and I sat down on some rocks and watched the surf come in and roll out. We talked about his sobriety and how his faith was helping him with it.

"Do you believe in . . . God?" Mike asked. This wasn't a conversation we had ever had before.

"Yeah," I said awkwardly. "I don't know if it's God, exactly, but—"

"More like the universe, nature, energy?" Mike said.

"Definitely a power greater than ourselves, yeah."

We sat there a long moment in silence.

Then Mike said, "I've been praying for you to finish, that you'll be okay."

I looked at him and grinned. "I've been praying for me too."

We both laughed, shaking off the uncomfortable subject.

"I'm so glad we're doing this together," Mike said.

"Thanks for being there for me. What a journey!"

"Love you, bro."

"Love you too, bro."

It was the first time, since that initial swim in the Pacific together that we'd acknowledged the healing that had gone on between us. Neither of us was the same person we'd been that first day when we'd waded into the choppy surf at Bompa's old swimming spot. This experience, this training, had changed us both, but more important, it had changed us together. We gave each other a long hug, never closer in our lives, and returned to the car.

We had a big dinner for forty people planned for that night. With my own money, I had rented a place a mile north of the pier for the final week. It was a multimillion-dollar spread, with a koi pond and a swimming pool like a lagoon, complete with waterfall. I spared no expense. I wanted someplace near the ocean where my family and friends could congregate without feeling on top of each other, and where I could relax and listen to the waves crashing. The back of the two-story house was almost completely glass, with huge sliding doors that opened out onto the patio. It was the bomb.

There I was in the early evening, waiting for everybody to arrive, chilling out on a lounge chair by the pool. There was a light breeze, and the surrounding palm trees made an almost hypnotic rustling. I was thinking of little Jake Robert. The thought sort of drifted away, and I put some Bob Marley on the stereo.

A few minutes later, one of the swivel chairs by the table on the opposite side of the pool started to turn in circles. It was the strangest thing. The other chairs around it were still, but this one kept rotating, counterclockwise, as if someone was perched on the edge.

Maybe it was the conversation with Mike, maybe it was the music and the palm trees and the crashing waves, but I did think for a brief moment that it might be Jakey, chilling with me. I felt very happy.

The dinner was a bit of a melee. LeFever cooked up burgers, and there were plenty of drinks, but I stuck to simple grilled chicken and rice, which would provide some good nutrients and not unsettle my stomach. I was incredibly grateful that everyone had come all this way to support me, but after so many questions— "Are you ready?" "How are you feeling?"—I simply wanted to retreat to my room.

Dilly gave me a pep talk, revving me up and saying he was there for whatever I needed. "I didn't come for the coconuts," he joked.

I also got to spend some time with Steve and Alison Robert. I told them about the swiveling chair I had seen earlier. The three of us were very emotional. "We're proud of you," Steve said. "Bring it home for Jakey."

Coming up on 10 P.M., Mike played bouncer and broke up the festivities. The house quieted down, and I got some restless sleep.

October 12, the day before the race, I followed Welchy's orders to a tee: "Do as little as possible and *stay off your feet!*" I was up early and had no trouble assuming the position. My feet up on an ottoman, I lounged on the patio with Michelle and my brothers, posted on Facebook, lingered over meals, and spent some time out by the ocean, mesmerized by the surf rushing through a blowhole worn into the lava rock.

In the early afternoon, I stepped into the pool. It was time to test out my shoulder. The pool was just about big enough to take a few strokes. A part of me didn't even want to know. If my shoulder hurt, I was still going to compete, so what was the difference? But Welchy wanted to know if the injury was still a problem, to see whether there were any last-minute adjustments that might be made. Mike watched from the side as I dipped below water and then took a couple of strokes. My shoulder was tight, but there was no pain. I swam back and forth a couple times. No pain. It might not bother me until I had swum half a mile, but that was not going to happen in this pool. After breathing a long sigh, relieved but by no means reassured that my shoulder was going to be okay, I climbed out of the water.

At 4 P.M., Mike and I drove into town to set up my race bike and to drop off my bags (with GU energy gels, Bonk Breaker nutrition bars, bike shoes, running shoes, jersey) to the transition areas. The chute and the tower at the finish had been set up, and I closed my eyes and imagined myself crossing the line, the digital clock still in the sixteenth hour. Into the rack I placed my bike, the same Cannondale Synapse frame, but now with high-end wheels and components, and then let some air out of the tires. Welchy had advised this, because the air in the tires would expand on the hot asphalt, and we didn't want the tubes to get overstressed and burst.

Later, I had a relaxed dinner with my family and a few friends. There was some gentle ribbing, like when I excused myself to go to the bathroom, and Matt joked, "Shouldn't you just piss yourself, you know, just to get used to it?" Afterward we hung out by the pool. My dad and brothers told me how proud they were of me, finish or no finish.

I headed up to my room before the gathering broke up. The closer to the race, the quieter I became, every ounce of focus and energy going toward keeping myself calm. After laying out everything I needed for the morning, I strapped on the plantar fasciitis boots and crawled into bed.

In the middle of the night, I woke up with a jolt. My first thought was that it was time to go, but the clock only read 1 A.M. I thought about the race, about how my shoulder would hold up in the swim, about what I needed to eat first thing in the morning and right before the starting cannon. Then I walked through every stage of the Ironman in my head, mapping out what could go wrong and how I would react to it.

During the swim, I might get kicked in the head or punched in the shoulder. I told myself to stay efficient, not to let the blows knock me off my game. For the bike, I imagined how it would feel—cramped muscles, the spasms in my back from maintaining a hunched-over position, the crick in my neck from holding up my helmeted head, hour after hour. I thought of the terrible heat and of the long, windy uphill climb to Hawi. I knew it would be awful, eight hours of agony. I told myself to suck it up and deal with it. For the run? Whatever I had left in the tank would have to do. I pictured the Energy Lab at night and swore to myself that I would not become one of those people who lost the race on that dark stretch of pavement.

Most of all, I imagined others coming up alongside or passing me, whether on the swim, bike, or run, and I told myself not to worry about it. *Maintain your pace, or you'll exhaust yourself. Run your race, Bonner. Don't let others distract you. Don't compete with "normal." Fight your fight.*

Over the next few hours, I drifted in and out of sleep, my mind occupied by every minute and mile of the race ahead. Then, giving up on getting back to sleep, I got out of bed and went downstairs. The house was silent. I saw that some friends had posted inspirational messages on the walls: "Now Take Your Place in History" and "You Will Triumph." I slid open the patio doors so I could hear the surf rushing through the blowhole. I made some gluten-free oatmeal with fresh fruit on top, the same breakfast I had had for the past six months, and some coffee. While I was eating, I e-mailed Welchy, thanking him for everything he had done to train and prepare me for the Kona Ironman.

His reply arrived within minutes. "I am a huge Bonner fan! I love you so, so much and have a careful way of showing it," he started. "Enough blowing hot wind under your lame-ass tail. . . . I want you to remember a few things. Don't get caught up in other people's pace, and don't get competitive! You have the job of staying on Bonner's pace!" He concluded, "I want you to know that I am happy for you. You deserve it, and I am . . . loaning you all my abundant energy for the day. . . . Good luck, my friend!" Reading his words, knowing how much he supported me almost left me in a pool of tears.

I recovered by reading a host of other e-mails and text messages, including one from Chrissie Wellington: "I know you will succeed. . . . Can't wait to meet you at the finish line!"

While I was in the middle of reading all these notes of love and support, Mike showed up downstairs, exactly on schedule: 4 A.M. Together we went through my gear, checking and double-checking everything, including my bottles of water with C5 mix and salt tabs. There was no need to speak, and I didn't feel like talking much anyway. I knew he had my back, and this settled me like nothing else. Soon enough, we were in the SUV headed for the start. I stared at the sliver of moon that hung in the pitch-dark sky, absentmindedly rubbing the top of my head.

"You're ready," Mike kept repeating, as he maneuvered through the traffic-bound streets. He slowed to a halt by the King Kamehameha Hotel for me to get out. We gave each other a big hug, an "I love you," and a "See you out there."

The start area was controlled mayhem. Music blared, drowning out the predawn chirps of unseen birds in the palm trees. Race volunteers in blue shirts pointed the athletes, all pumped and primed, to where they needed to go to check in, weigh in, and have their race numbers done. "Follow the crowd" was the general advice. I joined the herd, telling myself to stay calm, to breathe. When I emerged from the tents, now shirtless and with the number 1421 stamped in black on my arms, the sky was beginning to lighten.

I threaded my way through the bands of athletes to the transition area on the pier. I set up my bike computer, pumped up the tires, and placed my bottles of frozen water and C5 electrolyte mix that I had brought from the house this morning into their holders (two on the frame, two behind the seat). They would soon thaw. Then I headed over to the lawn beside the King K to stretch on the grass. My every movement was slow and deliberate, and I took care to breathe deeply. I nibbled on a Bonk Breaker bar and took a few sips of water from another water bottle.

Spectators were pouring into the area. Helicopters hovered overhead. A line of Hawaiians in tribal outfits beat on drums, ramping up the already high intensity. Every few minutes, the announcer's voice would boom out the race countdown. Already the waters of Kailua Bay were filling with swimmers, but following Welchy's advice, I remained on dry land.

"We are about ready with almost two thousand triathletes," boomed Mike Reilly, the legendary announcer of the Ironman

Championship, over the loudspeakers. "This is the hardest finish line on the planet, and you're going to get there today."

Ten minutes before the start, I joined the line of triathletes waiting to descend the narrow staircase off the pier into the water. I looked out at the sea of blue (for men) and pink (for women) caps bobbing in the bay. Many were crowded up against the wall of paddleboarders forming a start line at the opening of the bay. On the seawall surrounding the half-moon bay, thousands of spectators cheered and whistled.

This is it. No turning back now. Dig deep. Give it everything you got. This is it. This is it.

Moving slowly forward in the line, I found myself standing next to Kevin Robson, whom I had met through TYR, my swim sponsor. Although Kevin was suffering from terminal cancer, it had been his lifelong dream to race in the Ironman. Whenever I had bumped into him during the week, he had been the soul of calm. Now he looked like a man about to walk the plank. His eyes were huge, and he kept swaying back and forth, arms hugging his chest. I knew I probably looked the same. We gave each other a half smile.

"Anybody seen an ocean around here?" I asked.

Kevin laughed for a brief moment, and then Mike Reilly rang in with another countdown.

Stomach uneasy, throat dry, feeling as though I needed to urinate, when at last it was my turn, I headed down the stairs to the water. Someone called out my name. I looked up to see Chrissie Wellington, the four-time Ironman World champion, leaning over the railing and waving at me. I gave her a thumbs-up, and she shouted, "Today is your day, Bonner. Nothing will stop you. I believe in you."

I breathed deeply, wanting to believe her, and then I dropped into Kailua Bay.

13

Go Time

"Five minutes," Reilly announced over the loudspeakers. Kevin and I stood next to each other, knee-deep in the water, as we wetted our goggles and put them over our eyes.

"Who is ready to be an Ironman today?" Reilly asked. We held our arms over our heads and yawped.

"Today is *your* day," I said to Kevin, repeating Chrissie's words.

"You'll crush it," he replied. Then we hugged, wished each other luck, and said at the same time, "See you at the finish."

Then I turned, dove into the water, and swam out to find a starting spot. After I had taken a few strokes, my nerves settled somewhat. My shoulder felt okay, but I couldn't help but worry about what would happen if it flared up before the second buoy, as it had done before. I swam a hundred yards toward the shore, looking for a place away from the dense pack of swimmers, so I could avoid getting kicked and punched—especially in the shoulder.

"Avoid the scrum," Welchy had told me. "You're not going to win the race, mate, so just make sure you get to a place where you can settle in and be efficient."

I found a spot where there was nobody within an arm's length of me. From the seawall, spectators yelled and clapped. The drum line was booming with increasing intensity. Overhead, the helicopters whoop-whoop-whooped. My heart was pounding so heavily I could feel it in my temples. A minute, less, until the start.

"It's go time!" I chanted several times, the tension almost overwhelming.

I dipped down below the surface of the water and asked for strength from Bompa. The ocean was his home, and if there was any place he would hear me, it was here.

Let's do this, Bompa. You and me together.

When I emerged, an unusual calm fell over me. A peace. Four years ago, driven by fear, pain, anger, and a need to prove myself to others, I had faced down Mt. Kilimanjaro. Now, in Kona, at the Iron-man World Championship, I felt none of that negative emotion. The fun-house mirror showed a very different picture of me than before. I was there to prove to myself that there were no limits to what *I* could do. I was there to show the world that they should never put limits on children with disabilities. I was there to represent all those people who supported me, to represent the OM Foundation and all the kids it would help. And most of all, I was there to race my race, fight my fight.

The announcer was now counting down in seconds. Two thousand heads bobbed up and down in the water.

You have done all you can do to prepare for this. You belong here. It will be a brutal long day, but you can do this. You are going to do this. Nothing will stop you.

The cannon boomed, and I leaned forward to take my first stroke. It looked as if someone had dipped a giant hand blender into the bay. The clear water churned and quickly grew murky. I concentrated on staying away from other swimmers and maintaining my stroke—not too fast, not too slow. I reminded myself I had already swum this course. The key was to take it little by little, nothing more. Five buoys out, a total of roughly 1.1 miles. The turnaround by the catamaran, maybe another 0.2 miles. Then five buoys back to the pier for the complete 2.4 miles. My goal was to emerge from the water in an hour and a half.

A couple of hundred yards into the course, my body relaxed. I stroked easily; there was no pain in my shoulder, not even the slightest twinge. The ocean was calm, the swells at most 5 feet high, so I didn't have to worry too much about how far I angled my head out of the water to take a breath. I glided smoothly through the bay.

One, two, three strokes. Breathe on the left. One, two, three strokes. Breathe on the right.

I kept reminding myself to maintain form. Legs up. Don't let them be a rudder. Little kicks spaced out more than my strokes. Arms extended straight out from my shoulders. Pull back strong, hands relaxed. Roll easy, left and right, not too much. By the first buoy, I was feeling very strong. My goggles were beginning to fog up, but I told myself not to let it bother me. That always happened at the start, maybe because I was breathing more heavily. They usually cleared themselves. Keep the strokes going. One, two, three. Breathe.

Through the haze of my goggles, I identified some swimmers who were moving at the same pace I was and angled my way toward them. If I wedged myself in between them, they would guide my direction, and I could focus on maintaining my stroke. I zipped past the second buoy. It was a good 15 feet away, which meant that my two "guides" were not exactly leading me on the straightest path, but that was okay. I might be swimming a little farther than necessary, but since I didn't have to raise my head above water to take my line of sight, I was conserving energy. A fair trade-off.

One, two, three. Breathe. One, two, three. Breathe.

Between that point and the next couple of buoys, I found myself surging past one swimmer after another. It was obvious I was making good time, but this meant that I was catching up with the main body of competitors. Soon I was being crowded in by the scrum. A few times I had to slow up to avoid a kick in the head or surge ahead when someone hit my feet with their own strokes.

A part of me wanted to stay with the pack. But the constant back-and-forth was messing with my concentration and throwing off my rhythm. *Fight your fight, Bonner.* I needed to stick to my pace. After veering off, I reached the line of paddleboarders who followed the swimmers along the course in case anybody got into trouble. They maintained a fairly straight line, and I decided to switch to using them as my visual guide along the course.

Now completely clear of the other swimmers, I hit the groove with my stroke, moving effortlessly across the surface. For a spell, I almost forgot that I was only at the beginning of a very, very long race. Everything was peaceful. I observed the sun slanting through the crystal-clear water and the pools of colorful fish gliding through the deep below me. I thought again of Bompa, of how he used to look when he was moving in slow motion through the ocean. He was such a relaxed, efficient, and steady swimmer, and in that moment I became one too.

I soon reached the fifth buoy and readied to make the turn to the right around the catamaran sailboat. But when I lifted my head out of the water to spot the floating turnaround point, it was far ahead in the distance. I didn't understand. The catamaran should be right after the fifth buoy. I wondered if I had miscounted the number of buoys—or maybe the catamaran had drifted off course. Something was wrong. If I had been wearing a swim watch, I could have checked my time, but I had decided against one, my pace so ingrained after almost two years of training. But now my uncertainty threw me out of my rhythm. There was nothing to do but follow the others. *Don't let this bother you. Don't dwell on it. Keep swimming.*

Another stretch, and I closed in on the catamaran. Somewhere along the way I worked out that the race organizers must have added more buoys to mark the course better. The herd of swimmers tightened at the clockwise turn around the catamaran. I remained on the outside. It was a short swim to the next buoy, which was the final turn before the long straight return.

Halfway there now, and the swim back to the pier favored me. I was right-side dominant, and the strokes from my right arm always carried a little more force. On the return, this advantage would nudge me slightly away from shore, while the swells would push me in. The two would balance each other out, leaving me on a straight line without extra effort. I continued to track the position of the paddleboarders out of the corner of my eye.

Moving powerfully through the water, I imagined the booming music I would hear once we came back within earshot of the pier. The crowds would greet our return. The announcer would yell out the race numbers of the competitors emerging from the water. "Bonner Paddock, Number 1421." It would be a sweet sound, one-third of the Ironman done.

As I swam toward the next buoy, I took a few extra breaths now and again, but still I felt little strain. All the hours in the pool, fine-tuning my stroke and putting in the laps, were paying off. Thanks to Mike, I was perfectly at ease in the ocean, rolling naturally with the swells, not fighting against myself.

Fog began to creep along the edges of my goggles and then completely blurred my vision. Stopping to rinse them, I gazed around me. Competitors surged ahead all around me, chopping the water with their rhythmic strokes. The finish was three-quarters of a mile away and far out of sight. Still a long way to go. Goggles clear, I took a couple of long breaths and then got back to it. Not 20 yards later, I felt a little twinge in my right shoulder. *Put it out of your mind. It is nothing. You are on your way to the pier.*

With every minute, the pain in my shoulder grew worse. I tried to lengthen my strokes to minimize the number I would need to finish. I lightened up how much I pulled through the water as well. Both helped slightly, but I knew I would have to fight through to the end. It wouldn't be an issue for the bike and run, but I needed to make sure that the pain did not slow me down too much now, forcing me to speed up on the rest of the course. Everything was a balancing act, and any one thing could throw off the rest of the race. *Little victories. Just get to the next buoy, then the next. Don't let your mind wander beyond that.*

I needed to focus on the present moment, to make sure that my stroke, shoulder problem or no shoulder problem, was as efficient as it could be. I bore down, keeping my head in the water, not looking up to see if I was nearing the next buoy or the one after that. They could look after themselves.

One, two, three. Breathe. One, two, three. Breathe.

Eventually, I regained some rhythm with my stroke, forcing the pain into that good old place, deep inside me. Pain would do me no good. It was only a distraction. I swam on, losing myself in the steady stroke of my arms into the water. Left, right, left, right—the roll of my body between each. My shoulder was nothing. Insignificant. I could continue forever.

Then I turned my head to take a breath and heard music. The swells lessened, and I knew I was approaching the pier. Once inside the harbor, the surface flattened, and the music blaring by the transition area vibrated through the water. Only a tenth of a mile now. Eager to finish the swim, to get out of the water and hop onto my bike, I surged ahead, adrenaline carrying me. My goggles fogged up completely, and my right shoulder felt as if someone had plunged a knife into it, but none of that mattered now. The swim was at its end.

Before I reached the beach, I pulled up and stood for a moment in chest-level water. I had learned in training that it took me a few moments to regain my body balance after a long swim. The deep water kept me from pitching over. I cautiously walked to the beach and took off my goggles. As I climbed the steps, I heard my name being chanted somewhere in the sea of spectators. By a huge banyan tree stood a band of my supporters. I couldn't miss them, they were all wearing their big blue cowboy hats. They jumped up and down and shook their fists, going crazy at my arrival. My spirits soared at the sight of them, and I pumped my fist up and down. The swim was over, and my shoulder had held out to the finish.

At the top of the steps, I saw a big digital timer. It read one hour, twenty-four minutes. I didn't believe it. How could I have beaten my goal time by six minutes, particularly with my stroke thrown out so badly?

"Is that the race clock?" I asked the nearest race official. "Or some other timer?"

"That's the race clock," she said, with a happy smile.

"Yes!" I pumped my fist again and headed for the transition area.

I rinsed the saltwater off my body under a garden-hose shower. Then I headed toward the line of volunteers waiting with buckets of sunscreen. After the half Ironman, when I had almost baked the outline of my jersey permanently into my skin, I took my sweet time at this station.

"Don't be shy," I said. "Really lather me up. I'll be out there a *long* time."

"You'll do great," a female volunteer said encouragingly.

When I emerged from the sunscreen station, I looked as if I had taken a bath in the slick white paste. Everybody seemed to be running past me down the lanes to their bikes, grabbing them from the racks, and chugging out of there at top speed. My instinct was to follow them, but then I reminded myself again of what Welchy had told me: "This is you against the course. Do your best. Nothing else." Anyway, I had killed the swim course. On closer inspection, I realized that my bike, in all its Cannondale glory, was one of the few remaining. *Killed it, huh?* I chuckled to myself. *Okay, big boy.*

I sat down beside my bike and drank a small bottle of my C5 mixed drink, knowing I needed the nutrition after the long swim. Slowly, methodically, I put on my socks and clip shoes, turned on my bike computer, and then checked and double-checked that I had all my GUs, water bottles, and Bonk Breaker bars. Nothing could be left to chance. Then I donned my bike helmet and the red-and-white-framed sunglasses with the OM Foundation symbol etched on the left lens, which Oakley had made especially for me for this race.

Eleven minutes after leaving the ocean, I mounted my bike and clipped in my left shoe. In the distance, I could hear people chanting my name. I said a little prayer to Jake to give me the strength I needed for the brutal test ahead. Then, pushing off and clipping in my other shoe, I rode around the curving corridor lined with spectators. On either side of me was a small army of blue-hatted supporters, who went wild as I passed. The sight of them boosted my spirits, and I returned a big smile. I wanted to give them a thumbs-up—"Hey! I'm feeling good!"—but I kept both hands on the bars. As usual I was feeling a little wobbly on the bike.

Almost immediately I came to a hill, and I muttered, "Welcome to hell on earth." The next 112 miles would be hot, humid, and a real ass-buster. My target time was eight hours. Longer than that, and I would have to push too hard on the marathon to make it to the finish by midnight. A lot longer than eight hours, and I would miss the cutoff time to finish the bike course (5:30 P.M.) and be removed from the race altogether.

Fighting the instinct to charge up this first hill, I told myself to take it slowly, stick to an easy gear, and get settled in. Even now, after months on the RevMaster, then more than a year training on the open road, there was nothing comfortable for me about being on the bike. My feet locked into the clips, my legs never straightening out, my upper body hunched continuously over the handlebars—all of it was like kryptonite working against my cerebral palsy. Hour after hour, it would slowly break me down.

Added to this, I needed to focus completely on what I was doing to maintain my balance. "It's like riding a bike" meant something very different for me than for most people. The action—or scores of small actions that made up riding a bike—had never become second-nature to me.

After I crested the first hill, too pumped up on adrenaline to feel any burn, I began the loop through Kona that made up the first 8 miles of the bike course. My legs warmed up quickly in the already stifling heat at 9 A.M. On the sharp downhill curve leading from Palani Highway onto Kuakini Highway, I passed by another crowd of Bonner blue hats who whooped and hollered for me.

I rode a long, straight flat, then up another hill, and back along Kuakini. I kept reminding myself, *Cadence, cadence, cadence.* No matter

the terrain, Welchy wanted me to maintain the eighty to ninety rotations per minute. Feeling good, not straining too much, I passed
the first-aid station without stopping and returned past the string
of blue cowboy hats bouncing up and down at the intersection of
Palani and Kuakini. When I banked right, back up steep Palani, I
shifted down into "granny gear."

As I labored up the hill, Zach and Tyler Robert jogged beside me
on the grassy traffic island. "Go Bonner!" they yelled.

Soon I left them behind. Nearing the top of the climb, I was
breathing heavily and was finally feeling the effort in my legs. When
I turned onto Queen Ka'ahumanu Highway, I knew what was ahead:
100 miles of closed-down road, most of it away from the spectators.
No more of the Bonner army. My energy level took a hit, and I already felt lonely. Fortunately, there was a tailwind and a downhill
slope at the beginning of the highway. Crouched and resting my
forearms on my Aero handlebars, I settled into a rhythm.

I broke the course down into small segments, setting one goal
after the next. This made the ride much less intimidating. My first
goal was the Kailua-Kona International Airport, Mile 15. The highway gradually turned uphill, but it was a smooth, gentle slope,
helped by the wind on my back. I knew this same wind would be in
my face on the return to Kona, but at this point it did me no good
to think about that. I passed the Energy Lab and tried to push away
the thought of that point in the marathon, still so many, many hours
away. *Small bites. You can only chew a little at a time.*

By the airport, I stopped at an aid station and unclipped from my
pedals. Still straddling my bike, I asked for some ice. Welchy had
advised me to take an ice bath at every station to numb my hip
flexors and weary muscles and, more important, to lower my core

temperature in the blistering Big Island heat. "Keep the core cool, or it's game over."

A volunteer offered me a small cup of ice chips, but I shook my head.

"I need big chunks," I said.

Someone else pointed to a plastic bag–lined trashcan filled to the brim with ice. With my balance and rigid muscles, getting off my bike would not be easy. Instead, I lifted it up between my legs and awkwardly hobbled over to the trashcan. Dipping my hand deep into it, I found an oblong block, lifted it out with one hand, and with the other pulled out the waistband of my bike shorts. "Mate," Welchy had said, "your dick is going to hate you for the next eight hours, but if it works, then you won't feel it." I took a deep breath and lowered the ice into my shorts.

"Who-ah!" I exclaimed as the cold hit me. "Hello!"

I dumped more ice down the back of my shorts as well as down the front and back of my shirt and inside my helmet. One volunteer gave me a strange look, like "This guy is bat-shit crazy," but the more experienced ones staffing the station didn't give me a glance. I was sure they had seen stranger rituals than this one over the years. The ice bit into my skin, particularly in my more delicate regions, but it definitely cooled me down.

Over the next several miles, I kept up a good cadence. Passing the turnoff to the palatial grounds of the Four Seasons, I was surprised by a small cluster of Bonner blue hats who held up a sign that read, "Go, Bonner! Go!" This stoked me up for long enough to reach the next aid station.

After that, the temperature and trade winds off the coast picked up big-time. The Queen K now cut across an almost completely barren landscape. The two-lane highway crossed the fields of cooled lava that had flowed from Mauna Loa. Some stretches, the oldest flows, were brown in color, as the fields had broken down over time into clumps of rock and mud, where pockets of straw-colored grass grew. Other stretches, from more recent flows, were as black as coal and had the sheen of glass. The sun reflected sharply off this lava rock, which pulsed with the heat.

Breaking up the monotony of these fields were messages written with bits of white coral for passersby. Some were declarations of love: "NB + DB." Many others were for the Ironman racers: "Race Tracy Race" or "Go Bob Go. Move Your Fat Ass." I only saw a few of these messages. My head was down most of the time, looking only a few feet ahead of me on the asphalt.

On and on I rode, heading north, the extinct volcano Mauna Kea looming closer with each passing mile. Whenever I emerged from a cutout in the highway, the wind howled, trying to throw me from my bike. I held on tight and kept pedaling, forever pedaling. I crossed Wailua Bay off my to-do list at roughly the two-hour mark. Mile 32, done and dusted. Then Hapuna Bay, twenty minutes later, Mile 38.

The sun was now blasting down on me at 11 A.M. The chunks of ice I poured into my shorts and shirt at each aid station melted quickly. The runoff, mixed with my sweat, flooded down my legs and soaked into my shoes. Despite constant sips at my water bottle, I couldn't quench my thirst, and my hips and quads were beginning to burn.

Near Kawaihae Road, where I would turn off the Queen K, Kevin Robson passed me. I muttered some kind of hello. He turned back in his seat and offered encouragement. I knew I must now be the one who looked as though he was in deep trouble. It did not help that many of the elite athletes were now roaring past on their return from Hawi. I tried to look up to see who was in the lead, but they were blurs. The lucky bastards were on their way home, and I still had 80 miles more to go. *So be it. Keep moving.*

After turning onto Kawaihae, I started to get hungry—very hungry. Nibbling on a Bonk Breaker every quarter hour was just not doing the trick, and I stared ravenously at the GUs taped to my bike frame. Welchy had warned me not to have them until Mile 80, on the way back from Hawi. That seemed like an eternity away.

On the last downhill stretch before the long, brutally steep hill up to Hawi, I felt as if I were riding straight into an industrial-sized blow-dryer. The air was hot, humid, and gusting straight into my face. I hunkered down low on my Aero bars, but that did little but make my lower back tighten up. I was dreading the 17-mile straight uphill climb soon to come, and my thoughts started to turn black.

I pulled over at the aid station outside Kawaihae Village and got off my bike to stretch and go to the bathroom.

As I stood up straight for the first time in almost three hours, it seemed as though all my blood rushed down to my feet. I was suddenly lightheaded and wobbly. It took a few minutes before I recovered enough to do my stretches. These eased the spasms in my back and legs. All too soon I was straddling my bike again, ready to return to my tortured hunched position. Before clipping in, I closed my eyes, took a few deep breaths, and spoke quietly to myself. *Okay, Bonner. You're hurting. So what. Stop whining. This is going to suck. Fine.*

Not a mile into the ascent to Hawi, I was struggling. My stomach had tightened into a hard ball. The heat was messing with my body, and though desperate for food and water, I couldn't face either. I forced myself to eat and drink, which made me even more nauseous. It was a vicious cycle worsened by the inescapable heat. I continued to take my ice baths at the aid stations, but they no longer seemed to make a difference.

I crawled up the long hill, my speed half of what it had been earlier on the course. Frustrated at seeing the single miles-per-hour digits on my bike computer, I stopped looking. Instead, I focused on my bike frame and envisioned reaching the turnaround.

Pain started to creep around my toes and instep with each rotation of the pedals, soon enveloping both feet. I tried to figure out what the problem was. I had never experienced any blistering in my training or in my other races, but that was what it felt like—kind of. Water from the melting ice and sweat continued to run down my legs into my shoes, and I suspected that the problem might be something to do with my wet socks. There was nothing I could do about it now. I needed the ice to cool down my core, and I certainly didn't have a spare set of shoes or socks. *Pedal over pedal. Best as you can.*

Every single mile was harder than the one before. Halfway up to Hawi, I felt as though I was fighting my way up sheer rock face. The harder I drove on the pedals, the worse my feet hurt. I didn't know how much longer I could continue. For a moment, I thought maybe I should walk my bike up for a while, but then I pushed the idea away. If I got off now, that would be it for me. I churned onward, and then, like a gift from heaven, the scorching hot sun disappeared behind some clouds. The relief carried me for another quarter of a mile.

Then the winds picked up. The sky darkened, and all of sudden it started to rain. At first the shower felt cool on my hot skin, but then it started to pour. In the gusting winds, the rain pelted my face. I tried to turn my head away to avoid the onslaught, but the wind was blowing straight at me, and there was no escaping the deluge. Looking up at the sky, I laughed and shouted, "Really?! Are you kidding me? What are you going to throw at me next!?"

It didn't take long for me to find out.

14

Man of Iron

On the hillside leading up to Hawi, a scattering of skeleton trees, their trunks bleached white, had been permanently bent by the trade winds. My back and legs ached to be straight, but any time I tried to stand up on my pedals, those same winds tried to knock me off my bike, hurling little spikes of rain into my face while they were at it. Hawi was 4.1 miles away. Four miles. A little farther my bike computer indicated 3.9 miles.

All that training, all that distance, week after week, had now boiled down to counting down one-tenth of a mile, then another. To be assaulted by the elements on this, the steepest and windiest leg of the bike course was pure misery and frustration. I was going at a crawling pace too, and one racer after another passed me by coming down from Hawi. As much as I tried not to let them bother me, my spirits sank with each one who passed. *Time to fire up the furnace.*

Desperate to push onward but failing to find the strength, I reached for anger again, turning to thoughts of my youth, all the jabs and jibes, feeling different, outside the norm. I thought of my family, the years of separation and distance. All those memories had spurred me forward on Kilimanjaro, but now, as I called upon them once more, they didn't burn nearly as brightly or for as long. By accepting my cerebral palsy, by healing myself, I had also exhausted the power of these memories over me.

Searching for fuel, I thought then of my friend John Winn, who had passed away after a long battle with non-Hodgkin's lymphoma the year before. I thought about one day when I visited him at his house after yet another round of treatments. Sitting in his recliner, an IV drip by his side, he had no color in his face, and his shoulders shivered slightly. It was all right, he said. He promised to beat the cancer. He would have a full life with his wife and young son. I thought of the sunset on that October evening, walking into a charity concert headlined by Donavon Frankenreiter, whom John loved, and getting the call that he had died. Now 2.8 miles, 2.7. *Give me some strength, John. I need it, big man.*

I threw all the grief at John's death into the furnace, but what really stoked the flames was the thought of how he had promised never to give up his fight, the thought of the love and support he and his wife had shown each other. John had been sure he would see me race in Hawaii. Spurred on by his memory, I hunkered down over my bike frame and pushed my way up the final couple of miles to Hawi.

Mile 60. Only 52 to go. At the turnaround point by a small general store, there was an aid station and bag depot, where the day before I had left some fresh C5-mix bottles and a supply of Bonk Breaker bars and GUs. I unclipped and stopped my bike, but when I tried to dismount, my right leg wouldn't cooperate—it was too stiff. I was forced to lay my bike down to the ground to get clear of it. The soles of my feet felt like someone had been rubbing sandpaper on them for the past four hours.

As I moved toward the bag depot, I started with my calculations. It was 12:40 P.M., close to when I had hoped to reach Hawi. I wanted to be finished with the bike course by 5 P.M., which would give me a full seven hours to finish the marathon before midnight. That left me with a little over four hours to complete the bike course to be on target—and less than five hours to avoid the course cutoff time that would end my Kona Ironman ambition before I even got to the run. There was little room for error.

A father-and-son volunteer team handed me my bag, and as I put the new bottles into the rack on my bike, they were really encouraging. "You're doing great!"

"Do you want to drive me home?" I asked.

They laughed and waved me on, then turned to the next racer. A quick stretch, then I was back on my bike, mule-kicking my way on the pavement to get up some momentum. The rain stopped, and though the road was still wet, I hauled like a maniac down the hill for the next 6 miles. It was a great relief to cover those miles with no effort other than making sure I didn't go splat on any of the turns.

I passed a number of racers who were still on their way up to Hawi. Many were crawling. Others were pulled up on the side of the road and appeared to be in trouble. Farther down the hill, I came across the first pair of Grim Reapers and their van with its flashing lights. They were stopped beside a competitor who was bent over his bike. From the looks of concern on their faces, they were asking him if he wanted to continue, if he could even hope to finish the course before the cutoff.

Over the next 10 miles, I guzzled through my water faster than I had planned, and every couple of minutes a wave of nausea swept over me. I had long since exhausted the relief from going downhill, and now a terrible weariness sank into my bones. I struggled to reach the top of the hill before the turn back onto the Queen K. It hadn't seemed so steep on the way down, but now I realized that it was an absolute bear. The wind cut at me from right to left, and I gripped my handlebars tight. The road seemed empty of other racers, and I felt alone in the world. Halfway up, I couldn't continue and pulled over to the side.

I got off my bike and, leaning against the metal road barricade, I splashed some water on my face and took a few deep breaths. I could barely handle the weight of my body on my feet without wincing. "All right, Johnny boy, I need some more of that fighting spirit," I said. Just voicing the words seemed to help. I stretched again, trying to loosen my spasming hamstrings, and then I mounted my bike again. If I kept stopping like this, I wouldn't even make the cutoff, let alone my target time. I needed to keep going, whatever the suffering, whatever the price. "Jakey, I need you to give me your strength. Juliana. Paige. Ashley. I need you too. Come on guys. I can't do it alone."

I forced my way back up the hill, each and every rotation of the pedals a triumph. At last I made it to the Queen K; 35 miles left on the course. As long as I maintained an average speed of 12 miles per hour, I'd reach the finish of the bike course with a half-hour cushion before the 5:30 P.M. cutoff.

For the next three hours, I continued to check my bike computer constantly, calculating how much time I had left before the cutoff versus how many miles I had left and what speed I needed to maintain to make it on time. I broke the ride down into increments of a minute, maybe two. Just reach that hill, that tree, that cutout, that straightaway. I occupied my mind with calculations and little victories. At the least it distracted me from my lifeless legs and the spikes of pain in my feet.

I passed Mauna Lani, which is where the transition to the run had been in May for Honu, the half Ironman. I wished I were doing the half again, that I could just turn in there, run a half marathon, and be done. It made no sense, but I was wishing for a lot at that moment. More downhills. Less wind. Less heat. That my hands would ache less from gripping the handlebars. That my back didn't feel like a steel beam. There was nothing to be done about any of these wishes, so I kept my head down, kept drinking my mix and sucking down my GUs on schedule, and kept turning those pedals, one after the other.

I reached the top of another hill and spotted a new target: the airport. *Getting there now,* I thought. Given my latest fuzzy math, I had a cushion of thirty to forty minutes before the cutoff if I maintained my speed. An NBC camera crew rolled by my side for a spell, asking how I was doing, how I was feeling. I gave them a smile and a thumbs-up.

"Looking good," one of the crew said.

I knew I probably looked like death on wheels, but they were a welcome distraction. Then they sped off, and I was alone again, me, my bike, and the narrow white line at the center of the Queen K. *Just pedal those damn pedals.*

At the next aid station, by the airport, I took my final ice bath and sucked down some C5 mix, water, and GUs, in order, as Welchy had advised. It was 3:45 P.M. I had 17 miles to go. Continuing to average 12 miles per hour, I was sure I was going to make it now. I began passing people on the side of the highway who were holding up signs and cheering as we passed. This gave me a welcome lift. I came to the Energy Lab, where a stream of runners was filing in and a stream was filing out. I forced away the thought of that obstacle to come as well as the envy of those leaving the lab who were less than 10 miles from finishing the race, and I was still on my bike. *They had their race. I had mine.*

At Mile 110, approaching Kona, I allowed myself a smile. I would make my target time at least, and if not, then definitely the cutoff. Even if I got a flat, I'd ride into town on the rims. I'd carry the bike across the line if needed. Nothing was stopping me. Nothing.

When I turned into town, I saw a crowd of blue cowboy hats. They roared when they saw me, and I sat up on my saddle and roared back. The relief of approaching the finish of the bike course overwhelmed me. Several times I pumped my fist, not even thinking that I was risking a crash with only one hand on the bars. Mike called out, "Yeah, bro!" and was practically in tears as I passed him. He looked almost as relieved to see me as I was to see him. A woman blew a whistle and called out to each racer crossing her path, "You are fantastic! You are a winner!"

At 4:46 P.M., eight hours and two seconds after clipping into my pedals, I finished the bike course.

I unclipped from my pedals and dismounted. A blast of pain shot from my feet, exploding into my head. It completely took my breath away. To shake it off, I tried a few steps, but each was more crippling than the last. Race volunteers took my bike and passed me my running bag. I stumbled toward the transition tent, eager to take off my shoes to see what the problem was.

Inside the nearly empty tent, two volunteers led me to a chair. The buzz I had felt at completing the bike leg was already gone. I leaned over and slowly took off each shoe. This alone delivered jolts of pain from my throbbing feet. Now I needed to take off my socks, which were soaked with melted ice, sweat, and, judging by their pink color, blood as well.

"Anything we can do?" asked one volunteer.

"What do you have for pain?"

"Advil."

"As many as you can give me."

As he went off to get the ibuprofen, the other volunteer looked down at my feet. "Can I help you with those?" he asked.

It was difficult to lean over because of my stiff back, and whenever I did the blood rushed to my head. The muscles in my legs were also too locked up to bend one over the other. I took a deep breath and nodded. The volunteer kneeled down to peel off my left sock. There are no words for the level of agony I felt at the first movement of the sock. I grunted and groaned as he almost got the sock halfway off, but then it became too much to bear.

"Stop," I begged. "Stop."

The other volunteer returned with the Advil. I downed several and closed my eyes, worried about how I was going to get these socks off, but also, and more so, by what state my feet were in underneath the cotton. Added to this was a sense of urgency: I needed to hurry and get on that run course.

I waved to the volunteer to continue. Holding my breath, hands balled into fists, nails pressed into flesh, I stared up at the roof of the tent as he peeled off one sock, then the other.

When the two volunteers saw the state of my feet, they gasped. I looked down to see that the skin on the soles and sides of my feet and toes was bubbled, raw, and peeling off in several layers. Over the past eight hours, the combination of the wet socks and the awkward way I pushed down on the pedals had made a mess.

An ice towel was placed on the back of my neck, and I felt some momentary relief.

"Sweet baby Jesus, that is so good," I said before the horror of my feet returned.

Both volunteers looked at me in the way that said, "You've done great, buddy, but maybe your race, this race, is done."

"I need to get my shoes on," I said.

They gave me brave smiles and bent down to help me. Every time they touched my feet, no matter how gently, an eruption of pain followed. I leaned back in my chair, closed my eyes, and focused on pushing the pain so deep inside me that it had no impact. *It's just a feeling, and it's of no use to you. It's in your head. You can control it. Push it down and away, and don't ever let it up.*

"You're all set," said one of the volunteers. I opened my eyes to find that my shoes were on my feet. Now I needed to stand. I tried to push myself up in my chair, but my legs were locked. "Can you help me up?"

One volunteer lifted me up with a hand underneath my arm. The other pushed me from behind. The second I stood, a dozen razor blades were slicing away at my feet. I almost dropped back down to the chair, but I knew that if I did that, my Ironman would be over.

"Just give me a second," I said, a hundred expletives rushing into my head, and probably a few out my mouth as well. *It's just a feeling. It's of no use to you. You can control it.*

"Are you really going to do this?" asked one volunteer.

I nodded and took a step forward, barely lifting my foot off the ground. Slice, slash went the razor blades. Then another step. Slice, slash. After the third step, I stopped and put a hand on the table beside me, trying to muster up the courage to continue.

The idea of pain was so familiar, it was more than just a friend—it was a live-in roommate without a girlfriend or a job. It was always there, always unmistakable. This, however, was something else altogether. At once different from anything that I'd known, and yet somehow familiar. It was too great to simply bury it within myself, so I opened my arms and accepted it. As uncomfortable as it was, it was the only way I could make my body move.

The two volunteers stayed at my side, hands out, as if they expected me to fall at any moment. I wanted to, but I had a race to finish.

"All right," I said. "Time to go set a new world record in the marathon."

They didn't know whether to laugh or cry. "Go get 'em!" said one.

"Thanks."

I shuffled my way over to the exit. Slice, slash. Slice, slash. Each step was a horror, but I just pushed onward, accepting it.

Outside, I was stirred alive by the booming voice of Mike Reilly. The Ironman announcer stalked the finish line from the time the first elite athletes came through right up to the cutoff, heralding the arrival of each and every competitor with the words, delivered in his inimitable style, "You are an Ironman!" The finish was only a stone's throw from the transition area, and competitors were already coming in, one after the other.

It didn't matter to me that the elite triathletes had long since finished their race or that many more runners were completing their marathon when I hadn't even started mine. It didn't matter to me that the bike racks were full, that the transition area was nearly empty. I was probably in eighteen-hundredth place or something. As I made my way to the start of the marathon course, the only thing I could think of was how sweet it would sound for Mike Reilly to announce my name: "Bonner Paddock. You are an Ironman!"

When I emerged from the transition area, an army of blue hats chanted my name and cheered me on. I high-fived them down the line, the pain in my feet forgotten for a moment. My good friend Jesse accompanied me for a time, from behind the barrier fence, calling on me to keep going. Another friend, Carl, acting like a high-school football coach gone mad, shook his fist at me and screamed at the top of his lungs. "You are a badass, Bonner! A! Bad! Ass!" Mike trailed beside me as well, his voice far more calm and assured. "You have this, bro. You have this."

All too soon, though, I had left them behind, and I set off through Kona at a brisk walk. Other competitors ran past me on their last mile of the race.

My watch read 4:55 P.M., which gave me a little over seven hours to complete the marathon. With my calculations—always more calculations—I had to average sixteen-and-a-half-minute miles to cross the finish before the cutoff. That was not much more than a light jog, but with my feet, with the hours' exertion in the heat still to come, the continued strain on my muscles, and the possibility of losing my ability to continue no matter how strong my will to do so, nothing was certain. *Run your race. You've done the training. You have to finish.*

For the first half hour, heading south out of town for the 10-mile loop down Alii Drive along the coast, I barely endured the excruciation of my feet. Any time I tried to pick up my pace to a jog, the punishment became too much and I would slow back down to a walk. I would have wept from the pain, but as on Kilimanjaro, I knew that if I gave in to that emotion, I was done. My suffering was made even more pitiful because of the huge celebration erupting in Kona Village. The bars and restaurants were packed, and people, some of whom had competed earlier that day, were drinking and jamming to music on the balconies and outdoor patios.

All that fun—and the first taste of beer in six months—will be yours soon enough. Just cross the line before the stroke of midnight.

More and more I was talking to myself—any distraction to get me another hundred yards along the course. I focused on swinging my arms in a nice rhythm, back and forth, back and forth, to propel my body forward, just as Welchy had taught me. Slowly, my muscles loosened up after the long hours hunched over my bike, but the pain in my feet never dulled.

I thought about Juliana, how before her surgery she walked on her knees to get around and how much determination she must have had to endure such pain. I promised myself that I'd fight through any pain to finish.

At Mile 2, some friends, including a young woman named Karen, whose soccer team I used to coach with her father, joined me and kept me company from the opposite side of the road.

"You're doing great," Karen called out. "Looking good."

The distraction helped me settle into a rhythm. The ruby-red sunset over the water helped as well. My stride lengthened, and on the slight downhill I even picked up into a jog. This feel-good moment lasted for a couple of miles, but then my energy level sagged again, and all the agony returned.

Near the turnaround on Alii Drive, Mile 5, I stepped into a porta-potty, the first time I had needed to use the bathroom in a long while. My body, beginning to have a mind of its own, did not know what to make of the sudden stop, and as I tried to turn around, all my muscles locked up again. Scarcely managing to take care of business and free myself from the stinking green box, I knew I couldn't stop again—to use the bathroom, to take a drink, for anything. Everything would have to be done in motion.

On the return into town, Karen continued slightly behind me, but as a distraction it was losing its effect. I kept up a good pace, but my feet were being pummeled into bloody pulp. The sky darkened into night, and a race official on a scooter pulled up and handed me some glow necklaces to wear. I tried not to imagine that they could also be used to find me if I collapsed and stumbled off the road.

"Doing good," he said.

"Thanks," I muttered. Even the effort of speaking was too much.

I had hoped that the temperatures would ease with nightfall, but by Mile 6 I was scorching hot. My temples almost burned to the touch. I took off my hat to cool down, but this provided little relief. What was more, my stomach was grumbling badly. Twelve hours of eating nothing but GUs and Bonk Breakers was twisting my system into some horrific knots.

Turning to Karen, I said, "I'm not feeling so great."

"You are doing great. Just try and keep it up," she said.

I grimaced, eased down to a light jog, and prayed that this sudden fever was temporary. At the Mile-7 aid station, I downed some water, then some Coke, then some Perform drink, and then some more water. Not surprisingly, I was only a couple of hundred yards away when the urge to urinate came over me. There was no stopping, and on a dark patch on Alii Drive I pissed in my shorts for the first time. It was humiliating, disgusting, and satisfying all at once. *Everybody does it. That's what Welchy says.*

At Mile 9, just before entering town, I drank some more water, and another couple of hundred yards away I had to let it flow again. It was clear that my body was rushing through any liquids I gave it, and if this continued, I would dehydrate, overheat, and, even worse, bonk. Then I would be sure bait for the Grim Reapers, who were now following a couple runners heading south on Alii who had little chance of finishing before midnight.

Slowing to a walk, I headed back into town. I heard the distant boom of Mike Reilly announcing the most recent finishers. I tried to think again what it would be like to hear my name called, but at that moment in time I felt a very long way from being an Ironman. After turning off Alii, I lost Karen in the crowds gathering in Kona. Everything around me started to blur, and I forged onward, numbly, constantly looking at my watch as if it had answers to some question I was too delirious to ask. My walk became little more than a shuffle as I reached the steep climb up Palani Road.

Just like when I was heading out on the bike course, the Robert family was waiting for me on the traffic island that split the road. Zach and Tyler called out my name and gave me encouraging thumbs-up. Hurting bad, preoccupied by my slow pace and feverish heat, I barely uttered a word back to them. It was as if they were speaking to somebody else. I trudged up the hill, trying to reckon how long it would take me to finish the race at this sluggish seventeen-minute-mile pace. At the Queen K, I turned left and headed out toward the Energy Lab. *Ten miles down. You're in double digits.*

Running north on the highway, I sank into the pitch-black of night, my way lit only by the headlamp I carried in my hand. There were lava fields to either side of me, no cars, and only an occasional runner passing in the other direction. The only thing to listen to was my slow, erratic stride and my heaving breaths. I had never felt so alone and so isolated, and given my deteriorating physical state, I felt something I hadn't experienced all day: fear.

Any hope that my feet would somehow resolve themselves was now lost. Even at a slow jog, they were being hammered into a mash of bone and flesh. At times, it took every single ounce of focus I had left to shove down the agony. If I pulled back any more on my pace, I'd never make the midnight cutoff.

The aid stations were oases in the desert of the dark. Every time I passed one, I started yearning for the next. Not 50 yards after the Mile 15 aid station, I lost the fluids I had taken in only moments before. I still had so far to go, and I was yo-yoing between chills and fever.

"Hurry up, you lazy ass!" came a voice from behind. Welchy puttered up beside me on a scooter, his wife, Sian, holding him tight from behind. I was so glad to see them—to see anyone—that I could have bear-hugged them straight off their ride. But I kept moving. They parked the scooter on the side of the highway and then caught up with me. Both wore flip-flops and shorts, all healthy and flushed with energy. There was no doubt in my mind that I looked far from the same.

"We came out to find you," Welchy said. "To see how things are going."

"I'm hurting," I replied and told him that I wasn't able to hold onto any fluids.

"Your body's shutting down. Slow it down for a bit, and drink some chicken broth at the stations."

I nodded and loped along another few excruciating steps.

"And there's a murder scene going on in my shoes."

Welchy gave a halfhearted laugh, but he could see the pain in my eyes. "There's a ton of blue hats waiting for you to come back to town."

"Okay," I said, forcing my way forward.

For a while, Welchy and Sian chatted to me about the race: who won, in what time, how crazy the Bonner army was. I offered only a few words in reply, but it was so good to have them there. They were so positive, so sure that I had this race under control as long as I stayed smart, drank what I needed, and kept placing one foot in front of the other.

"Got to get back," Welchy said at last. After all, he was commentating on the race for the Ironman live webcast.

"I'll never quit on you," I said. "I'll never quit."

"Maintain pace. Run your race. Okay?"

I gave him a thumbs-up.

He and Sian turned back toward their scooter, and I was on my own once again. Almost instantly, I felt cold, and I zipped up my jersey.

Soon after, at Mile 16, I reached the entrance to the Energy Lab. Here it was at last. The breaker of champions, a 3-mile loop of roughly paved road, nothing to see in the inky darkness but some strange buildings silhouetted in faint yellow light and the rumble of some even stranger unseen machines. At the aid station, I drank some chicken broth as Welchy commanded and then made my way down toward the coast.

Fifty yards into the lab area, I pissed myself yet again. With each mile, nature was running its course more and more quickly. On the downslope, I had trouble swinging my legs out; my hip flexors felt shredded. This awkwardness, added to my already awkward gait, only made the punishment on my feet worse. They felt as if they were swelling inside my shoes, and I was afraid they might burst like balloons. There was also a rising burn in my ankles that I knew would only get worse with each minute that passed.

And those minutes were seeping away. By Mile 17, it was 9:05 P.M., leaving me less than three hours to finish the rest of the marathon before they turned off the lights and called it a day.

Bonner Paddock, you are an Ironman.

As I tried to pick up my pace, I kept repeating these words, imagining Mike Reilly intoning them. This carried me along a short way, but then pain and weariness swept back with a vengeance. I slowed to a crawl, unable to keep a straight line. My eyes blurred, and I felt as though I were slipping into some kind of half-consciousness, lulled by the pain, the inescapable pain, that constant drone in my head.

I shook myself awake and tried to ramp up the gears into a jog. I was in such a fog that I didn't know whether my body got the message.

Come on. You need to give more to this race. Everything. Dig deeper.

At last I felt my pace quicken as I headed north up the coast toward the Energy Lab turnaround. Just as soon as I felt I had command of myself again, I felt my energy levels sag.

"Keep the strides long, mate," Welchy said. He wasn't there. He had turned back to Kona. I was imagining him. But I needed him so badly. I needed everything, everyone.

"I'm running my race," I said.

"Yes you are, mate," Welchy said. "Me, Mike, we know you got this. We're here for you. And the blue hats, they're at the finish waiting for you."

I smiled at the thought and turned to Welchy. But as quickly as he had come, he was gone again.

I trembled at the thought of continuing out there alone. My body was useless to continue. I felt the light dying inside me. It was time to feed the furnace.

You are not alone. You never were. Welchy was just here, by your side. Mike. Steve. Alison. Tyler. Zach. John. Juliana. Ashley. Paige. Jake. They are all with you.

The thought of them, there, running by my side, cheering me on, fueled the furnace much brighter than any painful memories of the past. The renewed fire carried me through the darkness. At last I spotted the halo of light from the lab's turnaround point, and I was soon heading back toward the Queen K. Every few minutes, I rasped through my parched throat: "Bonner Paddock. You are an Ironman."

In the opposite direction came a Grim Reaper trailing after a runner who was staggering from one side of the road to the other. *They will never get me,* I promised myself, *not with everybody at my side.* These thoughts carried me back up the slope and onto the highway.

Getting out of the Energy Lab, that canyon of doom, took any reserve I had left. Spots began to form in front of my eyes. I slowed to a walk, but everything grew hazy again. In my mind, I imagined the hands of a clock closing in on midnight. My time to finish the race was dwindling now. I lost my balance trying to look at my watch and almost fell. It was just too dangerous to take my eyes off the pavement in this darkness. I might stumble into the lava field and never get up.

The volunteer at the Mile-20 aid station was cranking out some JayZ on a boom box. As I passed, he called out my number, "Hey, 1421. You got this big man. Home stretch now. Almost there."

I kept trudging, now favoring my right leg because of some mounting pressure in my left foot. My pace was all over the map, my body moving by some instinct of its own. A thirty-second jog here, a one-minute walk there, a forty-second jog here—too much—a two-minute walk there—too slow—a fifteen-second run, then back to a walk.

Somewhere past Mile 23, I took a step in the darkness, and my left foot simply exploded. It felt as though someone had taken a sledgehammer to it and broken every bone. I hobbled and came to a stop. I tried to suck it up, to ignore it, to force it away and take another step, to keep fighting, but my whole world had disintegrated into bright, red-hot flashes of pain. I howled into the night. After this release, I tried another step, this time with my left foot angled outward to relieve any pressure on it, but it didn't help. Panic followed. I would have to crawl to the finish line. The only part of this idea that did not work for me was that it would take too long. I was too far out. Three miles at a crawl? I would miss the cutoff.

Okay, so there is nothing left inside you. That furnace has gone cold. You're done.

My foot singing with pain and every muscle and fiber of my being aching and sagging with weakness, I accepted that there was no hope for me. Gasping for breath, I only wanted to sit down on the roadside, to let the Ironman go. *Let the Grim Reapers come. Stick out your thumb and hitch a ride.*

That second passed.

In the next second, I resolved to finish the race and hobbled forward. *You must keep moving. You are running out of time.*

One foot. Then the next.

And again. One foot. Then the next.

And again . . . and again . . . and again.

My watch battery was dying. Everything was dying. From my legs to my hip flexors to my head. Disconnected images passed through my mind. I think they might have been my subconscious trying to help me by throwing anything and everything, every last chunk of fuel, into the furnace to get me over the line.

I saw Jake, spinning back and forth on the chair by the poolside. I saw Ashley, weaving back and forth toward me on her own two feet. I saw Steve and Alison Robert running in the 2007 Orange County

Marathon with Tyler and Zach, keeping them company for a stretch. I saw my brother Mike, charting a course for me in the ocean, waiting in a Jeep for me to come by on my bike, walking beside me through the Energy Lab at sunset. I saw Welchy, leaning forward in his lawn chair, hashing over my game plan.

I will finish this race for everyone who supported me. I will finish this race to give every kid with a disability a fighting chance at life. I will finish this race, me, Bonner Paddock. I was born with cerebral palsy. It is a defining part of who I am. I represent everyone struggling every day to push past the limits the world has set on them. I am going to show them that there are no limits if you accept yourself for who you are. I am going to show myself. I am made of iron and more, and I will finish.

The next 2 miles passed in a blur. Then the lights of Kona grew brighter and brighter.

Approaching the end of the Queen K, I came upon Fireman Rob, one of the Inspired Athletes. Rob was running the marathon in full fireman's gear, raising money for firefighters with cancer. I wanted to stop, to help him along, but I knew if I lost my momentum I would be finished.

"Are you okay?" I asked.

"I'm fine," Fireman Rob said. "Keep going. See you at the finish line."

With Palani Road ahead, it started to sink in that I might very well make it across the line in time. I could hear the music cranking by the finish and the distant sound of Mike Reilly's voice, still calling names fewer and farther between in the final minutes before midnight.

Bonner Paddock, you are an Ironman. Force away the pain. Fight your fight. One more step. You are an Ironman.

At the turn down Palani, a crowd of blue cowboy hats greeted me with cheers that swelled my heart. I came to the final aid station, where I grabbed a quick drink of water.

As I made my way toward Alii Drive and the chute to the finish, more and more people patted me on the back, urging me forward. Their touch startled and unsettled me, and for a brief stretch I accelerated, feeling as if I were being chased. I'd left sanity behind long ago on the Queen K.

Then came the turn onto Alii Drive. My close friend Fitzy handed me a foam cowboy hat and passed me the blue OM Foundation flag as I swept into the chute lined on both sides with hundreds of spectators. They banged ThunderStix together to a steady beat and hollered and clapped and cheered.

Force away the pain. Fight your fight. One more step.

The bright lights of the finish were straight ahead. The roar from the crowd sounded like one long roll of thunder. All the weariness, all the pain drained away.

We did it! We did it! We did it!

"You are the man, Bonner!" someone yelled as I passed. I cracked my first smile in hours. Twenty-two minutes before midnight, I came down the final stretch. *This is happening. It's actually happening.*

Suddenly I found myself jumping and hopping and smiling and pumping my fist. I leapt, sidestepped, high-stepped, hollered, and stomped, total euphoria overcoming me like nothing I have ever known. I cried. I laughed. I pumped my fist again, raised my flag overhead, and crossed the finish line at last.

"Bonner Paddock, Newport Coast, California. You are an Ironman! Look out!" Reilly cheered over the loudspeakers, the clock reading sixteen hours, thirty-eight minutes. "Are you happy? Or what?" He slapped me on the arm in congratulation. "There he is. The only man to ever finish this race with cerebral palsy. Bonner has cerebral palsy. He battles it every day, but he just finished Ironman."

Right ahead of me stood Welchy, a big smile on his face. I staggered toward him and fell into his outstretched arms. My cowboy hat fell off. My legs gave out. But Welchy braced me.

"It's over. You did it," he said, holding me tight. "Well done, mate."

Tears coming down my face, I said. "No. We did it. We did it."

In victory, Welchy raised my left arm high into the air.

"One more time for Bonner Paddock," Reilly reveled. "You are an Ironman. Wow."

One Man, One Mission.

Moments after the finish, Welchy and a pair of Ironman volunteers pulled me toward the medical tent. Halfway there, Mike hopped a nearby barrier and helped haul me inside. His face was pure, raw emotion, doing the same kind of somersaults between joy and worry and relief that my body had crossing the line.

"I'm so proud of you," Mike said, tears streaming down his face.

"This is for both of us," I muttered as they lowered me onto a makeshift stretcher. "For everybody."

"You did it," Mike said. "You're an Ironman!"

We grasped hands, and then, after another second of triumphant elation, my body crumbled in on itself. My limbs shook. My teeth chattered. My eyes refused to focus.

"Where's Dr. Bob?" I mumbled, worried about what was happening to me.

Another doctor began speaking quietly to me. I couldn't understand his words and put my hands over my face, withered with exhaustion.

Someone brought my hands down and crossed my arms over my chest. Another elevated my feet and put a foil blanket over me.

Dr. Bob threaded through the tent toward me. In the mellow voice of a man who had seen every weakness of the human body revealed in the wake of Ironman's extreme punishment, he said, "Hi, Bonner. Congratulations. We have been waiting for you. Congratulations."

After those brief words, a flush of relief overcame me. "Thanks for believing in me."

"It's impossible not to believe in you," Dr. Bob said.

Under his guidance, the Ironman's medical team took my blood pressure, monitored my heart rate, and administered a few tests. They asked some questions to see if I was delirious. I certainly was. Once they removed my shoes, the pain returned. The bottoms of my feet looked as though someone had taken a cheese grater to them. Bright spots of light flashed across my eyes. Everywhere there was a searing, unstoppable pain. I felt as though I had gone five hundred rounds with Muhammad Ali and lost every damn one of them but the last.

To calm down, I forced myself to suck in air through my nose and expel it out my mouth. Mike kept a hand on my shoulder to ease me as well. A few minutes after they inserted a second bag of IV drip into my arm, my body settled. Occasional bursts of pain overcame me, stealing my breath and making my face tighten. But slowly these dissipated, and I recovered enough to speak again.

Turning to Mike, I asked, "Did you see my finish-line dance?"

Mike shook his head yes. He wiped a tear from his face and, through a clenched throat, said, "I'm so emotional."

A nurse stopped beside me. "Looking good. You're getting color back."

"I hear they're serving martinis in here," I joked before my tortured feet sent another jolt of pain splitting through my skull.

Over the next two hours, I remained on the stretcher, the words, "We did it. We did it," passing my lips over and over, as if I didn't quite believe them. Welchy and his wife stayed at my side a while. My dad and brother Matt stopped by for a hug and a cheer as well. After taking in two whole IV bags, I felt strong enough to sit up and then, after a few minutes, stand. My shoes were a mess, so Mike gave me his flip-flops and went barefoot himself. Leaning heavily on his arm and shoulder, I staggered from the tent, my Ironman journey complete at last.

Many months after Hawaii, my body continued to suffer the consequences of the triathlon. I wore orthopedic boots every night to heal my feet. Muscle spasms gripped my body. Numbness permeated my toes. And on the inside, blood levels and the like remained a mess. Even after a year, an attempt to do a short jog and light workout with weights left me almost incapacitated for days. My doctors expected it might take me three to five years to recover completely, and that was not even a guarantee. This diagnosis was sure proof of how close to the edge I had come.

Thankfully, the healing process with my family proved much smoother. After Kona, Mike and I were closer than we had been at any point in our lives. Even though we no longer had the crucible of the Ironman to bring us together, we looked to each other every day still for support—and companionship. It was amazing to think that in many ways he was now my best friend.

Through the course of Ironman, I came to realize that a lot of the damage in our relationship had come because we simply did not accept each other for who we were, faults and all. Further, I understood that in the past I had seen his absence from my life as a statement that he did not want me in his own, instead of considering that he might have had personal challenges that kept us at a distance. This might not sound like rocket science, but for a long time it was for me. This same new understanding brought me much closer to my father and spurred me to take the first steps to reconcile with my mother.

Six months after Ironman, I reached out to her for the first time in years. We met at a little vegan place on the Pacific Coast Highway for breakfast. On my approach, she smiled and then shuffled toward me for a big hug. Waiting in line to order, she told me of her church, her house, her neighbors—anything but the reason why we had not spoken really since Bompa's death. At the table outside, overlooking the ocean, I told her about my work, my foundation—again, anything but the heart of the matter.

At last, thirty minutes into our breakfast, I explained how my climb of Kilimanjaro, my Ironman journey, had forced me to take a look at myself, and my upbringing, and come to terms with it, both the good and the bad and the in-between.

"I'm the happiest I've ever been now," I said. "All the stuff that's happened between us, regardless of who was right or wrong, I want to get past it. I apologize for my part in our relationship breaking down, and I want you in my life again if you're open to it."

"I was waiting for that," she replied. "Now we can move on."

No apology came from her end, nor did I need one anymore. She was my mom. I would never walk away from her again, but I hoped one day she would do her own soul-searching so that we could be close in the way Mike and I had become. The breakfast was a start though.

After Kona, my mother, and pretty much every single person I met, asked me the same question: "What's next?" Any fun-house mirror ambitions I might have had to push my body to its breaking point again, to trek across the Sahara, to summit Everest, to swim in Antarctica—whatever madness I could find—were well and truly gone. Any demons I might have had about my cerebral palsy, any need to show the world that I was normal no longer remained.

I had a single purpose now: to support the building of centers across the world for children with disabilities. In Orange County, the one we had already supported was serving as a model for success, and the OM Foundation was partnering with Dr. Aminian to construct another center to serve more children with an even wider array of therapies. In Austin, with the leadership of Jake's dad, Steve Robert (who was on the foundation's board), we were hoping to break ground on another center. In Tanzania, we were also expanding our work, partnering with other organizations to bring relief to children abandoned by their families because of their disabilities as well as bringing surgeons over to provide life-changing surgeries similar to the one performed on Juliana.

In August 2014, I journeyed again to Africa. Stepping onto the tarmac, I felt that now-familiar mix of excitement and unease, as if the ground underneath me was not quite solid. The fact was my previous trips had changed me, making me see myself and my purpose in life differently, and I sensed the same would happen yet again. It was in Tanzania that I had first come to realize that I could no longer continue to neglect embracing my CP as a fundamental part of who I was. It was there that I had found the calling to start my foundation.

At the airport exit, a young man in his late twenties with a bright polo shirt, baggy pants, and sneakers waved a sign with my name on it. He introduced himself as Jabir, my driver for the week, then he quickly ushered me to his car. On the way to the hotel, we struck up a conversation, ranging from his country's politics, to my climb of Kilimanjaro, to his family, to the reason for my trip this year, to his Muslim beliefs. After he helped me check in with the half-asleep hotel staff, I invited him to breakfast the next day before we set out.

In the morning, he was already waiting at the table. We drove out to Machame Hospital on the slopes of Kilimanjaro where Dr. Aminian and a group of doctors had arrived several days before to begin surgeries and other procedures on children with disabilities—as well as instructing local doctors on the same to improve the overall level of care in the area. Jabir was intently curious about our work, and between my explanations, I drew out of him stories about his two young children, and his wife who he had met in this area. While courting her, he used to walk for hours through the bush to see her for just a few moments before returning all the way home.

Once at Machame, Jabir waited in the car as I met the hospital staff and patients with Dr. Aminian. In their short time in Tanzania, the crew of doctors had performed numerous amputations and corrective gait surgeries. They advised on physical therapy, heart defects, and high-risk pregnancies. They returned sight to five people who were medically blind and aided others to walk again. At the end of each day at the hospital, Jabir peppered me with questions, curious about the patients and their lives, which were both very much the same and yet very different from that of his own healthy kids.

After some days at the hospital, Jabir drove Dr. Aminian and me along a remote dirt road to the Faraja School. Started by the Tolmies, a retired American couple, the school provided a safe refuge for disabled children. Like the Usa River School, it was a place I hoped to assist in caring for their young charges. This time, I invited Jabir to come along with me on my tour. At first he was hesitant with the children, but soon he eased and then started acting as my translator, part of the team. When the children learned I had climbed Kilimanjaro, their eyes always seemed to drift to my legs in wonder that I could have done such a thing.

On the way to one classroom, Jabir and I crossed paths with a boy whose CP left him only able to spin the wheels of his wheelchair with the back of one hand (because of the spasticity in his limbs). The way he moved with such calm and resolute will reminded me of how much strength these kids had inside of them. Later Dr. Aminian called me into a therapy room where a teenage boy was being examined. Jabir joined me to translate.

Growing up, this boy had been burned severely in an accident. Doctors had amputated his left leg halfway down the shin, and he was barely ambulatory on his other leg. The trouble was he was growing, and the bone in his left leg was pushing out through the stump of his amputation (because the burned skin was not elastic enough). This left him in constant excruciating pain, and Dr. Aminian suggested a surgery to relieve his distress. At Machame, it would cost sixty dollars.

As I reached for my wallet, Jabir had already produced his own, forcing ten dollars into my hand. I told him to keep it, but Jabir insisted. Added with money of my own, this boy would get his surgery. It amazed me that only sixty dollars could dramatically change a life for the better. It amazed me more that Jabir would contribute money of his own (ten dollars was no small sum for his family).

"My wife and I want to help how we can," Jabir said.

Before leaving the Faraja School, I committed to helping them provide more therapy and medical care for their kids, as well as funds for once their charges left, whether it was to pursue secondary school or to learn a vocation.

Then Jabir took me to the last stop of my mission in Tanzania, the Usa River School, where in many ways it had started. To my joy, I found Juliana had come there to learn dressmaking. It was incredible to know that this young girl, who had first approached me by ambling along on her knees, was now on the path to self-sufficiency and would likely serve as a shining star to others. One life helps another, then another—that was the idea.

Afterward, I bid Jabir good-bye and flew to Zanzibar to decompress. Sitting on the beach, I thought of my time in Africa, why each trip left me with a better understanding of what was necessary and real in the world. Yes, the setting had an influence. The enormity of Kilimanjaro, the sight of elephants roaming the bush as they had for thousands of years, definitely put things into perspective. Most of all though, it was the people. Few were of any great means. Like Jabir or our guides on the mountain or the Masai warriors I met in Zanzibar (who wondered how many cattle I owned at home), most were simply trying to put food in their mouths and a roof over their heads, to care for and be with their families. It was life stripped of the things that I once thought would make me happy—the fancy car, the trendy clothes, the right friends, the big office, the lucrative career, the perfectly healthy body. Most of the Tanzanians I had met lived in the moment, the now, and they offered their community the best of what they had because, often, it meant the difference between survival or not for all of them.

It was not utopia, of course. People starved, suffered, and died in ways they unlikely would have in the United States. Further, their bare existence left little room for the disabled, who many considered a burden to be at best pushed aside—at worst, purged. It was my mission in Tanzania to provide this room and counter the idea that children like Juliana did not have a positive mark to make on their community. This was my contribution, but it was returned many times over to me through the gift of understanding of what was essential and important in life.

Only Jake had given me more. While in Tanzania, he was constantly with me. It was his story that truly gave impetus to my own. The Robert family, in their daily lives and annual run at the Orange County Marathon, kept his spirit alive as well. In 2014, my foundation joined with them to take on the mantle of Team Jake. Now we have volunteers sporting the team name who can raise funds by running a marathon, starting a lemonade stand, or even entering an amateur boxing ring for children with special needs. In 2016, the tenth anniversary of his passing, a huge crowd will gather to honor him at the Orange County Marathon again.

Soon after returning from Africa, I visited the hillside cemetery, overlooking the Pacific Ocean, where Jake rested. It was a bright, perfectly sunny California afternoon as I made my way up to his burial site, thinking of how his brothers earlier that summer had included Jake on their roster for baseball as a pinch hitter, to be called on when needed.

Dozens of marathon medals now hung from the branches of the willow tree over the gravestone, and someone had wrapped a wide bright multicolored ribbon around the tree's trunk as well. Sitting on the stone bench beside it, I stared down at the portrait of Jake's young face held within the stone, more grateful than ever at the journey of discovery his life had inspired in me.

I narrowly came through summiting Kilimanjaro. In striving to earn the title of Kona Ironman, I discovered a fuel that burned so much brighter and purer than physical and emotional pain. By putting my faith in others, accepting my weaknesses, embracing my normal, and racing my race, I powered through a test of endurance and will that would have broken me before. And when this was still not enough, I focused on the reason I was there, a purpose greater than myself. When I had nothing left, my mission to help every child with disabilities push beyond their own limits drove me through to the finish.

Looking out at the Pacific, the same ocean I'd learned to swim in, the same ocean I'd trained in, I was able to see clearly just how much he'd pushed me. None of this would have happened without Jake. He answered my call and from that I'd discovered a purpose I never thought possible. Walking back down the hill, I hoped my story, this one, would inspire the same kind of journey in others, so that ultimately they, too, would find the fight of their own lives.

Afterword

When I first met Bonner Paddock, he had just begun sharing his story with others, but in the years since, both Bonner and his story have grown by leaps and bounds. No longer the young man nervous to speak about his cerebral palsy, Bonner now embraces who he is. This book is a testament to how far he's come since he began his journey.

But there is another side to this story, one that is also important to share, because the impact of Bonner's efforts—running a marathon, climbing a mountain, racing in the Kona Ironman, and launching a foundation—goes far beyond him. Those close to him, my family especially, have been forever changed as well. His effect on our family has long been a tough conversation, knowing that what first set Bonner on his path was the tragic death of our son Jake, but I know beyond any doubt that we are in a better, higher, more understanding place because of our friendship with Bonner.

Ever since Bonner first began talking publicly about his story, I felt like our family was a part of it—even before we actually were.

Ours was a friendship that formed without ever speaking a word. In many ways Bonner instantly became a safe place for many of my greatest fears. Once it was clear that our son Jake would struggle to take a step, hold his head up, or communicate to us in any way, I became paralyzed by the thoughts of all the things he would never do. Bonner, simply by standing up and saying he had cerebral palsy, changed the way I thought about my son and his own diagnosis. Jake did not change. He did not stand up and walk, talk, or care for himself after I met Bonner. His diagnosis remained the same. I don't know why I needed a young man with CP to help me connect with my son, but I did. After meeting Bonner, I changed the way I thought about his CP, about what the future looked like in my head. My deepest fears subsided and my focus shifted from fear to one of celebration for the smallest things.

In the painful aftermath of Jake's death, Bonner offered our family something that all of us needed, but none of us knew how to ask for: a reason to keeping talking, to ourselves and to others, about the wonder that was Jake. Alison and I were told that if our boys continued to discuss Jake and keep his memory alive in the family, it would be a sign they were doing well after their loss. Talking about your brother who died is not "cool" or even acceptable at school, but Bonner, through his amazing accomplishments, has given our boys the context to keep talking about their brother Jake from a place of pride. Bonner carried our grief and turned it into a fuel that drives him, and our boys know that by extension Jake is running, climbing, and competing along with Bonner. Through this, he has been able to help them heal in ways that Alison and I struggled to, because we were still trying to recover ourselves. In this way, his efforts not only helped our kids, they helped our marriage.

Sometimes real kinship comes more naturally when not bound by familial ties. I know that Jake's brothers, all of them, feel a spirit with Bonner that they do not necessarily share with each other. Not better or worse, but born from a different place. My wife shares an understanding with Bonner and I have feelings of ease and gratitude and awe I do not have anywhere else. Bonner fills a space in our lives that we would not have the energy to pursue on our own.

Sometimes when you don't have the courage or the strength to capture all that someone means to you, it is easier to let someone else do the talking for you. Bonner has given us that—and so much more: keeping us a part of the special needs community; giving us a platform to support all the other "Jakeys" and their families; showing our boys that real men stand up front and take action; and finally, most of all, taking Jake well beyond his limits by carrying our boy's spirit with him in Orange County, Africa, Hawaii, and beyond.

In his four and a half short years, Jake Ryan Lee Robert taught us all the only language we need to say thank you to a man who heals us every day: love.

—Alison, Steven, Tyler, Zach, Brady, Cody, and
Our Sweet Angel Jake Ryan Lee Robert

Barnes & Noble Booksellers #2173
5709 Lone Tree Way
Antioch, CA 94531
925-978-1031

STR:2173 REG:002 TRN:5254 CSHR:Madison S

CUSTOMER ORDER PICKUP
ORDER NUMBER: 2173-211807

One More Step: My Story of Living with C
9780062295606   T1
  (1 @ 16.99)   16.99

Subtotal   16.99
Sales Tax T1 (8.750%)   1.49
TOTAL   18.48
CASH   18.48

A MEMBER WOULD HAVE SAVED   1.70

Connect with us on Social

Facebook- @BNAntioch
Instagram- @bnantioch
Twitter-   @BNAntioch

101.44A   07/16/2017 10:18AM

CUSTOMER COPY

Opened music CDs, DVDs, vinyl records, audio books may not be returned, and can be exchanged only for the same title and only if defective. NOOKs purchased from other retailers or sellers are returnable only to the retailer or seller from which they are purchased, pursuant to such retailer's or seller's return policy. Magazines, newspapers, eBooks, digital downloads, and used books are not returnable or exchangeable. Defective NOOKs may be exchanged at the store in accordance with the applicable warranty.

Returns or exchanges will not be permitted (i) after 14 days or without receipt or (ii) for product not carried by Barnes & Noble or Barnes & Noble.com.

Policy on receipt may appear in two sections.

Return Policy

With a sales receipt or Barnes & Noble.com packing slip, a full refund in the original form of payment will be issued from any Barnes & Noble Booksellers store for returns of undamaged NOOKs, new and unread books, and unopened and undamaged music CDs, DVDs, vinyl records, toys/games and audio books made within 14 days of purchase from a Barnes & Noble Booksellers store or Barnes & Noble.com with the below exceptions:

A store credit for the purchase price will be issued (i) for purchases made by check less than 7 days prior to the date of return, (ii) when a gift receipt is presented within 60 days of purchase, (iii) for textbooks, (iv) when the original tender is PayPal, or (v) for products purchased at Barnes & Noble College bookstores that are listed for sale in the Barnes & Noble Booksellers inventory management system.

Opened music CDs, DVDs, vinyl records, audio books may not be returned, and can be exchanged only for the same title and only if defective. NOOKs purchased from other retailers or sellers are returnable only to the retailer or seller from which they are purchased, pursuant to such retailer's or seller's return policy. Magazines, newspapers, eBooks, digital downloads, and used books are not returnable or exchangeable. Defective NOOKs may be exchanged at the store in accordance with the applicable warranty.

Acknowledgments

Steve: How can I possibly say a proper thank you to the first person who showed me that by telling my story I could give hope to someone? Still to this day, the most powerful and impactful email or conversation I have ever received. Our bond is for life and you have helped me more than any one person ever has. With the emotion and love you share all the time for Jakey and your family while still enjoying life to the fullest, you and Ali have demonstrated how a family truly stays together through the darkest hour any family could have.

    Ali: You have shown me how a mother truly loves their kids. So many would not have half the strength you display so often, and it has made a huge impact on how I have tried to work on me, to better reconnect with my family. Thank you for always including me as part of your family. You and Steve will always tell me how it is not what I want to hear and that and the love you show me are the greatest things I hope to share with those I love too.

    Tyler: The strength you have was evident even when you stood at the pulpit at Jakey's funeral. I knew then you would be an amazing person and to watch you grow into exactly that is just awesome! I love you like a li'l bro and will always be there for whatever you need. Thank you for showing me the courage even at such a young age that we all have in us.

Zach: Thank you for showing that calmness can show confidence and not have to always be bragging about our own talents and success! The gifts you hold are greater than most I have come across. The power you have will be immense to change this world for the better. You too are like a li'l bro to me and I love you and Tyler as part of my family.

Brady & Cody: Your lives are such a gift to me. Thankful of our early mornings when your brothers and parents were still sleeping, telling me all the facts of Dodgers, MineSweeper, and everything that is going on in your lives. The way you see the world is so refreshing to me; thankful for the perspective I get to see through your eyes.

Dad: Wow, what a roller coaster of a ride you and I have been on. From not talking to now one of my best friends . . . you were the first person to show me the path to forgiveness by your selfless acts in college when reconnecting with me. Even though the verbal is not always easy for you, your eyes and smile say it all. I am so proud to be your son and will continue to grow with you as an example of wisdom, strength, patience, and integrity. I am your #1 fan and honored that you are my dad! Love you, Pops!

Mike: Thank you for being you. I am so proud of the man you are. You have worked tirelessly, seen darkness that most in life never will, and you still stand tall and strong. You are my best friend in the world, and we share a bond that will never be broken. Your selfless sacrifices through my Ironman journey and your commitment to me even at a moment's notice were easily the highlight of those two years. I love you, bro!

LaDonna: It's never easy coming into the family of someone who has kids, and the strength and confidence you show is what I needed so bad to get from a female/mother figure. You have given me such great advice and never waver on your commitment to Dad and us. Couldn't of dreamed up a better woman for Dad and our family. Love you!

Welchy: My Australian brother from another mother! You threw yourself into this crazy World Record attempt and never backed off. You put your name on the line with your sponsors and that was the greatest honor given what you have accomplished. You have given me so much wisdom beyond just the Ironman training, teaching me that the true goal of any race in life is not the finish line but the journey there. As much as Ironman was the hardest physical challenge I have ever done by far, I loved so much of it because of you. Love your chicken legs, li'l brother!

Wendy: Thank you to someone who understands me so well and for all your patience. It's never easy coming into the situation you did at ADHC and you handled it with such class. We make a great team and you give me such balance in very intense situations. So grateful for all you have done for my foundation and the kids we serve. You and your family are such amazing people.

Dr. Aminian: To describe how admirable a person you are and how much you have changed my life would take an entire book. From walking across the courtyard and saying "you have CP don't you?" to the time you have spent in Africa for my foundation, you are so selfless. I have such respect for you and the countless things you have done to help these kids. You are nothing short of amazing, and the humility you show is unreal.

Ashley and The Arambulas: If I had Ashley's attitude with my lighter case of CP, I would have already climbed Everest, swam around the globe, and beat RedBull to jumping from space. Thank you for always knowing what's important—from your visits to our office to your beautiful view of life. You may be in a wheelchair for now, but you will be walking full time soon. Your parents and brother Joe are so fantastic. I think of you all every day and work so hard to be a better person because of what all of you have shown me.

Linda, The Beresfords and Disabled Community: I am so grateful for all the support the disabled community has shown me, especially the Beresfords. Linda, your dedication to Team Jake is paramount in the growth of OMF and will be the basis for how the foundation lives on. Thank you for including me in your beautiful family and showing me how challenges in your lives haven't let them get the best of you.

Matt: I can never thank you enough for including me in so much growing up when I wasn't finding a lot of close friends. Some of my loneliest times you let me tag along and made me feel special. Love ya, bro!

Mom: With some ups and many downs, I understand now why you are who you are. By Dad showing me the path to not holding grudges and to letting things go, it has led us to talking again. Thank you for trying your best when I was growing up to give us what you could. Life is a journey and sometimes very difficult, but you kept a smile and happy front as best you could. I love you xoxo

Vern Underwood, Chris Underwood, and my Young's Family: One of the most humble and generous families I have ever met or been a part of are the Underwoods and my Young's family. Right away, you accepted me and always made me a part of the family. To Vern, a man who is a legend in our industry but has stayed so humble and caring; you have been the guide I've needed as this journey has moved at such a rapid rate. Your humor and outlook are such true representations of all you have achieved. Chris, I love you like a brother and so enjoy all our talks on the road and working for you.

You push people to become better co-workers, but also better people. Thank you for everything you have done for me and my foundation. Young's is my family and I will never work anywhere else as long as you and your dad are running it.

The Samuelis and Anaheim Ducks Family: Thank you to Henry and Susan Samueli for showing me what generosity is. Your kindness has impacted so many people's lives. Thank you for the support you always showed, from coming to my charity events like the documentary premiere to allowing me to follow my dreams. You made the very difficult decision to leave the Ducks as easy as it could be. To my Ducks family—from the players, coaches, and staff—you always were so helpful and friendly to me both on the personal and professional sides.

Dane and my Oakley Family: Eternally grateful to Stan Chen for introducing us in 2008 and for you taking a risk to sponsor me. I'm honored to wear my Oakley gear with such pride. Dane, you were the initial person at Oakley who then introduced me to such exceptional people like Tanja, Postie, Pope, Cuan, and of course Postie going to talk to Welchy and asking him to be my coach for Ironman. With so many wonderful people in one place, I never could have dreamed of what having an endorsement deal with a brand like Oakley would do. Dane, you taught me we are all equals and that's what makes the Oakley family so special. We both knew I wasn't Shaun White, but you exposed me to so many things that are now such a huge part of my life. We have changed the world together and helped my confidence so much that I am in the Oakley family.

To OM Foundation Board: I admire you all so much, that you would give my foundation your valuable time. I can't do it alone and you all have always put the kids over anything personal. You have so many other things you could be doing but you spend so much time on this foundation. All of us working together has resulted in our huge success in such a short time. You are the future of this foundation.

Jesse Brewer: You are such a talented, caring, and hard worker, but most importantly a close friend. Many of the work things fall to you when I am gone at Young's and you handle it flawlessly. You will be everything you could possibly want to be—there is nothing stopping you but the brightness of your future. From finding me in the pitch-black Queen K Highway at the end of Ironman to make sure I was still okay to the time you put into everything, being around you makes me a better person. I never will forget the big part that you and your sacrifices have played—thank you.

Dilly and Iron Horse: Each of you stepped up to help me in my quest to climb Kili. Both of you are from such different upbringings, but I have learned so much from you. The fun we have when we all are together and the strength you have shown me is so empowering. I am eternally grateful for the sacrifices you have made for me and my foundation.

Mitch, Kent, and Jeff: To three of the most talented filmmakers around. You took a huge gamble and risk on my journey to capture the Kili attempt. You captured the hardest thing at the time in my life when I was just beginning to scratch the surface of my own personal growth. You poured so much time, energy, and money into making that movie, but then to donate the rights and proceeds from the film to my foundation says it all about how much character you have. I have been so proud of the success you have earned since then and can't wait to see all you do.

MCD: Two people who have had some of the biggest impact on my life were two people I literally knew for such a short time before their deaths, Jakey and Michael Clarke Duncan (MCD). Thank you

MCD for believing in me so much to donate your valuable talents to the documentary. Your life was so far different than mine but you never let fame change you. Your past was your reminder of where you came from and what made the person you were.

Greg LeFever: Going from a neighbor in Newport Coast to becoming such an integral part of my life journey, especially through some of both our darkest moments in our lives, I enjoyed our trainings so much. You selflessly donated all your time, came to races, had me over for dinners, and most importantly showed the confidence in me even when I was having doubts during training. You pushed me harder in those workouts than I ever thought was possible.

Friends: From my best friend of almost twenty-five years, Fitzy, to others who have come into my life briefly but with impact, thank you for loving me and including me with all my imperfections and mistakes. You make me laugh and keep me grounded and the crazier things are, the more I need that.

Billy and Cannondale Team: You all worked tirelessly, making sure everything was perfect for the ride of my life I would need to make the cutoff time at Ironman. We all knew it would come down to the bike portion, and you gave me the bike of my dreams. You reached out to all your contacts to make sure I had everything I needed at every race. I rode the bike with such pride. Billy, your positive attitude is so infectious. Steve, Murray, and gang, thank you for coming out to Kona to give me everything I needed. You are all a huge reason we conquered Kona. ☺

David Abrutyn and IMG: David you saw something in me before I did and took a big risk signing me at IMG. You have worked so hard to build your career and name and it is such an honor you have given me the chance. You are so talented and such a vision of so many things that have all come true for me. You are one of my mentors and I respect you for all you have accomplished in your life. Thank you for believing in me!

Ron Seaver and NSF Family: We both took a risk when you hired me and I left my job at ADP to chase what I thought was a dream to be in the sports industry. It was by far the greatest choice in my career and I came away with so much more than a career . . . I came away with my first family that is tied to work. Ron, you are so amazing in how you handled my coming out to you about my CP and showing me what true work ethic is. Dave Mullins, you helped me out so much at NSF. To all the others who gave me advice, encouragement, and love, it has been a journey of such happiness with your help. Thank you all for everything you do for me and my foundation.

My sponsors and donors: I can physically do Kili and Ironman, but truly the only way we are helping change the lives of so many children is through the generosity of my sponsors and donors. From Young's, many of our suppliers, Oakley, Cannondale, and so many others, I have turned down other offers because I only want to have people and brands associated with my foundation that embody the same character. You have changed so many lives with what you have done for me and my foundation.

Juliana: Thank you for showing me hope when life appears to have given you no chance of survival ... from walking on your knees for the first sixteen years of your life to still showing that amazing smile of yours during your darkest times. You will have everything you ever dreamed of if you want it!

Andrew Wabuko: Your sacrifices and generosity to be there for the doctors and Juliana, translating morning, noon, and night to allow for her to get the best care possible even under the toughest unforeseen circumstances. You always stayed true to the amazing person you are! *Asante sana!*

Kili Climbers: Thank you to all who spent so much energy on this amazing trip! From our team lead, Tim, to Turtle for her medical expertise, to Nancy for being so nurturing from the moment we set off on this journey. To all of the support team—Minja, Moody, Bariki, and all—you were first class and went so far above and beyond to help our team make it safely to the summit. I owe you a huge debt of gratitude. Every trip over to continue helping your country we talk about how that was the beginning of my love for Tanzania and the amazing people.

Ironman Family: From all the amazing pros who took time to give me advice and support but, most importantly, Chrissie Wellington for so many conversations and your friendship! To Diana, Dr. Bob, and the awesome team at Ironman and in Kona! Without you there would be no race and platform for so many athletes to show the character that lies within all of us but so few ever tap into. Thank you for allowing me to show mine in 2012 and for believing in me and my quest.

Lisa, Matt, and HarperCollins: Thank you for your trust in Neal and me to deliver this amazing project! You believed in us the most and have given such great guidance, advice, and now friendship. For someone who knew nothing about the book industry, you have been patient with and supportive of me. You understood what a sensitive subject this is for me and my family. Proud that you are our publisher!

Neal: When I met you to interview a ghost writer, I had no idea what to expect and if this journey was going to be best with someone who would be like a friend or a brother or dad. What I got was someone that I feel so comfortable with but so different than anyone I am close with. You are such a brilliant writer and researcher, but more than that you spent two years of your life eating, sleeping, and living my life. It's not easy to get that out of me and you handled it so well. You allowed me just the right leniency but had such a great way of pushing me past my limits and not letting me just gloss over some important things in my life. This was truly the hardest thing I have ever done with needing to go back into my childhood and some very unpleasant moments in my family's past. You wrote the truth but did not make it any harder on us than it needed to be.